I0009905

Copyright

Dedication

To every developer who:

- Read the docs, followed the rules, and still got an "Access Denied."
- Spent four hours fixing something that turned out to be a missing IAM permission.
- Deployed to production with confidence, only to be betrayed by an S3 bucket policy from 2018.
- Added /* to an IAM policy "just to test something"—and forgot to remove it.
- Googled "why Lambda doesn't work" at 2:47 a.m. with coffee in one hand and regret in the other.

You're not alone. This book's for you.

Acknowledgments

This book was born out of broken deployments, midnight outages, and postmortems that left more questions than answers.

Thanks to the devs who challenged assumptions, the teams who made the same mistakes twice so I didn't have to, and the AWS community that never stops digging deeper.

And to the readers—thanks for trusting me to help you through the chaos.

How to Use This Book

This book isn't meant to be read cover-to-cover—unless you're into that kind of pain.
Each chapter stands alone and targets a real AWS problem you're likely to hit in the wild.

You can:

- Jump to a chapter when something breaks
- Use the checklists to audit your setup
- Copy CLI examples and fix issues fast
- Skim "What You Probably Missed" to find the traps

If you're new to AWS, some content might move fast. That's okay. Bookmark it—because eventually, these issues will find you.

About This Book

Mastering AWS: Solving the Top Developer Challenges with S3, IAM, EC2, Lambda, and Cognito is a practical guide for developers and engineers who live in the trenches of cloud infrastructure—deploying, debugging, and defending systems built on AWS.

This is not a beginner's course or a documentation rewrite. It's a book built around the real problems teams face in production:

- Why S3 buckets go public without warning
- Why EC2 bills keep climbing even after instances are stopped
- Why your Lambda function times out without logs
- Why "Access Denied" happens even when your IAM policies look perfect
- Why Cognito sign-ups break—or tokens mysteriously expire

You'll find **real-world problem breakdowns**, **battle-tested AWS CLI fixes**, and **configuration examples**—all written from the perspective of developers who've been burned by vague errors, silent failures, and surprise costs.

Each chapter focuses on a specific, high-impact issue—explaining why it happens, how to detect it quickly, and what you can do to prevent it next time. There's no fluff, no theory dumps—just straight answers and proven patterns.

Whether you're building serverless apps, managing IAM for a growing team, optimizing cloud costs, or troubleshooting a production outage at midnight, this book is for you.

Written by a hands-on architect who's been through the chaos—this guide exists to save you time, money, and mistakes.

Contents

9

Part 1: Mastering Storage and Data Security

Chapter 1: The Accidental Exposure – Why S3 Buckets Go Public and How to Catch Them Before It's Too Late

S3 is secure by default, but that doesn't mean your buckets stay private. All it takes is one misstep—a wildcard `"Principal": "*"`, a forgotten ACL, or an automation script skipping Block Public Access—and your entire bucket contents are exposed to the internet.

In this chapter, we break down exactly how S3 exposures happen, how to detect them fast with CLI and Trusted Advisor, and how to lock your environment down tight.

Quick Exposure Checklist:

- Is Block Public Access fully enabled at both account and bucket level?

- Are any bucket policies using `"Principal": "*"` without restrictive conditions?

- Are object or bucket ACLs granting access to AllUsers or AuthenticatedUsers?

- Have you enforced Object Ownership (`BucketOwnerEnforced`) to kill ACLs?

- Are you using Access Analyzer or Trusted Advisor for visibility?

- Have you reviewed CloudTrail for recent `PutBucketPolicy` or `PutObjectAcl` events?

- Do you serve content via S3 static site hosting without CloudFront or signed URLs?

How This Happens in Real-World Environments

S3 is engineered for scale and openness. That's great for performance—but dangerous when developers overlook the subtle layers of access control. The most common pathways to accidental exposure include:

- Creating "temporary" testing buckets that never get cleaned up

- Enabling static website hosting with open `s3:GetObject` policies

- Copy-pasting wide-open bucket policies across projects

- Using automation tools that don't respect account-level Block Public Access

- Allowing IAM roles with `PutObjectAcl` permissions

Example: your team sets up a public image bucket for a frontend app. Days later, someone uploads a private report or credentials file to the same bucket. It inherits the same public ACL or bucket policy—and now your internal docs are being indexed by bots or search engines.

Root Causes of Exposure

Cause	Description
Wildcard Bucket Policy	A `"Principal": "*"` without IP, referer, or auth restrictions
Public ACLs	Object or bucket ACLs granting access to `AllUsers` or `AuthenticatedUsers`
Block Public Access Disabled	Block Public Access (BPA) not enforced
IAM Permissions to PutObjectAcl	IAM roles or services allowed to apply public ACLs
Legacy Static Website Hosting	Requires public read access, often leads to open buckets
ACLs Still Active	Default setting allows ACLs unless disabled via Object Ownership

How Developers Misread the Situation

- "The console says it's private."
  → The console only shows **bucket-level** public access, not object-level ACLs.

- "IAM roles are locked down."
  → IAM is only one part of the access model. ACLs and bucket policies can bypass it.

- "Block Public Access is enabled."
  → Is it at the **account** level, or just for some buckets?

- "We disabled ACLs."
  → Unless `BucketOwnerEnforced` is set, ACLs are still active.

Detecting Misconfigurations with AWS CLI

Step 1: Check Block Public Access

```
aws s3api get-bucket-public-access-block --bucket your-bucket-name
```

Expected output:

```
{
  "BlockPublicAcls": true,
  "IgnorePublicAcls": true,
  "BlockPublicPolicy": true,
  "RestrictPublicBuckets": true
}
```

Step 2: Scan for Wildcard Bucket Policies

```
aws s3api get-bucket-policy --bucket your-
bucket-name
```

Search for `"Principal": "*"` and validate if it's properly scoped with `Condition`.

Step 3: Audit Bucket and Object ACLs

```
aws s3api get-bucket-acl --bucket your-
bucket-name
aws s3api get-object-acl --bucket your-
bucket-name --key path/to/object
```

Look for this red flag:

```
"Grantee": {
  "URI":
"http://acs.amazonaws.com/groups/global/All
Users"
}
```

Killing ACLs with Object Ownership

```
aws s3api put-bucket-ownership-controls \
  --bucket your-bucket-name \
```

```
--ownership-controls
'Rules=[{ObjectOwnership=BucketOwnerEnforce
d}]'
```

This setting disables all ACLs, and enforces ownership by the bucket owner—even for cross-account uploads. It is the best-practice "kill switch" to prevent object-level public access.

Diagram: How Object Ownership Affects ACL Behavior

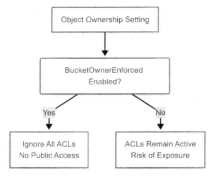

Use Access Analyzer and Trusted Advisor

Access Analyzer (Free):

- Detects external access to S3, IAM, and other AWS resources

```
aws accessanalyzer list-analyzers
```

```
aws accessanalyzer list-findings --
analyzer-name default --filter
type=PublicAccess
```

Trusted Advisor (Business/Enterprise):

- Go to: Security → S3 Bucket Permissions

- Flags any buckets with public read/write or anonymous access

---

Step-by-Step: Locking Down Your Buckets

1. Enable Full Block Public Access

```
aws s3api put-public-access-block \
  --bucket your-bucket-name \
  --public-access-block-configuration '{
    "BlockPublicAcls": true,
    "IgnorePublicAcls": true,
    "BlockPublicPolicy": true,
    "RestrictPublicBuckets": true
  }'
```

2. Enforce Object Ownership

```
aws s3api put-bucket-ownership-controls \
  --bucket your-bucket-name \
  --ownership-controls
'Rules=[{ObjectOwnership=BucketOwnerEnforce
d}]'
```

3. Remove `"Principal": "*"` from Bucket
   Policies

If public access is truly needed, scope it down like this:

```
{
  "Effect": "Allow",
  "Principal": "*",
  "Action": "s3:GetObject",
  "Resource": "arn:aws:s3:::your-bucket/*",
  "Condition": {
    "IpAddress": { "aws:SourceIp":
"203.0.113.0/24" }
  }
}
```

4. Reset ACLs on Buckets and Objects

```
aws s3api put-bucket-acl --bucket your-
bucket-name --acl private
```

```
aws s3api put-object-acl --bucket your-
bucket-name --key object --acl private
```

What You Probably Missed

- ACLs are still **enabled by default** unless you explicitly disable them with
  `BucketOwnerEnforced`

- Use **CloudTrail** to trace who changed a bucket policy or applied a public ACL

```
aws cloudtrail lookup-events \
  --lookup-attributes
AttributeKey=ResourceName,AttributeValue=yo
ur-bucket-name
```

- **Trusted Advisor is not real-time**. Use Access Analyzer and CloudTrail for faster detection

- **Static website hosting forces your hand**. It often pushes you toward public read policies—use CloudFront with signed URLs instead

- **Public buckets attract bots**. Even harmless logs or images can trigger massive data transfer charges

By locking down S3 access at every level—Block Public Access, ACLs, bucket policies, and ownership—you're not just protecting files. You're protecting your team, your compliance posture, and your company's reputation.

The best S3 bucket is invisible to the internet.

Chapter 2: The Silent Wallet Killer – Hidden Causes of Unexpected S3 Charges and How to Automate Detection & Cleanup

Quick Skim Checklist

- Are large files stored in S3 Standard that haven't been accessed in 30+ days?

- Do you have incomplete multipart uploads consuming GBs?

- Are old versions piling up in versioned buckets?

- Are logs or analytics reports stored indefinitely in Standard class?

- Is S3 Intelligent-Tiering set up *without* automatic archive transitions?

- Do lifecycle rules exist to delete or transition stale data?

- Have you reviewed S3 Storage Lens or Cost Explorer by prefix or tag?

How This Happens in the Real World

You're shipping fast, uploading backups, logs, images, and data pipelines into S3—because it's durable, scalable, and cost-effective. But months later, the bill spikes. What happened?

Common real-world oversights:

- A developer left a `logs/` prefix uncleaned for a data pipeline prototype

- Product screenshots were uploaded to `s3://web-assets-prod` but never deleted after product retirement

- A team used S3 Standard for archival documents due to a deadline, intending to "optimize later"

- A CI/CD job aborted during a multipart upload—repeatedly—leaving behind orphaned parts that still cost money

- A team enabled versioning to protect against overwrite... but never expired old versions

The result? A slow, silent accumulation of costs across buckets, prefixes, and storage classes.

Root Causes

Cause	Description
Stale Data in Standard Storage	Infrequently accessed data left in S3 Standard
No Lifecycle Rules	No automatic transition or expiration configured

Incomplete Multipart Uploads	Aborted or failed uploads leave orphaned storage
Versioning Bloat	Unexpired versions consume hidden space
Intelligent-Tiering Without Archiving	No automatic transition to Archive/Deep Archive tiers
Long-Term Log Retention	Logs (e.g., ALB, CloudTrail) stored indefinitely without pruning
Unused Backups or Snapshots	Backup processes dumping data to S3 but never cleaning it up
Forgotten Buckets or Prefixes	Orphaned projects with active buckets nobody monitors

Compliance & Financial Fallout

- **Wasted storage spend** – Hundreds or thousands in monthly charges from forgotten data

- **Cost overages** – Breaching budgets or tagging policies due to misallocated storage

- **Compliance violations** – Retaining data longer than policy or legal requirements

- **Slow security audits** – Larger-than-expected S3 footprints slow down analysis and reviews

- **Missed archive discounts** – Not using Glacier/Deep Archive when appropriate

How Developers Misread the Situation

- "S3 is cheap. We'll deal with optimization later."
  → It's cheap at scale *only if* you manage it.

- "We enabled Intelligent-Tiering, so we're fine."
  → Without infrequent access or archival transitions, you're still paying full price.

- "Versioning just helps us recover files. It's harmless."
  → Until you have 40 versions of 1GB files per object.

- "Lifecycle rules are too complex for now."
  → Ignoring them means manual cleanup—or no cleanup at all.

- "We use S3 for logs and backups, that's expected."
  → Retaining 12 months of ALB logs in Standard class? That's $10s–$100s/month.

Detection Steps (AWS CLI Preferred)

1. Check storage class distribution per bucket (via S3 Inventory + Athena):

Enable S3 Inventory (if not already set):

```
aws s3api put-bucket-inventory-
configuration \
  --bucket your-bucket-name \
  --id standard-inventory \
```

```
--inventory-configuration
file://inventory-config.json
```

Sample `inventory-config.json`:

```
{
  "Destination": {
    "S3BucketDestination": {
      "AccountId": "111122223333",
      "Bucket": "arn:aws:s3:::your-
inventory-bucket",
      "Format": "CSV"
    }
  },
  "IsEnabled": true,
  "Id": "standard-inventory",
  "IncludedObjectVersions": "All",
  "Schedule": { "Frequency": "Daily" },
  "OptionalFields": [ "StorageClass",
"LastModifiedDate", "Size" ]
}
```

Then analyze via **Athena** to detect:

- Standard storage used for >90 days

- Files larger than 100 MB not accessed recently

- Count of object versions per key

2. Detect incomplete multipart uploads

```
aws s3api list-multipart-uploads --bucket
your-bucket-name
```

Watch for UploadId entries with timestamps older than a few days.

3. Use AWS Cost Explorer (CLI) to check per bucket or prefix:

```
aws ce get-cost-and-usage \
  --time-period Start=2024-03-01,End=2024-
04-01 \
  --granularity MONTHLY \
  --metrics "UsageQuantity" "UnblendedCost"
\
  --group-by Type=DIMENSION,Key=SERVICE
```

Look specifically for Amazon Simple Storage Service costs.

4. S3 Storage Lens

Enable in the console or via:

```
aws s3control put-storage-lens-
configuration \
  --config-id org-lens \
  --account-id <account-id> \
  --storage-lens-configuration
file://lens.json
```

View daily object counts, bytes by storage class, and more in the console.

Diagram: S3 Cost Traps Flow

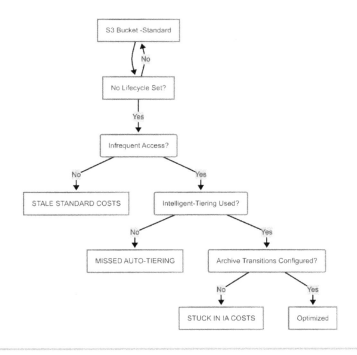

Fix Instructions

1. Set Lifecycle Rules to Transition or Delete

```
aws s3api put-bucket-lifecycle-
configuration \
  --bucket your-bucket-name \
  --lifecycle-configuration
file://lifecycle.json
```

Sample `lifecycle.json`:

```
{
  "Rules": [
    {
      "ID": "ArchiveOldData",
      "Prefix": "",
      "Status": "Enabled",
      "Transitions": [
        {
          "Days": 30,
          "StorageClass": "GLACIER"
        }
      ],
      "Expiration": {
        "Days": 365
      },
      "NoncurrentVersionExpiration": {
        "NoncurrentDays": 90
```

```
        }
      }
    ]
}
```

2. Configure automatic cleanup of incomplete uploads

```
aws s3api put-bucket-lifecycle-
configuration \
  --bucket your-bucket-name \
  --lifecycle-configuration file://abort-
multipart.json
```

Sample `abort-multipart.json`:

```
{
  "Rules": [
    {
      "ID": "AbortOldMultipartUploads",
      "Status": "Enabled",
      "AbortIncompleteMultipartUpload": {
        "DaysAfterInitiation": 7
      },
      "Filter": { "Prefix": "" }
    }
  ]
}
```

3. Use Intelligent-Tiering properly

Ensure transition to archive tiers is enabled:

```
aws s3api put-bucket-lifecycle-
configuration \
  --bucket your-bucket-name \
  --lifecycle-configuration
file://intelligent-tiering.json
```

What You Probably Missed

- **Storage class does not auto-adjust.** Standard storage keeps billing you even if nothing has accessed the data for a year.

- **Incomplete multipart uploads are not deleted automatically.** Unless you explicitly configure a lifecycle rule, they accumulate.

- **Versioning doesn't prune by default.** Each overwrite can create gigabytes of hidden cost.

- **Logs grow indefinitely.** ALB logs, CloudTrail logs, and data pipeline outputs will expand forever unless rotated and expired.

- **Tags can power cleanup automation.** Tag objects with `project=demo` or `env=dev` and expire them via lifecycle rules.

Chapter 3: CORS Carnage – Why Browsers Block Your S3 Assets and How to Fix It for Good

---

Quick Skim Checklist

- Are your CORS rules configured on the S3 **bucket**, not just your app?

- Is the request using `XMLHttpRequest`, `fetch()`, or an `img` tag across domains?

- Is your origin (`Origin` header) listed in the `AllowedOrigins` field?

- Does your method (`GET`, `PUT`, `POST`, etc.) match an allowed method?

- Are custom headers (like `Authorization`) listed under `AllowedHeaders`?

- Does your request trigger a **preflight OPTIONS** check that isn't allowed?

How This Happens in the Real World

You upload your JavaScript app, fonts, or media files to S3. It works fine locally. But in production, your browser screams:

```
Access to XMLHttpRequest at 'https://your-
s3-url' from origin
'https://yourdomain.com' has been blocked
by CORS policy...
```

Even worse, static websites hosted in S3 suddenly break on fetch requests, embedded images, or even third-party SDKs that expect CORS headers to behave a certain way.

Real-world scenarios include:

- React/Angular/Vue apps pulling API responses or assets from S3

- Fonts hosted on S3 for cross-site use

- Lambda frontends calling presigned S3 URLs

- SaaS apps using S3 via JavaScript but forgetting the preflight

In every case, the failure is silent in the backend—but explosive in the browser console.

Root Causes

Cause	Description
No CORS Config on Bucket	S3 returns no headers; browser blocks cross-origin request

Origin Mismatch	`Origin` header doesn't match any `AllowedOrigins` in the bucket
Method Not Allowed	HTTP method (`PUT`, `POST`, `DELETE`) not listed under `AllowedMethods`
Missing Preflight Support	Browser sends `OPTIONS` request, S3 returns 403 or no CORS headers
Header Not Allowed	Custom headers (e.g., `Authorization`, `x-api-key`) not whitelisted
Wildcard Headers with Auth	Using `"*"` in `AllowedHeaders` with `Authorization` is invalid
Wrong Resource	CORS config applied to wrong bucket or missing from origin bucket

Compliance & Financial Fallout

- **User experience breakage** – JavaScript apps silently fail or return opaque network errors

- **Increased support costs** – Frontend developers lose hours debugging browser-side issues

- **SDK malfunction** – Some AWS SDKs (especially JS-based) rely on proper CORS behavior for uploading/downloading objects

- **Lost functionality** – Presigned URLs, file uploads, and public access scenarios break without warning

- **Security confusion** – Misconfigured CORS can either overexpose or overrestrict access

36

How Developers Misread the Situation

- "It works with curl/Postman—so it's not a backend issue."
  → Browsers enforce CORS, not CLI tools.

- "We added * to everything."
  → Wildcards break when using credentials or custom headers.

- "S3 is public, so CORS shouldn't matter."
  → CORS is about cross-origin **JavaScript**, not public access.

- "We're allowing GET, that should be enough."
  → Did you allow OPTIONS too? The browser sends it before your actual request.

- "I put the policy on CloudFront."
  → If the origin is S3, that's where CORS has to be enabled.

Detection Steps (AWS CLI Preferred)

1. Check if the bucket has a CORS configuration:

```
aws s3api get-bucket-cors --bucket your-bucket-name
```

If the bucket has no configuration, you'll get:

```
An error occurred (NoSuchCORSConfiguration)
```

2. View the actual CORS policy (if present):

```
aws s3api get-bucket-cors --bucket your-bucket-name
```

Output example:

```
{
  "CORSRules": [
    {
      "AllowedOrigins":
["https://yourdomain.com"],
      "AllowedMethods": ["GET", "HEAD"],
      "AllowedHeaders": ["*"],
      "MaxAgeSeconds": 3000
    }
  ]
}
```

3. Use browser DevTools to inspect CORS error:

Look under the **Network** tab → click the failed request →
check the **Response headers** and **Console error** for
CORS blocks.

Diagram: CORS Behavior Flow (S3 Browser Access)

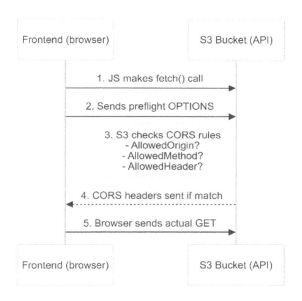

Fix Instructions

1. Set a proper CORS configuration for your bucket

```
aws s3api put-bucket-cors \
  --bucket your-bucket-name \
  --cors-configuration file://cors.json
```

Sample `cors.json`:

```json
{
  "CORSRules": [
    {
      "AllowedOrigins":
["https://yourdomain.com"],
      "AllowedMethods": ["GET", "HEAD",
"OPTIONS"],
      "AllowedHeaders": ["*"],
      "ExposeHeaders": ["ETag"],
      "MaxAgeSeconds": 3000
    }
  ]
}
```

Key Considerations:

- `OPTIONS` is **required** for preflight

- `AllowedHeaders` must list custom headers (not just `"*"`) if using credentials

- If using presigned URLs with `Authorization`, wildcard headers will fail

2. Test from the browser (not CLI)

40

```
fetch('https://your-
bucket.s3.amazonaws.com/some-object.jpg', {
  method: 'GET',
  headers: {
    'Content-Type': 'application/json'
  }
})
```

Inspect the **Network tab** in DevTools for returned headers:

```
Access-Control-Allow-Origin:
https://yourdomain.com
Access-Control-Allow-Methods: GET, OPTIONS
```

What You Probably Missed

- **S3 does not return CORS headers by default.**
  Every request without config will silently fail in the
  browser.

- **OPTIONS requests don't show up in normal
  logs.** If you're not watching preflight behavior, you'll
  miss it entirely.

- **Using `Authorization` or `x-amz-*` headers
  blocks** `*`. You must explicitly list these in
  `AllowedHeaders`.

- **CloudFront can strip or override CORS headers.** Always test with the origin directly.

- **MaxAgeSeconds can improve performance.** This reduces unnecessary OPTIONS preflight traffic.

Chapter 4: The Consistency Trap – Why Your S3 Object Isn't There (Yet) and How to Handle It Like a Pro

Quick Skim Checklist

- Are you uploading new objects and trying to read them immediately?

- Are deletes or overwrites followed by "phantom" GET results?

- Do you retry reads or deletes assuming eventual consistency?

- Are your systems assuming S3 returns 404 only when an object truly doesn't exist?

- Is your retry logic idempotent, backoff-aware, and context-specific?

- Are you using List operations and expecting the latest object version instantly?

How This Happens in the Real World

You upload an object to S3 via a Lambda, script, or application, then try to fetch it seconds later—and the GET request fails with a 404. Or you delete a file and another system still sees it. Even worse, a batch process lists objects and processes a file that should've been overwritten or removed.

This isn't a bug. It's a side effect of how **S3 consistency models** used to work—and still catch developers off-guard, especially in **cross-service orchestration** and **high-concurrency environments**.

Typical real-world issues:

- CI/CD pipelines uploading files then trying to validate presence immediately

- Applications uploading avatars or PDFs, redirecting users before object is visible

- Event-driven deletes not reflected when using `ListObjectsV2`

- Backup systems overwriting files that appear to not exist (but actually do)

Root Causes

Trigger	Description
Read-after-write gap	Delay between uploading and object being visible in subsequent GET
Read-after-delete delay	GET or HEAD can temporarily succeed after a delete
List inconsistency	`ListObjectsV2` may not reflect new or deleted objects immediately
Parallel writes	Simultaneous PUTs with the same key can cause confusion without versioning

| Misuse of 404 as final state | Assuming 404 = "object doesn't exist" rather than "object not visible yet" |
| No retry or jitter logic | Apps give up on the first failed read after write/delete |

Compliance & Financial Fallout

- **Data duplication** – Systems re-uploading data believed to be missing

- **False negatives** – Valid uploads failing validation due to timing

- **Overwrites of new data** – Mistaken assumption that object doesn't exist

- **User-facing bugs** – Broken downloads, missing thumbnails, failed previews

- **Lambda timeout costs** – Retrying fetches with no backoff results in wasted compute

- **Inconsistent reports** – Logs, backups, or exports with partial/inaccurate data

How Developers Misread the Situation

- "S3 is eventually consistent, right?"
  → As of 2020, **S3 offers strong consistency for all** operations—but only **under specific conditions**.

- "I uploaded the object, so GET should work immediately."
  → Not always. If using multipart uploads or cross-service writes (e.g., DataSync, S3 replication), delays can occur.

- "ListObjects will show what's there."
  → Not guaranteed. `List` is not strongly consistent—even today.

- "404 means it's gone."
  → It means it's **not available yet**—possibly still propagating.

- "Retrying blindly will fix it."
  → Only if your retries are exponential, limited, and don't cause race conditions.

Detection Steps (AWS CLI Preferred)

1. Test immediate read-after-write

```
aws s3api put-object --bucket my-bucket --key test-file.txt --body test.txt
aws s3api get-object --bucket my-bucket --key test-file.txt test-out.txt
```

If GET fails right after PUT, you're in a consistency gap.

2. Test read-after-delete

```
aws s3api delete-object --bucket my-bucket
--key test-file.txt
aws s3api get-object --bucket my-bucket --
key test-file.txt test-out.txt
```

Sometimes S3 still returns 200 for a brief window after delete.

3. Test list delay

```
aws s3api put-object --bucket my-bucket --
key test-listing.txt --body test.txt
aws s3api list-objects-v2 --bucket my-
bucket --prefix test-listing
```

The new key may not appear right away. Always use GetObject to confirm existence—not List.

Diagram: S3 Consistency Model – Modern vs. Legacy

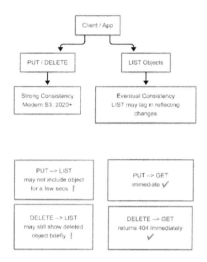

Explanation of the Diagram:

- **PUT, DELETE, and GET operations** now benefit from **strong read-after-write consistency**. This means that once a PUT or DELETE returns success, a subsequent GET or HEAD will immediately reflect the change.

- **LIST operations (like `ListObjectsV2`)** remain **eventually consistent**. You may **not** see a newly uploaded or deleted object reflected in the listing for a few seconds to minutes, especially in high-throughput environments or with large buckets.

Fix Instructions

1. Design with retry logic

Always implement exponential backoff with jitter when performing GETs after PUT or DELETE.

Sample pseudocode (Python-style):

```python
import time
import random
import boto3

s3 = boto3.client('s3')

def safe_get(bucket, key, retries=5):
    for attempt in range(retries):
        try:
            return s3.get_object(Bucket=bucket, Key=key)
        except s3.exceptions.NoSuchKey:
            wait = (2 ** attempt) + random.uniform(0, 0.5)
            time.sleep(wait)
    raise Exception("Object not available after retries")
```

2. Never trust List to verify existence

```
# Bad practice:
aws s3api list-objects-v2 --bucket my-bucket --prefix my-key
```

```
# Good practice:
aws s3api head-object --bucket my-bucket --
key my-key
```

3. Use Versioning for overwrite safety

```
aws s3api put-bucket-versioning \
  --bucket my-bucket \
  --versioning-configuration Status=Enabled
```

This avoids race conditions where objects are overwritten due to false assumptions about state.

4. For critical flows, use ETag confirmation

After upload, retrieve ETag and confirm it matches the expected hash of the object.

What You Probably Missed

- **List operations are still eventually consistent** even after S3's 2020 strong consistency improvements.

- **Cross-region replication can lag**, and the target region may show outdated data even with strong consistency at the source.

- **Multipart uploads are more prone to post-write inconsistency**, especially without finalization confirmation.

- **Lambda or Step Functions workflows** can trigger read-before-visible race conditions if not designed with delay/retry.

- **Batch delete events may result in read-after-delete anomalies**—triggering false alarms in cleanup jobs.

Chapter 5: Encryption Enforcement – Locking Down S3 with Bucket Policies and Service Control Policies

Quick Skim Checklist

- Are objects uploaded to S3 encrypted with SSE-S3 or SSE-KMS?

- Does your S3 bucket policy deny unencrypted PUT requests?

- Are you enforcing KMS key usage via condition keys?

- Is your organization using SCPs to prevent bypassing encryption via CLI or SDK?

- Are AWS SDK users or Lambda functions correctly configured to use SSE?

- Are you monitoring S3 for unencrypted objects using Config or S3 Inventory?

How This Happens in the Real World

Your dev team configures an S3 bucket for uploads. Encryption is recommended but not enforced. Some services, like AWS Lambda or scripts using the CLI, upload data without specifying encryption headers. The result? Sensitive objects land in S3 **unencrypted**, and no one notices—until an audit or breach.

Common real-world examples include:

- Mobile apps or web clients uploading files to presigned URLs with no enforced encryption

- Batch jobs using outdated SDK versions that omit SSE headers

- Cross-account uploads where the uploader doesn't honor the destination's KMS key

- Developers assuming default settings provide encryption (they often don't)

Root Causes

Trigger	Description
No bucket policy enforcement	S3 allows uploads without encryption headers by default
Missing SSE-S3 or SSE-KMS headers	Client doesn't include encryption in PUT or multipart upload requests
Presigned URLs	Uploads via presigned URLs bypass encryption unless specifically required
Incorrect KMS key usage	Clients use the wrong key, or no key, despite bucket expectations
SCP gaps	Organization-level policies don't prevent non-encrypted object PUTs
Lack of monitoring	No Config rules or S3 Inventory to detect encryption gaps

Compliance & Financial Fallout

- **Regulatory violations** – Failing encryption-at-rest requirements (HIPAA, PCI-DSS, GDPR, FedRAMP)

- **Audit failures** – Unencrypted files discovered in production buckets

- **Increased attack surface** – Plaintext S3 objects become a liability if access controls are compromised

- **Expensive remediations** – Mass object rewrites and key re-encryptions across thousands of files

- **Reputation loss** – Disclosing weak data storage practices erodes trust

How Developers Misread the Situation

- "We enabled default encryption on the bucket—so it's safe."
  → That doesn't **require** encryption. It only defaults it *if no header is sent*.

- "KMS is too complex; SSE-S3 is fine."
  → SSE-S3 is better than nothing, but many compliance frameworks demand KMS.

- "We use presigned URLs, they don't need extra config."
  → Presigned uploads can **bypass encryption** unless enforced at the bucket level.

- "It's encrypted once it's in the bucket."
  → If the PUT was accepted unencrypted, the object lands unencrypted—even with default encryption enabled.

- "We'll just scan later with S3 Inventory."
  → Good for detection, but not **prevention**. Prevention requires policy enforcement.

Detection Steps (AWS CLI Preferred)

1. Check bucket encryption settings:

```
aws s3api get-bucket-encryption --bucket
your-bucket-name
```

Expected output (SSE-KMS):

```
{
  "ServerSideEncryptionConfiguration": {
    "Rules": [
      {
```

```
"ApplyServerSideEncryptionByDefault": {
        "SSEAlgorithm": "aws:kms",
        "KMSMasterKeyID":
"arn:aws:kms:region:account-id:key/key-id"
        }
      }
    ]
  }
}
```

2. Audit existing objects for encryption status:

Using S3 Inventory with Athena or CLI:

```
aws s3api head-object --bucket your-bucket-
name --key your-object-key
```

Look for:

```
"ServerSideEncryption": "aws:kms"
```

3. Check if encryption enforcement exists in bucket policy:

```
aws s3api get-bucket-policy --bucket your-
bucket-name
```

Look for a Deny statement with this condition:

```
"Condition": {
  "StringNotEquals": {
    "s3:x-amz-server-side-encryption":
"aws:kms"
  }
}
```

Diagram: Encryption Enforcement Layers

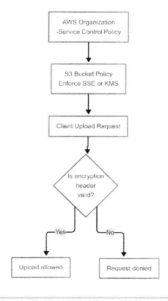

Fix Instructions

1. Enforce SSE-KMS or SSE-S3 in your bucket policy

Example bucket policy requiring KMS:

```
{
  "Version": "2012-10-17",
  "Statement": [
    {
      "Sid":
"DenyUnEncryptedObjectUploads",
      "Effect": "Deny",
      "Principal": "*",
      "Action": "s3:PutObject",
      "Resource": "arn:aws:s3:::your-
bucket-name/*",
      "Condition": {
        "StringNotEquals": {
          "s3:x-amz-server-side-
encryption": "aws:kms"
        }
      }
    }
  ]
}
```

For SSE-S3, change the value to `"AES256"`.

2. Add SCP to enforce encryption across your AWS Org

```json
{
  "Version": "2012-10-17",
  "Statement": [
    {
      "Sid": "DenyUnencryptedS3Uploads",
      "Effect": "Deny",
      "Action": "s3:PutObject",
      "Resource": "*",
      "Condition": {
        "StringNotEqualsIfExists": {
          "s3:x-amz-server-side-encryption": "aws:kms"
        }
      }
    }
  ]
}
```

3. Set default bucket encryption as fallback

```
aws s3api put-bucket-encryption \
  --bucket your-bucket-name \
  --server-side-encryption-configuration '{
    "Rules": [
      {

"ApplyServerSideEncryptionByDefault": {
        "SSEAlgorithm": "aws:kms",
```

```
        "KMSMasterKeyID": "your-kms-key-
arn"
          }
        }
      ]
    }'
```

What You Probably Missed

- **Default encryption does not enforce**
  encryption—it only applies when the request lacks
  an SSE header.

- **Multipart uploads** must include SSE headers on
  every part, not just initiation.

- **Presigned URLs require explicit configuration** to
  include encryption constraints.

- **Cross-account uploads can silently ignore your
  KMS key**, unless denied by policy.

- **Encryption enforcement doesn't retroactively
  apply**—scan existing objects with S3 Inventory or
  Config.

Chapter 6: The Silent Drop – Why S3 Event Notifications Fail and How to Troubleshoot Them

Quick Skim Checklist

- Is the event notification configuration attached to the correct bucket ARN?

- Are the event types (`s3:ObjectCreated:*`, `s3:ObjectRemoved:*`) defined correctly?

- Is the destination (Lambda, SNS, SQS) policy allowing S3 to invoke it?

- Are IAM roles and trust relationships correctly configured?

- Is object versioning affecting event delivery?

- Are there CloudWatch Logs or metrics from the destination (Lambda, SQS, SNS)?

- Are filtering rules (prefix/suffix) too restrictive?

- Did you check for overlapping event configurations?

How This Happens in the Real World

An application uploads a file to S3 expecting it to trigger downstream processing via Lambda or SQS—but nothing happens. No logs. No errors. Just silence.

This is a common trap in event-driven architectures using S3. Developers configure the event notifications but overlook permissions, filter rules, or even the differences between **PUT vs. multipart upload completion**, causing key processing pipelines to silently break.

Common scenarios include:

- Lambda isn't invoked after `PutObject`

- SNS topic is never triggered for large file uploads

- SQS queue remains empty even though objects are added

- Notification works in dev but fails in staging due to different prefixes

---

Root Causes

Trigger	Description
Destination policy blocking S3	The SNS topic, Lambda function, or SQS queue doesn't allow S3 as a sender
Misconfigured event types	Using unsupported or incorrectly formatted event types
Prefix/suffix filter too strict	Filter rules don't match actual object keys
Missing object write completion	Event fires only after the full upload completes (not on multipart initiation)

Permissions issue on S3 side	Bucket has no permission to invoke destination
Overlapping or duplicate configs	Multiple overlapping notification rules can cause non-deterministic behavior
Versioning interactions	Some events behave differently if versioning is enabled
Region mismatches	Destination and bucket are in different regions or wrong ARNs are used

Compliance & Financial Fallout

- **Missed processing** – Files uploaded but not parsed, converted, or scanned

- **Business downtime** – No data flowing to consumers due to broken automation

- **Data loss** – Systems depending on real-time triggers fail silently

- **Increased support/debugging time** – Developers chase ghosts across systems

- **Delayed compliance checks** – Logs, reports, or audits that rely on timely events fail to generate

How Developers Misread the Situation

- "I added the notification, so it should just work."
  → S3 doesn't validate destination IAM policies

during config—it silently drops if it can't deliver.

- "The Lambda is fine—it works when I test it manually."
  → S3 must have permission to invoke it, and filtering rules must match exactly.

- "We added a prefix filter to narrow events."
  → You narrowed it too much, and no object matches it anymore.

- "I see the PUT success in S3 logs—so the event must've fired."
  → Not necessarily. The event fires **after full object creation**, not just initiation.

- "We use `s3:ObjectCreated:*` so we're covered."
  → Not if the object was uploaded with a process that doesn't trigger that event type (e.g., CopyObject or multipart upload without proper completion).

Detection Steps (AWS CLI Preferred)

1. Inspect the bucket notification configuration

```
aws s3api get-bucket-notification-
configuration --bucket your-bucket-name
```

Expected output:

```json
{
  "LambdaFunctionConfigurations": [
    {
      "LambdaFunctionArn":
"arn:aws:lambda:us-east-
1:123456789012:function:ProcessImage",
      "Events": ["s3:ObjectCreated:*"],
      "Filter": {
        "Key": {
          "FilterRules": [
            {
              "Name": "prefix",
              "Value": "uploads/"
            }
          ]
        }
      }
    }
  ]
}
```

2. Check if the Lambda has a resource-based policy allowing S3

```
aws lambda get-policy --function-name
ProcessImage
```

Look for a statement like:

```
{
  "Sid": "s3-invoke",
  "Effect": "Allow",
  "Principal": {
    "Service": "s3.amazonaws.com"
  },
  "Action": "lambda:InvokeFunction",
  "Resource":
"arn:aws:lambda:region:account-
id:function:ProcessImage",
  "Condition": {
    "ArnLike": {
      "AWS:SourceArn": "arn:aws:s3:::your-
bucket-name"
    }
  }
}
```

3. Check CloudWatch Logs for the Lambda (if attached)

```
aws logs describe-log-groups | grep
ProcessImage
aws logs get-log-events --log-group-name
/aws/lambda/ProcessImage --log-stream-name
<latest-stream>
```

66

If no logs are present, the Lambda was never invoked—
meaning the S3 event didn't fire or wasn't delivered.

4. Test upload path and event filter match

Upload a test file matching the prefix and suffix:

```
aws s3 cp test.jpg s3://your-bucket-
name/uploads/test.jpg
```

Ensure it matches the `prefix` and `suffix` filters exactly.

Diagram: S3 Event Notification Delivery Flow

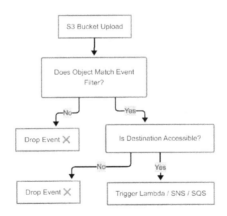

Fix Instructions

1. Add permission to Lambda to allow S3 to invoke

```
aws lambda add-permission \
  --function-name ProcessImage \
  --principal s3.amazonaws.com \
  --statement-id s3invoke \
  --action "lambda:InvokeFunction" \
  --source-arn arn:aws:s3:::your-bucket-
name
```

2. Apply a notification configuration to the bucket

```
aws s3api put-bucket-notification-
configuration \
  --bucket your-bucket-name \
  --notification-configuration
file://notification.json
```

Sample notification.json:

```
{
  "LambdaFunctionConfigurations": [
    {
      "LambdaFunctionArn":
"arn:aws:lambda:us-east-
1:123456789012:function:ProcessImage",
      "Events": ["s3:ObjectCreated:*"],
      "Filter": {
        "Key": {
```

```
      "FilterRules": [
        { "Name": "prefix", "Value":
"uploads/" }
      ]
    }
  }
}
]
}
```

3. For SNS or SQS, add topic/queue policy to allow S3

SNS topic policy example:

```
{
  "Version": "2012-10-17",
  "Statement": [
    {
      "Sid": "AllowS3Publish",
      "Effect": "Allow",
      "Principal": { "Service":
"s3.amazonaws.com" },
      "Action": "SNS:Publish",
      "Resource":
"arn:aws:sns:region:account-id:your-topic",
      "Condition": {
        "ArnLike": { "AWS:SourceArn":
"arn:aws:s3:::your-bucket-name" }
      }
```

```
      }
   ]
}
```

What You Probably Missed

- **S3 silently drops undeliverable events**—you won't see errors in the S3 console or logs.

- **Filters are case-sensitive and exact**—a prefix of `"uploads/"` won't match `"Uploads/"`.

- **You can't mix Lambda and EventBridge on the same bucket**—they're separate configurations.

- **Multipart uploads** only trigger events after a `CompleteMultipartUpload` call.

- **Event order is not guaranteed**—especially important if you rely on exact sequencing.

Chapter 7: Uploads Under Siege – Securing S3 from Malicious Files and Payload Abuses

Quick Skim Checklist

- Are presigned URLs restricted by file size and content-type?

- Is there a validation layer (Lambda, API Gateway, WAF) before S3 upload access?

- Do you scan uploaded files for malware or executables?

- Are S3 object uploads blocked for disallowed MIME types or extensions?

- Are client-side validations enforced via upload forms?

- Is lifecycle configuration in place to clean up unvalidated or unscanned files?

- Are CloudTrail and access logs enabled to audit upload behavior?

How This Happens in the Real World

You allow users to upload images, documents, or media through your application. To make things fast, you use presigned URLs so users can upload directly to S3. Then one day:

- Someone uploads a `.php` script into a public bucket.

- An oversized `.zip` upload silently bloats your storage bill.

- A malicious file passes through and ends up processed or downloaded by another user.

- Virus scanners are overwhelmed with 2GB video files where only PNGs were expected.

Presigned URLs are powerful—but without validation or constraints, they're a wide-open upload surface for abuse.

Root Causes

Trigger	Description
No file type validation	Users can upload `.exe`, `.php`, `.zip`, or binary files
Missing size constraints	Presigned URLs allow uploads of any size unless restricted explicitly
No virus/malware scanning	Files are not scanned before being used or distributed
Presigned URL misuse	URL reused to upload different file than intended
Public upload buckets	Combined with open PUT access, this enables total abuse
No extension/MIME type filtering	S3 doesn't validate file types unless configured externally

No cleanup process	Abandoned or unvalidated files linger indefinitely

Compliance & Financial Fallout

- **Malware injection risk** – Unscanned payloads exposed to internal systems or customers

- **Data exfiltration vectors** – Attackers upload and retrieve via compromised URLs

- **Storage cost spikes** – Oversized file uploads left unmonitored

- **Audit failure** – Lack of antivirus scanning or input validation control

- **Account abuse** – Attackers flood S3 with junk via leaked presigned URLs

- **Brand damage** – Users download malicious files from your domain

How Developers Misread the Situation

- "Presigned URLs are secure because they expire."
  → Expiration doesn't prevent malicious content within the valid window.

- "We trust users to upload only certain file types."
  → That's a policy, not an enforcement.

- "We'll validate after upload."
  → Damage may already be done (e.g., file auto-triggered downstream).

- "S3 won't serve it unless we link to it."
  → If public or indirectly accessed, it's still reachable.

- "It's HTTPS, so it's safe."
  → Transport security ≠ upload integrity or payload trustworthiness.

Detection Steps (AWS CLI Preferred)

1. Review presigned URL constraints

Presigned URLs must include conditions for file size, type, etc. Example generation snippet:

```
import boto3
import datetime

s3 = boto3.client('s3')

presigned_post =
s3.generate_presigned_post(
    Bucket='my-bucket',
```

```
    Key='uploads/${filename}',
    Fields={
        "acl": "private",
        "Content-Type": "image/png"
    },
    Conditions=[
        ["content-length-range", 0,
1048576],  # 1 MB
        {"Content-Type": "image/png"}
    ],
    ExpiresIn=300
)

print(presigned_post)
```

2. Check uploaded object content type

```
aws s3api head-object --bucket my-bucket --
key uploads/badfile.exe
```

Look for suspicious ContentType like:

```
"ContentType": "application/x-msdownload"
```

3. List large files over expected size

```
aws s3api list-objects-v2 \
```

```
--bucket my-bucket \
--query "Contents[?Size >
`5242880`].[Key, Size]"
```

Diagram: Validated Upload Flow (Presigned URL + Lambda Scanner)

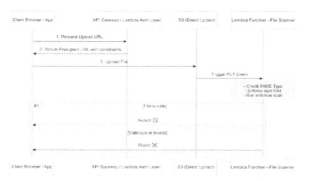

Fix Instructions

1. Generate presigned URLs with strict constraints

Ensure you restrict:

- File size (`content-length-range`)

- Content-Type (`image/png`, etc.)

- Prefix or object key patterns

- Expiry (use short durations: 5–15 mins max)

2. Add a Lambda trigger to scan uploads

Attach to the S3 bucket:

```
aws s3api put-bucket-notification-
configuration \
  --bucket your-bucket \
  --notification-configuration
file://notification.json
```

Example notification.json:

```
{
  "LambdaFunctionConfigurations": [
    {
      "LambdaFunctionArn":
"arn:aws:lambda:region:acct:function:ScanUp
load",
      "Events": ["s3:ObjectCreated:*"],
      "Filter": {
        "Key": {
          "FilterRules": [
            { "Name": "prefix", "Value":
"uploads/" }
          ]
        }
```

```
      }
    }
  ]
}
```

3. Use Amazon Macie, GuardDuty, or open-source AV

Use Macie for sensitive content detection or integrate ClamAV with Lambda containers for malware scanning.

4. Block disallowed content-types or extensions in Lambda

Example (Node.js):

```
if (!["image/png",
"image/jpeg"].includes(object.ContentType))
{
  throw new Error("Disallowed content
type");
}
```

5. Apply S3 Lifecycle Rules to auto-delete unverified files

```
{
  "Rules": [
    {
      "ID": "DeleteUnverifiedAfter1Day",
```

```
      "Prefix": "uploads/",
      "Status": "Enabled",
      "Expiration": {
        "Days": 1
      }
    }
  ]
}
```

What You Probably Missed

- **Presigned URLs don't validate file content—
  only metadata.** If the client lies about the content-
  type, S3 won't stop it.

- **Multipart uploads bypass some constraints** if
  not verified at each step.

- **Reused URLs = massive security hole.** Always
  generate per-upload and scope tightly.

- **No built-in malware scanning.** S3 never inspects
  the payload—you must do it.

- **Temporary files pile up.** Without lifecycle rules,
  unvalidated uploads can live forever.

Chapter 8: The Lifecycle Black Hole – Why Your S3 Rules Aren't Transitioning or Deleting Objects

---

Quick Skim Checklist

- Are lifecycle rules applied to the correct prefix or object tag?

- Is object versioning enabled, and are noncurrent version rules configured?

- Are transitions aligned with the object's current storage class?

- Are the specified days (Days or NoncurrentDays) sufficient for object age?

- Did you double-check for conflicting or overlapping rules?

- Are the rules in Enabled status and properly structured?

- Have you waited at least 24 hours for the rule to apply (S3 applies lifecycle once daily)?

How This Happens in the Real World

You configure lifecycle rules to move older files to Glacier or Deep Archive, or to delete files after 90 days. Then you wait.

And wait.

But files remain in S3 Standard, nothing transitions, and storage bills grow. Or worse—files that should've expired stick around for years, bloating your compliance exposure.

This is a frustrating—and common—problem, especially in environments using prefixes, versioning, multipart uploads, or tag-based rules.

Root Causes

Trigger	Description
Prefix or tag mismatch	Rule doesn't match actual object path or tag filter
Object age too young	Transition or deletion set to occur after N days, but object isn't old enough
Versioning enabled without NC rules	Noncurrent versions aren't affected unless explicitly defined
Overlapping or conflicting rules	Multiple rules may cancel or override each other
Invalid or incomplete rule format	Misconfigured JSON structure silently prevents application
Missing rule status	Rule is defined but `Status` is not `"Enabled"`
Transition to invalid storage class	Invalid class transitions (e.g., Glacier Deep Archive from Standard-IA)

AWS lifecycle timer delay	Lifecycle transitions run daily, not instantly

Compliance & Financial Fallout

- **Unmanaged data retention** – Files stay indefinitely, violating retention policies

- **Regulatory exposure** – Failure to meet data lifecycle or deletion requirements (e.g., GDPR, HIPAA)

- **Storage cost inflation** – Objects remain in expensive classes like Standard instead of Glacier

- **S3 bill surprises** – You expect transitions and deletions, but nothing happens

- **Failed internal audits** – Data lifecycle documentation doesn't match implementation

How Developers Misread the Situation

- "I set a rule to delete after 30 days—why is the file still here?"
  → S3 only runs lifecycle once per day. Also, was the object uploaded 30 *calendar* days ago?

- "The rule looks correct in the console."
  → Check if it's `"Enabled"` and if the filters match

your object prefixes or tags.

- "It's been a week, and no transitions to Glacier."
  → Lifecycle transitions don't apply to objects under the age threshold—even by one second.

- "We turned on versioning, so it should still delete."
  → Only current versions are affected unless you also define noncurrent version rules.

- "All our logs go to `/logs/`, so our prefix rule covers it."
  → If logs go to `logs/yyyy/mm/dd/`, your prefix might be mismatched.

Detection Steps (AWS CLI preferred)

1. Inspect current lifecycle rules

```
aws s3api get-bucket-lifecycle-
configuration --bucket your-bucket-name
```

Example output:

```
{
  "Rules": [
    {
      "ID": "TransitionToGlacier",
```

```
      "Prefix": "archive/",
      "Status": "Enabled",
      "Transitions": [
        {
          "Days": 30,
          "StorageClass": "GLACIER"
        }
      ]
    }
  ]
}
```

2. Check object prefix and age

```
aws s3api list-objects-v2 --bucket your-
bucket-name --prefix archive/
```

Look at the LastModified timestamps—are the objects older than the threshold (e.g., 30 days)?

3. Check if versioning is enabled

```
aws s3api get-bucket-versioning --bucket
your-bucket-name
```

Expected:

```
{
  "Status": "Enabled"
}
```

If versioning is enabled, check if your lifecycle rules handle **noncurrent** versions:

```
"NoncurrentVersionExpiration": {
  "NoncurrentDays": 60
}
```

4. Verify storage class for transition eligibility

```
aws s3api head-object --bucket your-bucket-
name --key archive/data.json
```

Check the StorageClass field—some transitions (e.g., from Standard-IA to Deep Archive) require explicit paths.

Diagram: S3 Lifecycle Rule Evaluation Flow

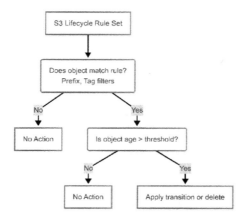

Fix Instructions

1. Create a working transition rule

```
aws s3api put-bucket-lifecycle-
configuration \
  --bucket your-bucket-name \
  --lifecycle-configuration
file://lifecycle.json
```

Example lifecycle.json:

```
{
  "Rules": [
    {
      "ID": "TransitionLogs",
      "Prefix": "logs/",
```

```
    "Status": "Enabled",
    "Transitions": [
      {
        "Days": 30,
        "StorageClass": "GLACIER"
      }
    ],
    "Expiration": {
      "Days": 365
    }
  }
 ]
}
```

2. Add noncurrent version rules (if versioning is on)

```
"NoncurrentVersionTransitions": [
  {
    "NoncurrentDays": 60,
    "StorageClass": "DEEP_ARCHIVE"
  }
],
"NoncurrentVersionExpiration": {
  "NoncurrentDays": 180
}
```

3. Add tag-based filters (if using tags)

```
"Filter": {
  "Tag": {
    "Key": "archive",
    "Value": "true"
  }
}
```

Make sure the object has this tag:

```
aws s3api put-object-tagging \
  --bucket your-bucket-name \
  --key your-key \
  --tagging
'TagSet=[{Key=archive,Value=true}]'
```

What You Probably Missed

- **Transitions aren't instant.** S3 lifecycle policies run once every 24 hours.

- **Prefix filters are case-sensitive and exact.** A typo or mismatch breaks the rule.

- **Rules must explicitly include noncurrent version actions**—they're ignored otherwise.

- **Tag-based rules require exact tag-value match.** No partial or wildcard matches.

- **S3 doesn't alert you about misapplied lifecycle rules.** Silent failure is the default.

Chapter 9: Watching the Watchers – Detecting Data Exfiltration and Suspicious IPs with S3 Access Logs

Quick Skim Checklist

- Are S3 access logs enabled and targeting a secure, dedicated bucket?

- Do you collect logs across all high-risk or public-facing buckets?

- Are you analyzing access logs for high-volume downloads or unknown IPs?

- Are object access patterns from unexpected regions or times being flagged?

- Do you correlate logs with CloudTrail for identity and action context?

- Are logs ingested into Athena, GuardDuty, or SIEM tools for active monitoring?

How This Happens in the Real World

S3 is the data hub of AWS workloads—but it's also a tempting target for internal misuse and external exfiltration. Maybe a dev accidentally makes a bucket public. Or a stolen IAM key is used to download 100GB of logs at 3 a.m. from a foreign IP.

Access logging is the last line of forensic defense. But most teams don't use it until after an incident. Worse, when enabled, logs are dumped into buckets no one queries.

Real-world scenarios include:

- Threat actors using presigned URLs to mass-download sensitive files

- Insider misuse—devs bulk downloading production exports before departure

- Public buckets being crawled by botnets or indexed by threat intel platforms

- Leaked access keys used from unfamiliar IP ranges or geographies

---

Root Causes

Trigger	Description
No access logging enabled	No historical record of object-level requests
Logs not analyzed or ingested	Logs are written but not reviewed, parsed, or alerted on
Open buckets	Public access leads to untracked downloads from anonymous IPs
Presigned URL misuse	URLs reused or leaked—difficult to trace to original requester

Lack of IP/geolocation monitoring	Unexpected IPs or regions aren't flagged in time
Overreliance on CloudTrail only	CloudTrail tracks API calls, but not **object access via signed URLs**

Compliance & Financial Fallout

- **Undetected breaches** – Data silently exfiltrated with no alerting

- **Non-compliance with regulations** – Lack of access tracking violates standards like HIPAA, PCI, SOC 2

- **Costly egress** – Large unauthorized downloads inflate network transfer costs

- **Incident response delays** – Lack of logs delays breach analysis and containment

- **Brand and trust damage** – Breaches discovered by third parties, not internal teams

How Developers Misread the Situation

- "We have CloudTrail—so we're logging everything."
  → CloudTrail logs API actions, not **actual object-level downloads** (e.g., via signed URLs or anonymous public GETs).

- "The bucket isn't public, so we're fine."
  → A leaked IAM key or presigned URL gives access without public bucket policies.

- "We'll check logs if there's ever an issue."
  → Without alerting or regular analysis, you won't know there *is* an issue.

- "S3 Access Logs are too noisy."
  → Only if you don't filter intelligently—Athena, CloudWatch Logs, or ELT tools help.

- "We can't afford the logging cost."
  → S3 logs are cheap (Standard-IA or Glacier eligible), and **not** logging is more expensive in a breach.

Detection Steps (AWS CLI preferred)

1. Enable access logging on your S3 bucket

First, create a **dedicated log bucket** (do **not** log to the same bucket you're monitoring):

```
aws s3api put-bucket-logging \
  --bucket your-data-bucket \
  --bucket-logging-status '{
    "LoggingEnabled": {
      "TargetBucket": "your-log-bucket",
      "TargetPrefix": "access-logs/"
```

```
        }
     }'
```

2. Confirm logs are being written

After some time (logs may take 1–2 hours to appear), list logs:

```
aws s3 ls s3://your-log-bucket/access-logs/
```

Look for files like:

```
2024-04-08-12-00-123456ABCDEF
```

3. Query logs using Athena

First, define a table with this DDL:

```
CREATE EXTERNAL TABLE s3_access_logs (
   bucket_owner STRING,
   bucket STRING,
   request_datetime STRING,
   remote_ip STRING,
   requester STRING,
   request_id STRING,
   operation STRING,
   key STRING,
   request_uri STRING,
```

```
  http_status INT,
  error_code STRING,
  bytes_sent BIGINT,
  object_size BIGINT,
  total_time INT,
  turn_around_time INT,
  referrer STRING,
  user_agent STRING,
  version_id STRING
)
ROW FORMAT SERDE
'org.apache.hadoop.hive.serde2.RegexSerDe'
WITH SERDEPROPERTIES (
  "input.regex" = "([^ ]*) ([^ ]*)
\\[([^\\]]*)\\] ([^ ]*) ([^ ]*) ([^ ]*) ([^
]*) ([^ ]*) ([^ ]*) ([^ ]*) ([^ ]*) ([^ ]*)
([^ ]*) ([^ ]*) \"([^\"]*)\" \"([^\"]*)\"
([^ ]*)"
)
LOCATION 's3://your-log-bucket/access-
logs/';
```

Then run queries like:

```
-- Identify most active IPs
SELECT remote_ip, COUNT(*) as request_count
FROM s3_access_logs
WHERE request_datetime > current_date -
interval '1' day
```

```
GROUP BY remote_ip
ORDER BY request_count DESC
LIMIT 10;


-- Look for large downloads
SELECT key, remote_ip, bytes_sent
FROM s3_access_logs
WHERE bytes_sent > 100000000
ORDER BY bytes_sent DESC
LIMIT 20;
```

Diagram: Access Logging Flow for Threat Detection

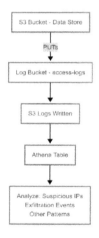

Fix Instructions

1. Enable logging on all critical buckets

- Centralize logs in a dedicated log bucket

- Use prefix filters to separate per-bucket logs (`"TargetPrefix"`: `"logs/bucketA/"`)

2. Tag high-risk objects for focused monitoring

Use object tags like `sensitivity=high` and track access to those keys in queries.

3. Set up Athena queries on a schedule (or use Amazon QuickSight)

Schedule saved queries to:

- Alert on foreign IP access

- Flag anonymous/public requests

- Highlight large or bursty downloads

4. Correlate S3 logs with CloudTrail and GuardDuty

Use CloudTrail for identity tracing and GuardDuty to detect anomalous download behaviors, e.g., unexpected geographies or credential misuse.

5. Automate response with Lambda or EventBridge

Set up EventBridge rules or Step Functions to:

- Notify security teams on access from known bad IPs

- Quarantine buckets or revoke IAM keys

- Block presigned URL access by invalidating permissions or setting restrictive conditions

---

What You Probably Missed

- **S3 Access Logs don't log presigned URL creation—only usage.** Use CloudTrail to monitor who *created* the URL.

- **Signed URLs used after expiration may still hit S3**—but will show 403s in logs.

- **Logs can get huge.** Use S3 Lifecycle policies to transition to Glacier after 30 days.

- **No logging on request failure types unless access reaches S3.** WAF or CloudFront blocks won't be logged here.

- **Logs are delayed.** Don't expect real-time feeds— use GuardDuty or VPC logs for faster detection.

- **No automatic anomaly detection.** You must build detection logic with Athena, Lambda, or a SIEM tool.

Chapter 10: Versioning Chaos – Mastering S3 Object Versions Without Losing Control

Quick Skim Checklist

- Is S3 versioning enabled for the bucket you're working with?

- Are lifecycle rules in place to expire noncurrent versions?

- Do your delete operations use version IDs (or unintentionally create delete markers)?

- Are replication and object lock policies aware of versioning?

- Have you accounted for the cost of storing all versions, including unreferenced ones?

- Are applications or users unintentionally duplicating objects by re-uploading with the same key?

How This Happens in the Real World

You enable versioning on an S3 bucket "just in case." It sounds like a great insurance policy: deleted or overwritten files are recoverable. But then a simple image file has 47 versions. Your storage bill spikes. Your backup scripts fail because they don't handle version IDs. And your delete scripts stop working—because instead of deleting objects, they just add **delete markers**.

This is versioning without discipline—and it's more common than you think.

Real-world examples include:

- Web or mobile apps re-uploading files every few minutes under the same key

- Teams mistakenly thinking a delete call will remove the file (it doesn't—it adds a delete marker)

- Backup or sync scripts that copy entire buckets without considering versioning behavior

- Lifecycle rules missing noncurrent version management

- Replication rules unexpectedly replicating deleted versions or old files

---

Root Causes

Trigger	Description
Versioning enabled without lifecycle	Old versions accumulate indefinitely, increasing cost
Misunderstanding delete markers	Delete removes "latest version visibility," not the object itself
Applications unaware of versioning	Uploads unintentionally create hundreds of versions

No `DeleteMarkers` handling	List operations show deleted objects unless delete markers are filtered
No version-aware backups/restores	Data recovery or sync logic fails to include versioned objects
Replication not scoped to versioning	Extra versions or delete markers get replicated unless explicitly filtered

Compliance & Financial Fallout

- **Storage bloat** – Multiple old versions of logs, documents, or large media files inflate costs

- **Data retention violations** – Without lifecycle rules, sensitive data remains in past versions

- **Broken recovery workflows** – Restore tools fail to recover the intended version

- **Compliance blind spots** – Old versions may still hold deprecated PII or secrets

- **Accidental deletions** – A delete marker makes a file invisible without actually removing it

How Developers Misread the Situation

- "I deleted the file—it's gone."
  → It's not. You just added a delete marker. All previous versions still exist.

- "We have versioning in case we need rollback."
  → Do you know which version to roll back to? Are you tracking version IDs?

- "We'll just sync the bucket to Glacier."
  → Without handling version IDs, you may miss entire versions—or archive redundant data.

- "Our lifecycle rule deletes after 90 days."
  → Does it delete **noncurrent versions**? If not, they stay forever.

- "Replication copies new files only."
  → Not true. S3 can replicate delete markers and older versions unless configured otherwise.

Detection Steps (AWS CLI preferred)

1. Check if versioning is enabled

```
aws s3api get-bucket-versioning --bucket
your-bucket-name
```

Expected result:

```
{
  "Status": "Enabled"
}
```

2. List versions of a specific object

```
aws s3api list-object-versions --bucket
your-bucket-name --prefix
path/to/object.jpg
```

Look for multiple VersionIds, including IsLatest: false entries and possible DeleteMarker: true.

3. List delete markers

```
aws s3api list-object-versions --bucket
your-bucket-name --prefix your-key \
  --query "DeleteMarkers"
```

4. Check object size growth from versions

```
aws s3api list-object-versions \
  --bucket your-bucket-name \
  --query "Versions[].Size"
```

Sum the results to understand storage impact of old versions.

Diagram: How S3 Versioning Works with Deletes and Lifecycle

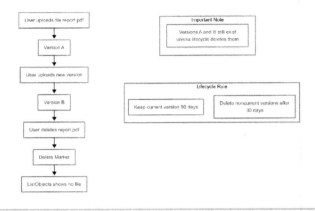

Fix Instructions

1. Enable versioning only when needed

```
aws s3api put-bucket-versioning \
  --bucket your-bucket-name \
  --versioning-configuration Status=Enabled
```

2. Add lifecycle rule for noncurrent version cleanup

```
{
  "Rules": [
    {
      "ID": "ExpireOldVersions",
      "Status": "Enabled",
      "Prefix": "",
      "NoncurrentVersionExpiration": {
        "NoncurrentDays": 30
```

```
        }
      }
    ]
}
```

Apply with:

```
aws s3api put-bucket-lifecycle-
configuration \
  --bucket your-bucket-name \
  --lifecycle-configuration
file://lifecycle.json
```

3. Delete specific object versions (not just latest)

To truly delete an object version:

```
aws s3api delete-object \
  --bucket your-bucket-name \
  --key report.pdf \
  --version-id "3HL4kqtJlcpXroDTDmUMLUo"
```

4. Remove delete markers when needed

```
aws s3api delete-object \
  --bucket your-bucket-name \
  --key report.pdf \
```

```
--version-id "<delete-marker-version-id>"
```

What You Probably Missed

- **ListObject calls ignore versions**—you must use `list-object-versions` to see everything.

- **DeleteMarker ≠ object deletion**—files may still consume storage and show up in metrics.

- **Storage metrics include all versions**—billing reflects every byte, not just latest.

- **Glacier and Deep Archive can't delete noncurrent versions easily**—you must lifecycle them before transition.

- **Object Lock + versioning can make deletes impossible**—be careful with governance modes.

Chapter 11: The Silent Split – Diagnosing S3 Replication Failures in Cross-Region Setups

Quick Skim Checklist

- Is versioning enabled on both the source and destination buckets?

- Are IAM permissions correct for the replication role?

- Are the replication rules in an `"Enabled"` state?

- Are object prefixes and tags matching the replication filters?

- Is replication time control (RTC) used, and are metrics configured?

- Are failures visible in CloudWatch metrics or S3 Inventory?

- Is KMS encryption preventing replication due to missing grants?

How This Happens in the Real World

You set up cross-region replication (CRR) to protect against region-level failure. The setup looks good in the console, so you upload files to the source bucket... and wait.

But days later, the destination bucket is still empty.

This is one of the most painful kinds of S3 failures— because there's **no error, no alert**, and no visible indication that replication has broken. Unless you're actively tracking replication status or reading logs, it fails completely silently.

Real-world scenarios include:

- Replication rules silently skipping encrypted files due to missing KMS grants

- Files excluded by prefix filters or tag-based rules without your knowledge

- Versioning disabled on destination bucket after initial setup

- Large objects (>5GB) being uploaded in ways that CRR doesn't support

- Buckets being manually renamed, reconfigured, or deleted mid-replication

Root Causes

Trigger	Description

Versioning not enabled on **both** buckets	CRR requires versioning to track object state
Missing IAM permissions	The replication role lacks `s3:GetObjectVersion` or `s3:ReplicateObject`
Encryption barriers (SSE-KMS)	Destination bucket lacks access to source KMS key
Rule status is `"Disabled"`	Replication rules exist but aren't active
Prefix or tag filters don't match	Replication rules exclude uploaded objects due to key mismatch
Destination deleted or changed	Rule points to a non-existent or misconfigured destination
Multipart uploads not finalized	CRR only replicates after complete upload
Object lock configuration issues	Governance mode or legal hold may block replication silently

Compliance & Financial Fallout

- **Backup gaps** – Files assumed to be protected are missing in the destination region

- **Business continuity risk** – Region failure renders data unrecoverable

- **Regulatory violations** – Multi-region replication required by compliance (e.g., ISO, FedRAMP)

- **Incident response delays** – Assumptions about data availability delay failover actions

- **Billing discrepancies** – You're paying for CRR but not getting the redundancy

---

How Developers Misread the Situation

- "The rule was created—replication is active."
  → Check that the rule is `"Enabled"`, and versioning is still on.

- "The file was uploaded, so it must be replicated."
  → Not if the rule filters don't match the object's prefix or tags.

- "The IAM role is correct—I copied it from a blog."
  → Missing `kms:Decrypt` on the source key? You won't see any replication error.

- "There were no errors in the upload."
  → S3 doesn't warn you about replication failures during upload.

- "I saw the replication metrics once."
  → Metrics won't show files *skipped* by rules—they just disappear.

Detection Steps (AWS CLI preferred)

1. Check versioning status on both buckets

```
aws s3api get-bucket-versioning --bucket
your-source-bucket
aws s3api get-bucket-versioning --bucket
your-destination-bucket
```

Expected result for both:

```
{
  "Status": "Enabled"
}
```

2. Retrieve the replication configuration

```
aws s3api get-bucket-replication --bucket
your-source-bucket
```

Look for:

- "Status": "Enabled"

- Matching Prefix and TagFilters

- Correct destination ARN

3. Confirm the replication IAM role exists and has necessary permissions

Policy should include:

```
{
  "Effect": "Allow",
  "Action": [
    "s3:GetReplicationConfiguration",
    "s3:ListBucket",
    "s3:GetObjectVersion",
    "s3:GetObjectVersionAcl",
    "s3:ReplicateObject",
    "s3:ReplicateDelete",
    "s3:ReplicateTags"
  ],
  "Resource": "*"
}
```

4. If using SSE-KMS, check KMS permissions

```
aws kms get-key-policy --key-id your-key-id
--policy-name default
```

Ensure the replication role is allowed to use kms:Decrypt (source) and kms:Encrypt (destination).

5. Search for replication metrics

Enable Replication Time Control and use CloudWatch to track delivery:

```
aws cloudwatch get-metric-data \
  --metric-data-queries file://replication-
metrics.json
```

Example query:

```
[
  {
    "Id": "repStatus",
    "MetricStat": {
      "Metric": {
        "Namespace": "AWS/S3",
        "MetricName":
"BytesPendingReplication",
        "Dimensions": [
          { "Name": "BucketName", "Value":
"your-source-bucket" },
          { "Name": "StorageType", "Value":
"AllStorageTypes" }
        ]
      },
      "Period": 300,
      "Stat": "Average"
    },
    "ReturnData": true
  }
]
```

Diagram: How Replication Can Fail Silently

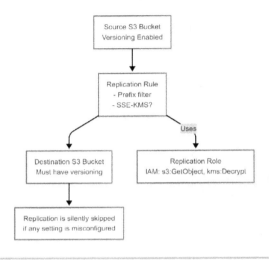

Fix Instructions

1. Enable versioning on both buckets

```
aws s3api put-bucket-versioning \
  --bucket your-source-bucket \
  --versioning-configuration Status=Enabled

aws s3api put-bucket-versioning \
  --bucket your-destination-bucket \
  --versioning-configuration Status=Enabled
```

2. Grant the replication role correct IAM permissions

Attach a policy like:

```
{
  "Version": "2012-10-17",
  "Statement": [
    {
      "Effect": "Allow",
      "Action": [
        "s3:GetObjectVersion",
        "s3:ReplicateObject",
        "s3:ReplicateDelete",
        "s3:ReplicateTags"
      ],
      "Resource": ["arn:aws:s3:::your-
source-bucket/*"]
    },
    {
      "Effect": "Allow",
      "Action": "s3:PutObject",
      "Resource": ["arn:aws:s3:::your-
destination-bucket/*"]
    }
  ]
}
```

3. Allow KMS access (if using SSE-KMS)

Update the KMS key policy to allow the replication role:

```
{
```

```
  "Sid": "AllowReplicationRole",
  "Effect": "Allow",
  "Principal": {
    "AWS": "arn:aws:iam::account-
id:role/replication-role"
  },
  "Action": [
    "kms:Decrypt",
    "kms:GenerateDataKey"
  ],
  "Resource": "*"
}
```

4. Test replication with known prefix and object

```
aws s3 cp testfile.txt s3://your-source-
bucket/replication-test/testfile.txt
```

Check for replication:

```
aws s3 ls s3://your-destination-
bucket/replication-test/
```

What You Probably Missed

- **Replication doesn't retry forever.** Failed objects
  are not automatically re-queued after a role or key

change—re-upload them.

- **Deleted objects can replicate delete markers** unless explicitly excluded.

- **S3 doesn't raise alerts on replication failures.** You must monitor CloudWatch or S3 Inventory.

- **Prefix filter matching is exact.** A missing trailing slash (`"prefix": "logs/"` vs `"prefix": "logs"`) can block replication.

- **Large objects must complete multipart upload before replication starts.**

Chapter 12: Legacy Permissions, Modern Risks – Auditing and Managing S3 ACLs the Right Way

Quick Skim Checklist

- Have you identified all buckets using ACLs instead of bucket policies?

- Have you checked for `AllUsers` or `AuthenticatedUsers` grants?

- Are object-level ACLs exposing data even if the bucket is private?

- Is the bucket configured with Object Ownership `BucketOwnerEnforced`?

- Have you run an audit using AWS CLI, Inventory reports, or Access Analyzer?

- Are ACLs still needed—or can they be disabled entirely?

How This Happens in the Real World

Before bucket policies became the standard, **Access Control Lists (ACLs)** were the go-to way to manage permissions in S3. Many organizations still have legacy buckets from years ago—some migrated, some created by third-party tools—that silently rely on ACLs.

The risk? These ACLs are often **invisible in your main IAM audits**, **easily misconfigured**, and can **grant public access at the object level**—even when a bucket's public access block is enabled.

Real-world situations include:

- Buckets created before 2015 still using `public-read` ACLs for assets

- Data migration tools adding object-level ACLs without permission boundaries

- Web apps where images or assets were manually uploaded with loose ACLs

- Buckets created by old CloudFormation stacks with default ACLs intact

---

Root Causes

Trigger	Description
Legacy bucket defaults	Buckets created before 2013 may have ACLs granting broad access
Object-level ACLs	Individual files have `public-read` or ACLs granting `AllUsers` access
Incomplete ownership enforcement	BucketObjectOwnership not set to `BucketOwnerEnforced`

Third-party tools using `put-object-acl`	Backup tools, CDNs, or apps applying unsafe ACLs
IAM blind spots	IAM roles may be restricted, but ACLs override with direct access
Lack of auditing/monitoring	ACLs aren't monitored unless specifically queried

Compliance & Financial Fallout

- **Public exposure** – Files available to the world despite bucket-level restrictions

- **Audit failures** – Unscanned ACLs lead to gaps in permissions reporting

- **IAM policy bypass** – ACLs can override expected identity-based access rules

- **Access confusion** – Devs struggle to debug "invisible" permissions

- **Reputation damage** – Security disclosures or GitHub issues revealing open assets

How Developers Misread the Situation

- "Block Public Access is on, so ACLs can't make things public."
  → Wrong. Block Public Access only blocks *new* public ACLs—not existing ones, unless fully

configured.

- "The bucket is private, so objects are secure."
  → Not if individual objects have their own ACLs granting public read or cross-account access.

- "ACLs and bucket policies do the same thing."
  → No—they're parallel systems. ACLs apply at the object level, often bypassing policies.

- "ACLs are outdated, so they must not be active anymore."
  → They remain fully supported unless explicitly disabled via Object Ownership.

- "We use IAM roles, so we don't need to worry about ACLs."
  → IAM doesn't control ACL-based access—ACLs are enforced separately.

Detection Steps (AWS CLI preferred)

1. List all buckets and check if Object Ownership is enforced

```
aws s3api list-buckets --query
"Buckets[].Name"
```

Then for each bucket:

```
aws s3api get-bucket-ownership-controls --
bucket your-bucket-name
```

Expected result to eliminate ACLs:

```
{
  "OwnershipControls": {
    "Rules": [
      {
        "ObjectOwnership":
"BucketOwnerEnforced"
      }
    ]
  }
}
```

2. Check bucket ACLs directly

```
aws s3api get-bucket-acl --bucket your-
bucket-name
```

Look for:

```
"Grantee": {
```

```
"URI":
"http://acs.amazonaws.com/groups/global/All
Users"
}
```

This means public read access is granted.

3. Check object-level ACLs (especially in legacy paths)

```
aws s3api get-object-acl --bucket your-
bucket-name --key path/to/object.jpg
```

Even if the bucket ACL is private, this command may show:

```
"Grantee": {
  "Type": "Group",
  "URI":
"http://acs.amazonaws.com/groups/global/All
Users"
}
```

4. Use AWS Config for ACL-based compliance

Enable managed rule:

```
s3-bucket-public-read-prohibited
```

This flags buckets with public ACLs.

Diagram: Where ACLs Interact with Access Logic

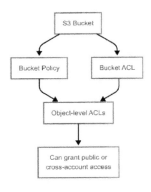

Fix Instructions

1. Set Object Ownership to `BucketOwnerEnforced`

This disables **all ACLs**, new and existing.

```
aws s3api put-bucket-ownership-controls \
  --bucket your-bucket-name \
  --ownership-controls '{
    "Rules": [
      { "ObjectOwnership":
"BucketOwnerEnforced" }
    ]
  }'
```

2. Clean up existing bucket and object ACLs

Make bucket private:

```
aws s3api put-bucket-acl --bucket your-
bucket-name --acl private
```

Clean up object ACLs:

```
aws s3api put-object-acl \
  --bucket your-bucket-name \
  --key path/to/object.jpg \
  --acl private
```

You can automate this with a script iterating through `list-objects` + `put-object-acl`.

3. Block new public ACLs at the bucket level

```
aws s3api put-bucket-public-access-block \
  --bucket your-bucket-name \
  --public-access-block-configuration '{
    "BlockPublicAcls": true,
    "IgnorePublicAcls": true,
    "BlockPublicPolicy": false,
    "RestrictPublicBuckets": false
  }'
```

4. Migrate to bucket policies and IAM roles

Replace ACLs with centralized policies:

```
{
  "Effect": "Allow",
  "Principal": { "AWS":
"arn:aws:iam::123456789012:role/AppAccess"
},
  "Action": "s3:GetObject",
  "Resource": "arn:aws:s3:::your-bucket-
name/*"
}
```

What You Probably Missed

- **ACLs are still active by default**—even on buckets created today.

- **Object Ownership is the only way to fully disable ACLs**.

- **IAM cannot restrict ACL-based access**—they operate on separate enforcement paths.

- **Public object ACLs bypass block public policy settings** unless you use `IgnorePublicAcls: true`.

- **Cross-account ACLs are invisible to IAM audits**—only object ACL inspection will show them.

Chapter 13: Latency Across the Map – Optimizing S3 Performance in Multi-Region Architectures

Quick Skim Checklist

- Are users accessing S3 buckets located far from their region?

- Are S3 buckets replicated or cached across multiple AWS regions?

- Do you use Amazon CloudFront to serve global access to S3-hosted content?

- Is latency-critical data stored in the region closest to compute or users?

- Are transfer acceleration or multi-region reads implemented where needed?

- Do your apps handle regional failover gracefully for S3 access?

- Are you monitoring S3 access latency with CloudWatch metrics or X-Ray?

How This Happens in the Real World

You deploy a multi-region app for resilience and global reach. Compute runs in us-west-2 (Oregon), but the app reads files from an S3 bucket in us-east-1 (N. Virginia). Or worse, a customer in Europe fetches images from your only bucket in the US.

Users report slow downloads. Upload APIs timeout. And edge services that rely on near-instant read access start misbehaving.

Why? Because **S3 latency across regions isn't predictable**, and relying on a single bucket for global workloads is a classic trap.

Root Causes

Trigger	Description
Centralized bucket design	Only one S3 bucket in a single region leads to cross-region latency
No caching layer	Public assets not fronted by CloudFront or CDN
No replication or read-local strategy	Apps in one region reading from a remote S3 bucket
Transfer acceleration not used	Uploads from distant geos take longer without acceleration
Data not geo-partitioned	Region-agnostic design leads to read inefficiencies
S3 used for transactional storage	S3's eventual consistency (for LIST) and latency don't suit all workloads

---

Compliance & Financial Fallout

- **Poor user experience** – Slow content delivery in non-primary regions

- **Time-sensitive job failures** – Analytics pipelines, Lambda calls, or API uploads timeout

- **Unexpected egress charges** – Cross-region data transfer is billed per GB

- **Disaster recovery failures** – Incomplete or stale data if replication is delayed

- **Customer dissatisfaction** – Downloads, previews, or file access fail silently for global users

---

How Developers Misread the Situation

- "S3 is globally available, right?"
  → No—**S3 is regionally isolated.** A bucket in `us-east-1` doesn't serve `ap-southeast-2` users with low latency.

- "It's just a few MB—how much latency could there be?"
  → Cross-region S3 access can add **100–300ms+** roundtrip latency, depending on network paths.

- "We'll just replicate everything."
  → CRR helps, but doesn't provide real-time **read-local** access unless architected carefully.

- "CloudFront is optional."
  → For global asset distribution, **CloudFront isn't optional—it's essential**.

- "Latency only affects images and videos."
  → Wrong. Many S3 workloads involve config files, ML models, or critical app state.

Detection Steps (AWS CLI preferred)

1. Check S3 bucket region

```
aws s3api get-bucket-location --bucket your-bucket-name
```

Output example:

```
{
  "LocationConstraint": "us-east-1"
}
```

2. Test cross-region access time

From a compute instance in a different region (e.g., eu-west-1):

```
time aws s3 cp s3://your-bucket-
name/somefile.dat /dev/null
```

Compare with download times from a local region.

3. Identify egress costs from S3 across regions

```
aws ce get-cost-and-usage \
  --time-period Start=2024-04-01,End=2024-
04-30 \
  --granularity DAILY \
  --metrics "UnblendedCost" \
  --filter '{"Dimensions": {"Key":
"USAGE_TYPE", "Values": ["DataTransfer-Out-
Bytes"]}}'
```

Diagram: S3 Latency Paths in Multi-Region Architecture

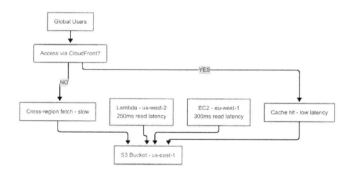

Fix Instructions

1. Use CloudFront in front of S3 for global reads

Set S3 bucket as origin and enable caching:

```
aws cloudfront create-distribution \
  --origin-domain-name your-bucket-
name.s3.amazonaws.com \
  --default-root-object index.html
```

2. Enable S3 Transfer Acceleration for uploads

```
aws s3api put-bucket-accelerate-
configuration \
  --bucket your-bucket-name \
  --accelerate-configuration Status=Enabled
```

Then upload using:

```
aws s3 cp file.jpg s3://your-bucket-name/ -
-endpoint-url https://your-bucket-name.s3-
accelerate.amazonaws.com
```

3. Set up Cross-Region Replication (CRR) for regional reads

Example: replicate from us-east-1 → eu-west-1

```
aws s3api put-bucket-replication \
  --bucket source-bucket \
  --replication-configuration
file://replication.json
```

replication.json:

```
{
  "Role":
"arn:aws:iam::123456789012:role/s3-
replication-role",
  "Rules": [
    {
      "ID": "eu-copy",
      "Status": "Enabled",
      "Destination": {
        "Bucket": "arn:aws:s3:::eu-bucket"
      },
      "DeleteMarkerReplication": {
"Status": "Disabled" },
      "Filter": { "Prefix": "" }
    }
  ]
}
```

4. Consider architecture patterns like

- **Geo-partitioned buckets**: Store EU user uploads in `eu-west-1`, US in `us-east-1`, etc.

- **S3 Multi-Region Access Points (MRAP)**: Use a single global access point (requires careful policy control)

What You Probably Missed

- **CloudFront caching requires explicit TTLs**—set `Cache-Control` headers on S3 objects to tune performance.

- **S3 Transfer Acceleration doesn't help with downloads**—only uploads.

- **Cross-region replication adds latency**—it's not synchronous.

- **Multi-Region Access Points help read routing, but don't reduce egress charges**.

- **Not all S3 regions support Transfer Acceleration or MRAP.** Check AWS Regional Services List (https://aws.amazon.com/about-aws/global-infrastructure/regional-product-services/).

Part 2: Navigating IAM and Permissions

Chapter 14: The Hidden Dangers of Over-Permissive IAM Policies

---

Quick Skim Checklist

- Do you see `Action: "*"`, `Resource: "*"` in your policies?

- Are IAM roles or users granted `AdministratorAccess` without justification?

- Did Access Analyzer generate findings showing unintended access?

- Are inline policies used heavily without peer review?

- Have you skipped reviewing CloudTrail activity before assigning permissions?

How This Happens in the Real World

In fast-paced environments, developers often get over-permissive just to "make it work." A team might grant `s3:*` when they only needed `s3:GetObject` for a Lambda function. Or, in a CI/CD pipeline, engineers might use `iam:PassRole` too broadly, accidentally enabling lateral privilege escalation. Without a systematic review of IAM policies, these temporary shortcuts turn into permanent risk factors—especially when copied across accounts.

A classic scenario: A developer writes a policy to allow a role access to DynamoDB but uses `dynamodb:*` because they're unsure which actions are required. This role ends up with permissions to delete tables and write access to all data, far beyond the read-only intention.

Root Causes

Root Cause	Description
Wildcard actions (`*`) or resources	Grants excessive power by default, rather than least privilege.
Reused policies across environments	Dev/test policies copied into production without reduction of scope.
Over-reliance on `AdministratorAccess`	Quick fix for access errors, but grants full AWS access.
Lack of policy versioning	No rollback or change tracking leads to permission creep.
No policy validation tools used	Policies are manually written and lack syntax/security checks.
Misuse of `iam:PassRole`	Allows unintended access escalation if not scoped with `Condition`.
Inline policies overused	Policies not centrally managed or reviewed.
Missing usage-based pruning	Permissions not refined using CloudTrail or last accessed data.

Compliance & Financial Fallout

- **PCI DSS Violation:** Broad access to data stores like S3 or RDS can violate data security standards.

- **SOC 2 & ISO 27001 Issues:** Excessive permissions contradict the principle of least privilege.

- **Cost Leakage:** Unauthorized users accessing expensive services like SageMaker or EC2 Spot Instances.

- **Security Incidents:** Attackers exploit IAM misconfigurations to escalate privileges or exfiltrate data.

- **Audit Failures:** Unused and undocumented policies raise red flags in compliance checks.

How Developers Misread the Situation

- "It's just temporary—I'll fix the policy later." (Later never comes.)

- "It needs full access to work." (It only needed 2 actions.)

- "That's an AWS-managed policy, so it must be secure." (Some are intentionally broad.)

- "I'm using a role, so it's safer than a user." (Only if the role's permissions are scoped correctly.)

- "If it breaks, I'll debug it by giving * access." (A major anti-pattern.)

Detection Steps (AWS CLI preferred)

To detect over-permissive policies using IAM Access Analyzer:

1. Create an analyzer (once per region/account):

```
aws accessanalyzer create-analyzer \
  --analyzer-name permission-checker \
  --type ACCOUNT
```

2. List current findings:

```
aws accessanalyzer list-findings \
  --analyzer-name permission-checker
```

3. Get detailed info about each finding:

```
aws accessanalyzer get-finding \
  --id [FINDING_ID]
```

4. Generate a policy based on actual CloudTrail usage:

```
aws accessanalyzer start-policy-generation
\
  --policy-generation-details
'{"principalArn":"arn:aws:iam::123456789012
:role/MyRole","cloudTrailDetails":{"accessR
ole":"arn:aws:iam::123456789012:role/CloudT
railAccessRole","startTime":"2024-03-
01T00:00:00Z","endTime":"2024-04-
01T00:00:00Z"}}'
```

This process generates least-privilege suggestions based on access history.

Diagram: How IAM Policies Lead to Over-Permission

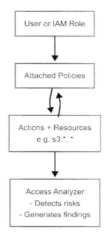

Fix Instructions

Step 1: Validate the problematic policies

```
aws accessanalyzer validate-policy \
  --policy-document file://bad-policy.json
\
  --policy-type IDENTITY_POLICY
```

Step 2: Review Access Analyzer findings and generate remediation plan

Step 3: Generate least-privilege policies

```
aws accessanalyzer get-generated-policy \
  --job-id [JOB_ID]
```

Step 4: Replace old policies Detach the old policy:

```
aws iam detach-role-policy \
  --role-name MyRole \
  --policy-arn
arn:aws:iam::123456789012:policy/OverPermis
sivePolicy
```

Attach the new policy:

```
aws iam put-role-policy \
  --role-name MyRole \
  --policy-name LeastPrivilege \
  --policy-document file://least-priv.json
```

Step 5: Archive resolved findings

```
aws accessanalyzer apply-archive-rule \
  --analyzer-name permission-checker \
  --rule-name resolved-perms
```

What You Probably Missed

- **IAM Access Analyzer runs regionally.** If you don't create an analyzer in each region, findings are incomplete.

- **Policy generation only works with recent CloudTrail data.** If CloudTrail logging was disabled, results may be empty.

- **Some AWS-managed policies are not least privilege.** For example, `AdministratorAccess` or `AmazonS3FullAccess` should be avoided for general use.

- **The `iam:PassRole` permission is a major escalation risk.** Always constrain it with conditions like `Resource` and `Condition`.

Chapter 15: The Root of All Risk — Why the AWS Root Account Should Be Locked Down

Quick Skim Checklist

- Do you see the root account used in CloudTrail logs?

- Is the root account the only one with billing access or admin privileges?

- Are there active access keys associated with the root user?

- Is MFA enabled on the root account?

- Are console sign-ins with the root account happening regularly?

How This Happens in the Real World

It starts innocently. An AWS account is set up using the founder's email. A team wants to deploy quickly, so they use the root credentials because it "has access to everything." Months go by, and that same root account is still used to make IAM changes, spin up EC2 instances, and even manage production billing.

In startups and even mature companies, engineers might save the root credentials in a password manager and treat it like a master key—logging in when "nothing else works."

This leads to zero visibility, no permission boundaries, and a high-value target for attackers.

The worst-case scenario? The root account is compromised and has no MFA. There's no support fallback, no granular permission control—just complete, irrevocable access.

Root Causes

Root Cause	Description
No delegation of permissions	Teams never created proper IAM roles or users with scoped permissions.
Root account email is shared	Root credentials distributed via email, shared vaults, or insecure storage.
No MFA enabled	Root access left vulnerable to password-based attacks or credential stuffing.
Used for automation	Scripts and pipelines use root credentials instead of IAM roles or users.
Single point of failure	Root user is the only account with billing or admin access.
Ignored AWS best practices	Teams unaware of or disregarding AWS guidance to restrict root usage.

Compliance & Financial Fallout

- **SOC 2 and ISO 27001 Non-Compliance:** Root access usage without justification or controls fails basic audit criteria.

- **PCI DSS Violations:** Lack of least privilege and root use for operational tasks breaches security mandates.

- **Compromised Root = Total Breach:** All services, data, and billing could be hijacked with zero ability to revoke access.

- **Support Lockout:** AWS Support actions (like account recovery) are limited without secure root control.

- **Billing Hijack:** Malicious use of the root account can result in massive, irreversible charges.

How Developers Misread the Situation

- "Only I have access to the root credentials, so it's fine."

- "We don't use the root account that often."

- "I need root to create users and roles."

- "It's too risky to change it—we might lose access."

- "We'll set up MFA later, after deployment."

Detection Steps (AWS CLI preferred)

1. List root user usage events in CloudTrail:

```
aws cloudtrail lookup-events \
  --lookup-attributes
AttributeKey=Username,AttributeValue=root
```

Expected Output: Events with Username: root indicate root activity that should not occur under normal operations.

2. Check for root account access keys:

```
aws iam get-account-summary
```

Look for these summary keys:

- AccountAccessKeysPresent

- AccountMFAEnabled

3. Verify MFA is enabled on the root account:

```
aws iam get-account-summary | grep
AccountMFAEnabled
```

Expected Output: Value of 1 means MFA is enabled.

4. Use AWS Config (if enabled) to detect root usage:
Check for compliance rule:

```
aws config describe-compliance-by-config-
rule \
  --config-rule-names "root-account-mfa-
enabled"
```

Diagram: The Risk Surface of a Root Account

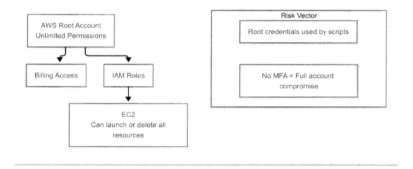

Fix Instructions

Step 1: Enable MFA on the root user (if not done):
Follow the AWS guide or:

```
aws iam create-virtual-mfa-device \
  --virtual-mfa-device-name RootMFA \
  --outfile QRCode.png \
  --bootstrap-method QR
```

Scan the QR code with an authenticator app, then:

```
aws iam enable-mfa-device \
  --user-name root \
  --serial-number arn:aws:iam::<account-
id>:mfa/root-account-mfa-device \
  --authentication-code1 123456 \
  --authentication-code2 654321
```

Step 2: Create a delegated IAM admin group:

```
aws iam create-group --group-name Admins
aws iam attach-group-policy \
  --group-name Admins \
  --policy-arn
arn:aws:iam::aws:policy/AdministratorAccess
```

Step 3: Create IAM users and add to admin group:

```
aws iam create-user --user-name devadmin
aws iam add-user-to-group --user-name
devadmin --group-name Admins
aws iam create-login-profile --user-name
devadmin --password 'TempPass123!'
```

Step 4: Remove access keys from the root user:

```
aws iam list-access-keys --user-name root
```

```
aws iam delete-access-key --user-name root
--access-key-id ABCDEFGHIJ1234567890
```

Step 5: Tag and monitor root use (set up CloudTrail alerts): Use EventBridge rule to detect root activity and trigger a notification or Lambda response.

What You Probably Missed

- **Billing Access Must Be Delegated Manually:** Use the AWS Billing console to assign billing permissions to IAM users.

- **No Service Control Policy (SCP) Can Restrict Root:** In AWS Organizations, the root user always has full control.

- **CloudTrail Can Miss Root Activity If Disabled:** If CloudTrail wasn't configured early, prior root use is invisible.

- **Password Recovery Tied to Root Email:** Make sure the root email is monitored and secured, preferably with a group address.

- **Root Cannot Be Deleted:** So minimizing its use is the only security option.

Chapter 16: The "Access Denied" Trap — When Policies Look Right but Still Fail

Quick Skim Checklist

- Did you check **both identity and resource-based policies**?

- Is the **resource ARN** exact, including wildcards and suffixes?

- Are you using `iam:PassRole` without a `Condition` or properly scoped resource?

- Is there a **permissions boundary**, SCP, or session policy in play?

- Did you assume a role and forget **session tags** or **context constraints**?

- Is the **resource in another region or account**?

How This Happens in the Real World

A developer deploys a Lambda function and gives it a policy with `s3:GetObject` access to a specific bucket. But every invocation fails with `AccessDenied`. They double-check the IAM role and policy — it looks perfect. Hours are wasted scanning JSON, assuming a bug in AWS.

In another case, a CloudFormation template works in dev but fails in prod. The IAM user can call `iam:CreateRole` in staging, but not in the production account, even with what seems like identical policies.

These aren't just rookie mistakes. Even experienced teams stumble when invisible constraints—like permission boundaries, SCPs, or cross-account mismatches—interfere with apparently correct policies.

Root Causes

Root Cause	Description
Resource ARN mismatch	Wildcards don't match specific resources, or resource names include suffixes (e.g., `/*` vs `/my-folder/*`).
Missing permissions in resource policies	For services like S3, Lambda, or KMS, the resource must *also* allow the action.
`iam:PassRole` not scoped correctly	Lacking `PassRole` permission for a role you're trying to use (e.g., with Lambda or ECS).
Permission boundaries	Permissions are further restricted by boundaries that override IAM policy grants.
Service Control Policies (SCPs)	In an AWS Organization, SCPs may silently deny actions, even if IAM allows them.
Session policies or conditions	Temporary credentials might be scoped with extra policies or session tags.
Region mismatch	Attempting actions in the wrong AWS region where resources or permissions differ.

| Trust relationship misconfigurations | Role assumption fails because the trust policy blocks the identity. |

Compliance & Financial Fallout

- **Blocked Deployments:** Lambda functions, EC2 roles, or ECS tasks fail silently, delaying releases.

- **Production Downtime:** Automation relying on role assumptions can break unexpectedly due to hidden constraints.

- **Costly Debugging Time:** Hours wasted on invisible permission constraints increases engineering costs.

- **Security Risks:** In frustration, developers may broaden policies dangerously to "fix" the error.

- **Audit Failures:** Misconfigured permissions can lead to unintended privilege escalation or access denial during incident response.

How Developers Misread the Situation

- "The IAM policy allows it—why doesn't it work?"

- "It works in staging, so it must be fine in production."

- "I checked the role trust policy; it's good."

- "The action is listed in the policy, so it should work."

- "The resource is mine—why would I need extra permission?"

Detection Steps (AWS CLI preferred)

1. Simulate the policy using IAM's `simulate-principal-policy`:

```
aws iam simulate-principal-policy \
  --policy-source-arn
arn:aws:iam::123456789012:role/MyLambdaRole
\
  --action-names s3:GetObject \
  --resource-arns arn:aws:s3:::my-
bucket/my-object.txt
```

Expected Output: `"decision": "allowed"` or `"decision": "explicitDeny"` (this will help you pinpoint if IAM policy is the issue).

2. Check if a permissions boundary is applied to the user/role:

```
aws iam get-role --role-name MyLambdaRole
```

Look for the `PermissionsBoundary` block in the output.

3. Check for SCPs at the organizational level:

```
aws organizations list-policies --filter
SERVICE_CONTROL_POLICY
```

Then check if any are attached to your account:

```
aws organizations list-policies-for-target
\
  --target-id <ACCOUNT_ID> \
  --filter SERVICE_CONTROL_POLICY
```

4. Validate resource-based policy (e.g., S3 or KMS):

```
aws s3api get-bucket-policy --bucket my-
bucket
```

Ensure the principal (user/role) is granted the required action.

5. Confirm trust policy for role assumption errors:

```
aws iam get-role --role-name
MyAssumableRole
```

Make sure the `Principal` block includes your identity
and the correct `sts:AssumeRole` action.

Diagram: Policy Layers That Can Deny Access

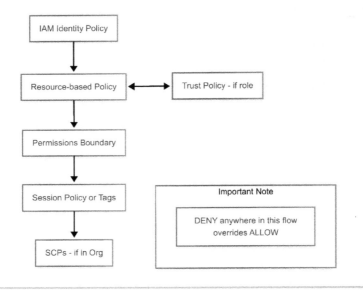

Fix Instructions

Step 1: Use simulation to find the actual denial point

```
aws iam simulate-principal-policy \
```

```
  --policy-source-arn
arn:aws:iam::123456789012:user/DevUser \
  --action-names dynamodb:PutItem \
  --resource-arns arn:aws:dynamodb:us-east-
1:123456789012:table/MyTable
```

Step 2: Validate the resource ARN and wildcards
Double-check formatting like:

```
arn:aws:s3:::my-bucket/my-folder/*
```

vs.

```
arn:aws:s3:::my-bucket/*
```

Step 3: Check and adjust resource policies Update your
bucket, key, or Lambda permissions:

```
aws s3api put-bucket-policy --bucket my-
bucket --policy file://policy.json
```

Step 4: Add missing `iam:PassRole` permissions If
invoking a Lambda or ECS task:

```
{
  "Effect": "Allow",
```

```
 "Action": "iam:PassRole",
 "Resource":
"arn:aws:iam::123456789012:role/MyExecution
Role"
}
```

Step 5: Remove or modify overly strict boundaries
Use:

```
aws iam delete-role-permissions-boundary \
  --role-name MyLambdaRole
```

Step 6: Fix the trust policy for role assumption

```
{
  "Effect": "Allow",
  "Principal": {
    "Service": "lambda.amazonaws.com"
  },
  "Action": "sts:AssumeRole"
}
```

What You Probably Missed

- **Session Tags May Be Required:** If access relies on a tag condition like `"aws:RequestTag/Project": "X"`, **assume-**

```
```

role needs to pass it.

- **Case Sensitivity in ARNs:** S3 bucket names and IAM resource names are case-sensitive in policies.

- **Missing KMS Decrypt:** For S3 downloads using SSE-KMS, `kms:Decrypt` permission is required even if `s3:GetObject` is granted.

- **Region-Specific Resources:** Some permissions may appear denied if the request is made in a region the resource doesn't exist in.

- **Cross-Account Access Needs Resource Policy:** Your role might have permissions, but the other account's resource doesn't trust it.

Chapter 17: The Art of Restraint — Writing Safe, Read-Only S3 Policies Without Wildcards

---

Quick Skim Checklist

- Are you using **specific bucket and object ARNs**, not `"*"`?

- Does your policy restrict access to `s3:Get*` **and** `s3:List*` actions only?

- Are **bucket-level and object-level permissions** both included?

- Have you tested the policy with a **simulated principal policy**?

- Is access limited by **conditions**, like IP range or VPC endpoint?

How This Happens in the Real World

You want to give a developer or application read-only access to a specific S3 bucket. You find an online example, plug it into the policy editor, and it works. But the policy looks like this:

```
{
```

```
  "Effect": "Allow",
  "Action": "s3:*",
  "Resource": "*"
}
```

It's a security nightmare. That user or role now has full read/write/delete access to *all* S3 buckets in the account— and maybe in other accounts if resource-based policies allow it. This kind of over-permissioned policy is how data breaches begin.

Security teams later scramble to audit access, or a compliance review flags the wildcard use. Fixing it retroactively becomes painful—especially when the bad pattern has already propagated to multiple environments or templates.

Root Causes

Root Cause	Description
Overuse of `"*"` in resources	Grants access to all buckets or objects, not just intended targets.
Using `s3:*` instead of scoped verbs	Includes write, delete, and ACL-related permissions.
Lack of understanding of ARN syntax	Many policies forget to separate bucket and object ARNs.
Copy-paste from generic examples	Blogs or forums often suggest unsafe wildcard templates.
Not accounting for separate permissions	`ListBucket` and `GetObject` require different ARNs.

Compliance & Financial Fallout

- **Failing Security Reviews:** Use of wildcards in S3 access triggers findings in audits or penetration tests.

- **Data Breaches:** Unintended access to sensitive or production data due to broad read permissions.

- **CloudTrail Noise:** Over-broad permissions result in larger event volumes, harder investigations.

- **Cross-Environment Risk:** Dev credentials might read production buckets if wildcards are used.

- **Legal Liability:** Leaked data due to improper IAM scoping may breach data privacy laws (GDPR, CCPA).

How Developers Misread the Situation

- "I thought `s3:*` just meant 'read-only' access."

- "The policy worked, so I assumed it was correct."

- "It's just a dev bucket, so no big deal."

- "I need `s3:ListAllMyBuckets` to see anything, right?"

- "Isn't `Resource: "*"` safe if I don't use `s3:PutObject`?"

Detection Steps (AWS CLI preferred)

1. Review attached policies for wildcard use:

```
aws iam list-attached-user-policies --user-
name ReadOnlyUser
```

2. Get the full policy details:

```
aws iam get-policy-version \
  --policy-arn
arn:aws:iam::123456789012:policy/ReadOnlyS3
Access \
  --version-id v1
```

Look for:

- `"Action": "s3:*"` or `"s3:Get*"` (bad)

- `"Resource": "*"` (bad)

- Missing `s3:ListBucket` (bad)

3. Simulate the policy to verify least-privilege:

```
aws iam simulate-principal-policy \
  --policy-source-arn
arn:aws:iam::123456789012:user/ReadOnlyUser
\
  --action-names s3:PutObject \
  --resource-arns
arn:aws:s3:::mybucket/myfile.txt
```

Expected Output: `"decision": "explicitDeny"`

Diagram: What a Proper Read-Only S3 Policy Covers

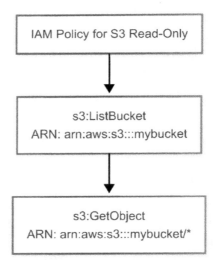

Fix Instructions

Step 1: Define exact ARNs for your target S3 bucket
Let's say your bucket is named `myapp-logs` and you want read-only access to its contents.

Step 2: Write the minimal, safe policy

```
{
  "Version": "2012-10-17",
  "Statement": [
    {
      "Sid":
"AllowListingOfSpecificBucket",
      "Effect": "Allow",
      "Action": [
        "s3:ListBucket"
      ],
      "Resource": "arn:aws:s3:::myapp-logs"
    },
    {
      "Sid":
"AllowReadOnlyAccessToObjects",
      "Effect": "Allow",
      "Action": [
        "s3:GetObject",
        "s3:GetObjectVersion",
        "s3:GetObjectAcl"
      ],
```

```
    "Resource": "arn:aws:s3:::myapp-
logs/*"
    }
  ]
}
```

Step 3: Attach the policy to a user or role

```
aws iam put-user-policy \
  --user-name ReadOnlyUser \
  --policy-name ReadOnlyS3Policy \
  --policy-document file://readonly-s3.json
```

Step 4: Validate with simulation

```
aws iam simulate-principal-policy \
  --policy-source-arn
arn:aws:iam::123456789012:user/ReadOnlyUser
\
  --action-names s3:GetObject \
  --resource-arns arn:aws:s3:::myapp-
logs/logs/app.log
```

Expected Output: `"decision": "allowed"`

What You Probably Missed

- `s3:ListBucket` **is separate from** `s3:GetObject` — and must reference the *bucket ARN*, not objects.

- **Omitting** `s3:GetObjectVersion` **may block versioned object access.**

- **Never use** `s3:*` **or** `Resource: "*"` **unless absolutely required and justified.**

- **KMS-encrypted buckets need** `kms:Decrypt` **permission on the key.**

- **Cross-account access needs bucket policy to allow the principal**, even if IAM allows it.

Chapter 18: Tracing the Shadow – How to Track Down the Role Assumption Behind a Breach

Quick Skim Checklist

- Did you enable **CloudTrail logging** across all regions?

- Are **assume role events** (`sts:AssumeRole`) visible in the logs?

- Have you extracted the **source identity or session name** from the event?

- Is **role session tagging** in use for better traceability?

- Are **CloudTrail insights or AWS Config** helping correlate activity?

How This Happens in the Real World

Imagine this: you detect unauthorized changes in your AWS environment—maybe S3 objects were accessed unexpectedly, or EC2 instances were terminated. You check IAM policies and see everything is locked down. Yet something or someone got through.

What happened? A role was assumed—maybe from a trusted third-party service, a CI/CD pipeline, or even another AWS account. Because the session name was generic (e.g., "Session"), you can't easily trace back who did it.

Security engineers are left digging through hundreds of CloudTrail events without clear evidence. Without proper tagging, naming, or guardrails, tracking down who assumed a role is like trying to find a single shadow in a pitch-black forest.

Root Causes

Root Cause	Description
Incomplete CloudTrail coverage	Logging wasn't enabled in all regions or for all management events.
Generic role session names	Developers or automation used nondescript names like `default` or `jenkins`.
No session tags	Roles were assumed without tagging for user or project identity.
Cross-account access poorly audited	External accounts assumed roles without a trail of who initiated it.
Lack of access boundaries	Roles were assumed and misused because `sts:AssumeRole` wasn't scoped or monitored.

Compliance & Financial Fallout

- **Security Incident Response Delays:** Tracing misuse may take hours or days without proper logs and identifiers.

- **Auditing Failures:** Compliance checks (e.g., for SOC 2, ISO 27001) may fail without proof of traceability.

- **Data Breaches:** If a role is misused and the identity behind it is unknown, impact assessment is impossible.

- **Excessive CloudTrail Costs:** A poorly scoped investigation across regions and accounts leads to bloated log processing bills.

- **Legal Exposure:** Without attribution, you may be unable to demonstrate due diligence in breach disclosure.

How Developers Misread the Situation

- "It's just a temporary session; why name it?"

- "Only our team can assume this role."

- "CloudTrail logs all this by default, right?"

- "We'll know who did it from the service or application."

- "The trust policy is restricted—we're good."

Detection Steps (AWS CLI preferred)

1. Search for `AssumeRole` events in CloudTrail

```
aws cloudtrail lookup-events \
  --lookup-attributes
AttributeKey=EventName,AttributeValue=Assum
eRole \
  --max-results 10
```

Look for entries with `eventSource:`
`sts.amazonaws.com` and note:

- `userIdentity.arn`

- `userIdentity.sessionContext.sessionIss`
  `uer.arn`

- `requestParameters.roleArn`

- `requestParameters.roleSessionName`

2. Use Event ID to dig deeper

```
aws cloudtrail get-event-selectors \
  --trail-name <your-trail-name>
```

Ensure management events are captured. Then:

```
aws cloudtrail lookup-events \
  --lookup-attributes
AttributeKey=EventId,AttributeValue=<event-
id>
```

3. Extract the source identity from the session

If the session used tags:

```
"userIdentity": {
  "type": "AssumedRole",
  "sessionContext": {
    "sessionIssuer": {
      "userName": "MyAppRole"
    },
    "attributes": {
      "mfaAuthenticated": "true",
      "creationDate": "2024-04-
01T12:00:00Z"
    },
    "tags": {
      "user": "jane.doe",
      "project": "billing-api"
    }
  }
}
```

4. Correlate with other suspicious activity

```
aws cloudtrail lookup-events \
  --lookup-attributes
AttributeKey=Username,AttributeValue=MyAppR
ole
```

Diagram: IAM Role Assumption and Traceability Layers

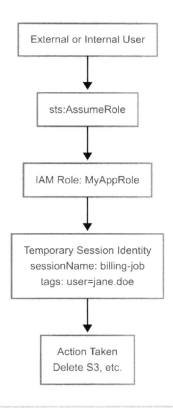

Fix Instructions

Step 1: Ensure CloudTrail is logging across all regions

```
aws cloudtrail update-trail \
  --name my-org-trail \
  --is-multi-region-trail
```

Step 2: Use structured session names for clarity

```
aws sts assume-role \
  --role-arn
arn:aws:iam::123456789012:role/MyAppRole \
  --role-session-name jane-daily-check
```

Step 3: Add session tags when assuming roles

```
aws sts assume-role \
  --role-arn
arn:aws:iam::123456789012:role/MyAppRole \
  --role-session-name ci-job-1243 \
  --tags Key=project,Value=api
Key=owner,Value=jane.doe
```

Step 4: Require `sts:TagSession` and enforce tags with conditions

Update the trust policy:

```
{
  "Effect": "Allow",
  "Principal": {
    "AWS":
"arn:aws:iam::111122223333:role/CICDRunner"
  },
  "Action": "sts:AssumeRole",
  "Condition": {
    "StringEquals": {
      "aws:RequestTag/owner": "jane.doe"
    },
    "StringLike": {
      "aws:TagKeys": ["owner", "project"]
    }
  }
}
```

Step 5: Analyze IAM role usage with Access Analyzer

```
aws accessanalyzer list-findings \
  --analyzer-name my-analyzer
```

Look for findings related to role trust policies, external access, or unintended sharing.

What You Probably Missed

- **Session names are optional but critical.** Without them, you'll only see generic "AssumedRole" identities.

- **Cross-account roles need stricter trust policies.** Even if your IAM is locked down, other accounts may not be.

- **Not all CloudTrail logs go to the same region.** Management events can span multiple regions, so use a multi-region trail.

- **Lack of `sts:TagSession` permission blocks session tags.** Grant this explicitly in calling identities.

- **Session tags can enforce business logic.** Combine with ABAC (Attribute-Based Access Control) for stronger security boundaries.

Chapter 19: Trust but Verify — Fixing Misconfigured Service-Linked Roles

Quick Skim Checklist

- Are **service-linked roles (SLRs)** missing or manually edited?

- Did a recent delete or policy change break a trusted service?

- Is a service like Lambda, ECS, or Auto Scaling **failing to assume its default role**?

- Do you see `AccessDenied` or `InvalidIdentityToken` in CloudTrail for a service action?

- Have you validated the **trust relationship and permissions** of your SLR?

How This Happens in the Real World

You deploy a new Auto Scaling group, and it fails to launch instances. Or, your ECS task definitions won't start. You check permissions and everything *looks* right. But buried in CloudTrail is a silent error: the service-linked role couldn't be assumed.

Sometimes the role is missing altogether—accidentally deleted in a cleanup script or cloudformation rollback. Other times, developers modify the trust policy to "fix" something, unknowingly breaking the relationship required by AWS.

Services like AWS Lambda, ECS, CloudWatch, and Auto Scaling depend on tightly scoped, preconfigured roles. When those are misconfigured, core infrastructure stops working—and the error messages are anything but clear.

Root Causes

Root Cause	Description
Role deleted manually	Developers or IaC tools delete default SLRs during cleanup.
Trust policy manually edited	Changing the `Principal` breaks the service's ability to assume the role.
Custom name used instead of default	Some services require specific role naming formats.
Not using supported AWS regions	The service and the SLR must both exist in a supported region.
Wrong or missing permissions in policies	Replacing attached AWS-managed policies causes the role to lose required permissions.

Compliance & Financial Fallout

- **Service Outage:** ECS tasks, ASGs, or Lambda functions may fail to launch or execute.

- **Incident Misdiagnosis:** Errors may appear unrelated, leading to wasted engineering hours.

- **Audit Failures:** Custom policies replacing SLRs may introduce broader-than-needed permissions.

- **Security Risks:** Replacing a tightly-scoped SLR with a manually created one can result in excessive permissions.

- **Resource Waste:** Failed service actions may still incur partial costs (e.g., ASG retries, ECS task storage).

How Developers Misread the Situation

- "It's just another IAM role—I can customize it."

- "I'll delete unused roles to clean things up."

- "That trust policy looks fine... it says 'ec2.amazonaws.com'."

- "Why is the role name so weird? I'll rename it to something clearer."

- "The service should recreate the role automatically."

Detection Steps (AWS CLI preferred)

1. List all service-linked roles:

```
aws iam list-roles --query
"Roles[?contains(RoleName,
'AWSServiceRole')].RoleName"
```

2. Check trust relationship for a specific SLR:

```
aws iam get-role --role-name
AWSServiceRoleForAutoScaling
```

Expected Output:

```
"AssumeRolePolicyDocument": {
  "Statement": [
    {
      "Effect": "Allow",
      "Principal": {
        "Service":
"autoscaling.amazonaws.com"
      },
      "Action": "sts:AssumeRole"
    }
  ]
}
```

3. Verify required permissions are attached:

```
aws iam list-attached-role-policies --role-
name AWSServiceRoleForAutoScaling
```

Check that the attached policy matches AWS-managed policies for that service.

4. Confirm recent errors in CloudTrail:

```
aws cloudtrail lookup-events --lookup-
attributes
AttributeKey=EventName,AttributeValue=Assum
eRole
```

Look for:

- `"errorCode": "AccessDenied"`

- `"userIdentity.type": "Service"`

- `"recipientAccountId"` and `roleArn` mismatches

5. Recreate a deleted service-linked role:

```
aws iam create-service-linked-role --aws-
service-name autoscaling.amazonaws.com
```

Diagram: SLR Trust Flow and Risk Points

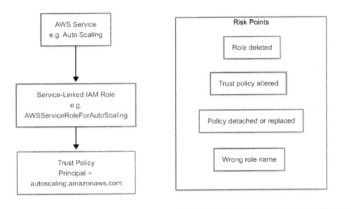

Fix Instructions

Step 1: Recreate the missing SLR

```
aws iam create-service-linked-role \
  --aws-service-name
autoscaling.amazonaws.com
```

If you're not sure which service caused the error, refer to:

```
https://docs.aws.amazon.com/IAM/latest/User
Guide/reference_aws-services-that-work-
with-iam.html
```

Step 2: Validate trust policy of the SLR

Compare to AWS docs or recreate to reset:

```
aws iam get-role --role-name
AWSServiceRoleForAutoScaling
```

Step 3: Reattach the correct AWS-managed policy

```
aws iam attach-role-policy \
  --role-name AWSServiceRoleForAutoScaling
\
  --policy-arn arn:aws:iam::aws:policy/aws-
service-role/AutoScalingServiceRolePolicy
```

Step 4: Enable CloudTrail to catch future misuse

Ensure you're logging management events:

```
aws cloudtrail get-event-selectors --trail-
name my-org-trail
```

Step 5: Prevent deletion with IAM SCP or tag guardrails

Tag the SLR:

```
aws iam tag-role \
```

```
  --role-name AWSServiceRoleForAutoScaling
\
  --tags Key=DoNotDelete,Value=true
```

What You Probably Missed

- **Some SLRs require service enablement first.**
  For example, you must first use ECS or Auto
  Scaling for AWS to provision the SLR.

- **SLRs are named and scoped by AWS.** If you
  rename or modify them, services may fail silently.

- **Custom policies don't always replicate AWS-
  managed policy scope.** Your replacement may
  lack required permissions.

- **SLRs exist in a *per-region* context for some
  services.** Don't assume they're global.

- **CloudTrail errors may appear generic.** Look for
  `InvalidIdentityToken` or `AccessDenied`
  from assumed role events as your clue.

Chapter 20: IAM Logic Unlocked — How AWS Resolves Conflicting Allow and Deny Statements

Quick Skim Checklist

- Do your IAM policies mix `Allow` and `Deny` from different sources?

- Are you using **both identity-based and resource-based policies**?

- Do you apply **permission boundaries** or **session policies**?

- Have you seen unexpected `AccessDenied` results, even with `Allow` present?

- Are **SCPs or organizational units** involved?

How This Happens in the Real World

A developer grants an IAM user `s3:PutObject` permissions using an inline policy. The team tests it, but the user still gets an `AccessDenied` error when uploading a file. The IAM policy *clearly* says `Allow`.

What no one noticed: there's an explicit `Deny` in a resource-based policy attached to the bucket—or a permission boundary that filters out the action. Other times, developers assume a single `Allow` overrides all other blocks. It doesn't. Not in AWS.

IAM evaluation logic is a powerful but nuanced engine. It considers multiple layers: identity policy, resource policy, session policies, permission boundaries, and service control policies (SCPs). Misunderstanding how they interact causes painful, silent failures.

Root Causes

Root Cause	Description
Implicit Deny misunderstood	Everything is denied by default unless explicitly allowed.
Explicit Deny overrides Allow	A single `Deny`, from *any* policy type, blocks access—no exceptions.
Multiple policy sources not evaluated together	Identity and resource policies are independently evaluated, leading to overlooked conflicts.
Boundaries limit allowed actions	Permission boundaries or session policies filter down the allowed set.
SCPs silently deny actions	Organization-level SCPs deny access even if the IAM policy grants it.
Conditions break Allow statements	An `Allow` may silently fail if the `Condition` is not met.

Compliance & Financial Fallout

- **Security Misconfiguration:** Deny policies used incorrectly can block critical operations.

- **Broken Deployments:** Apps fail silently when a single Deny overrides expected permissions.

- **Unnecessary Escalation:** Engineers broaden permissions ("just give admin") to bypass Deny.

- **Audit Failures:** Incorrect assumptions about IAM logic lead to over-provisioning or unnecessary access.

- **Downtime and Support Cost:** Confusing IAM behavior results in time-consuming investigations and support cases.

How Developers Misread the Situation

- "If there's an `Allow`, that action should succeed."

- "My IAM policy says it's allowed, so it can't be denied."

- "Only one policy type is evaluated at a time, right?"

- "Explicit `Deny` only matters in resource policies."

- "If it's failing, it must be a bug in IAM."

Detection Steps (AWS CLI preferred)

187

1. Simulate permissions using `simulate-principal-policy`:

```
aws iam simulate-principal-policy \
  --policy-source-arn
arn:aws:iam::123456789012:user/MyUser \
  --action-names s3:PutObject \
  --resource-arns arn:aws:s3:::my-
bucket/uploads/file.txt
```

Expected Output:

```
"decision": "explicitDeny"
```

Or:

```
"decision": "allowed"
```

2. Simulate with resource-based policy context:

```
aws iam simulate-custom-policy \
  --policy-input-list file://resource-
policy.json \
  --action-names s3:PutObject \
  --resource-arns arn:aws:s3:::my-
bucket/uploads/file.txt
```

3. Simulate with permissions boundary:

```
aws iam simulate-principal-policy \
  --policy-source-arn
arn:aws:iam::123456789012:user/MyUser \
  --action-names s3:PutObject \
  --resource-arns arn:aws:s3:::my-
bucket/uploads/file.txt \
  --permissions-boundary-policy
file://boundary-policy.json
```

4. Check for SCP restrictions (if in an Org):

```
aws organizations list-policies-for-target
\
  --target-id <account-or-ou-id> \
  --filter SERVICE_CONTROL_POLICY
```

Then fetch policy contents:

```
aws organizations describe-policy --policy-
id <policy-id>
```

Diagram: IAM Evaluation Flow

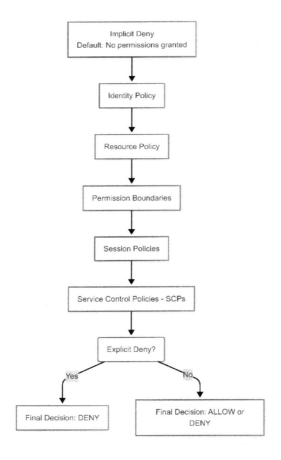

Note: A single explicit Deny at *any* stage overrides all Allow.

Fix Instructions

Step 1: Identify conflicting Deny statements

Use simulation to pinpoint which policy causes the explicitDeny.

Step 2: Review all attached policies

```
aws iam list-attached-user-policies --user-
name MyUser
aws iam list-user-policies --user-name
MyUser
```

Check for:

- Overlapping policies with Deny

- Policies with conflicting conditions

Step 3: Inspect permission boundaries

```
aws iam get-user --user-name MyUser
```

Look for a PermissionsBoundary field, then:

```
aws iam get-policy-version \
  --policy-arn <boundary-arn> \
  --version-id v1
```

Step 4: Validate resource-based policies (e.g., S3, KMS)

```
aws s3api get-bucket-policy --bucket my-
bucket
```

Step 5: If using session policies, evaluate those too

Session-based policies often come from temporary roles or federated users:

```
aws sts assume-role --policy
file://session-policy.json ...
```

Step 6: In Org environments, inspect and update SCPs

Use only the required services and actions in SCPs. Avoid overly broad Deny.

What You Probably Missed

- **Conditions can silently block access.** A policy might have Allow, but with a StringEquals on a tag that doesn't match.

- **SCPs apply across all IAM entities.** Even the root user is subject to SCP restrictions.

- **Session policies are easy to forget.** They come with temporary credentials or `assume-role-with-policy`.

- **Permission boundaries override identity policy** `Allow`. Think of them as "ceilings" for what a user or role can do.

- **Multiple** `Allow` **policies don't override a single** `Deny`. That `Deny` always wins, regardless of how many `Allows` you have.

Chapter 21: Tag, You're It — Safely Controlling Who Can Tag and Untag AWS Resources

Quick Skim Checklist

- Are `TagResource` and `UntagResource` permissions scoped to specific **resource ARNs**?

- Does the IAM policy **limit which tags** can be added or removed?

- Are `aws:TagKeys` and `aws:RequestTag` conditions used?

- Is tagging permission **restricted by service**, such as only allowing EC2 or Lambda tags?

- Are there guardrails for **what tag keys** users are allowed to modify?

How This Happens in the Real World

A company wants its developers to tag EC2 instances with a `Project` key for cost tracking. A well-meaning admin gives out `tag:*` permissions with `"Resource": "*"`. Now any IAM user with that policy can apply or remove tags from **any resource**, in **any region**, including things like IAM users or encrypted KMS keys.

194

Worse, developers can remove security-relevant tags like `Owner=SecurityTeam`, breaking audits and attribution. Without proper constraints, even tagging—something that seems harmless—becomes a subtle vector for **privilege escalation**, **data loss**, or **compliance failure**.

Root Causes

Root Cause	Description
Wildcard permissions on tagging	Using `tag:*` or `"Resource":` `"*"` allows unrestricted tagging.
No tag condition keys (`aws:TagKeys`)	Tag keys can be added or removed freely, including sensitive ones.
Over-permissive cross-service access	Permissions are not limited to specific resource types (e.g., EC2 only).
No `aws:RequestTag` conditions	Users can assign misleading tags, like `Environment=Prod`.
Missing resource constraints	IAM roles can tag resources outside their intended scope (e.g., prod instead of dev).

Compliance & Financial Fallout

- **Cost Attribution Failures:** Incorrect tags skew billing and budget reports.

- **Security Policy Bypass:** Removal of security-related tags disables alerts or automation.

- **Audit Discrepancies:** Tags used for access control (ABAC) become unreliable.

- **Unauthorized Changes:** Dev users accidentally (or maliciously) tag sensitive resources.

- **Violation of Least Privilege:** Broad tag permissions become a backdoor to other actions.

How Developers Misread the Situation

- "It's just tagging—it doesn't need tight security."

- "I didn't realize removing a tag could break things."

- "We need to let devs tag for cost tracking, so we gave full tag access."

- "Why does tagging an IAM role matter? It's just metadata."

- "We can't restrict tagging per key, can we?"

Detection Steps (AWS CLI preferred)

1. List IAM policies that grant tagging permissions

```
aws iam list-policies --query
"Policies[?PolicyName.contains(@, 'Tag')]"
```

2. Get the contents of a specific policy

```
aws iam get-policy-version \
  --policy-arn
arn:aws:iam::123456789012:policy/TagAccessP
olicy \
  --version-id v1
```

Look for:

- `Action: "tag:*"` (overly broad)

- `Resource: "*"` (unscoped)

- **Missing** `Condition` **blocks using** `aws:TagKeys` **or** `aws:RequestTag`

3. Simulate tagging access

```
aws iam simulate-principal-policy \
  --policy-source-arn
arn:aws:iam::123456789012:user/DevUser \
  --action-names tag:TagResource \
```

```
  --resource-arns arn:aws:ec2:us-east-
1:123456789012:instance/i-0abc1234def567890
\
  --context-entries
key=aws:RequestTag/Project,value=Demo
```

Expected Output:

```
"decision": "allowed"
```

4. Audit CloudTrail for suspicious tag modifications

```
aws cloudtrail lookup-events \
  --lookup-attributes
AttributeKey=EventName,AttributeValue=TagRe
source
```

Look for unexpected or unapproved tag keys or resources being modified.

Diagram: IAM Policy Conditions for Tagging

Fix Instructions

Step 1: Define allowed tagging actions and scoped resources

Example for EC2 instance tagging only:

```
{
  "Effect": "Allow",
  "Action": [
    "ec2:CreateTags",
    "ec2:DeleteTags"
  ],
```

```
  "Resource": "arn:aws:ec2:us-east-
1:123456789012:instance/*",
  "Condition": {
    "StringEqualsIfExists": {
      "aws:RequestTag/Environment": "dev"
    },
    "ForAllValues:StringEquals": {
      "aws:TagKeys": ["Environment",
"Project"]
    }
  }
}
```

Step 2: Apply this as an inline or managed policy

```
aws iam put-user-policy \
  --user-name DevUser \
  --policy-name TagOnlyEC2 \
  --policy-document file://tag-ec2-
only.json
```

Step 3: Test with policy simulation

```
aws iam simulate-principal-policy \
  --policy-source-arn
arn:aws:iam::123456789012:user/DevUser \
  --action-names ec2:CreateTags \
```

```
  --resource-arns arn:aws:ec2:us-east-
1:123456789012:instance/i-0abc1234 \
  --context-entries
key=aws:RequestTag/Environment,value=prod
```

Expected Output: `"decision": "explicitDeny"` due to mismatch on allowed tag key value.

Step 4: Use SCPs or permission boundaries for guardrails

In organizations, restrict access to high-impact tag keys using SCPs to prevent sensitive changes:

```
{
  "Effect": "Deny",
  "Action": [
    "tag:TagResource",
    "tag:UntagResource"
  ],
  "Resource": "*",
  "Condition": {
    "StringEquals": {
      "aws:TagKeys": ["SecurityOwner",
"Environment"]
    }
  }
}
```

What You Probably Missed

- **Tagging IAM roles affects ABAC.** If users can add/remove identity tags, they can influence permission grants.

- `CreateTags` **and** `TagResource` **are different.** Some services use `CreateTags`, others use the `tag:` namespace API.

- `aws:RequestTag` **is evaluated** *before* **a resource is created.** Great for restricting launch tags on EC2, Lambda, etc.

- `aws:TagKeys` **restricts the keys, not the values.** Pair it with `aws:RequestTag` to validate tag content.

- **Removing a tag can break billing or automation.** Treat `UntagResource` with the same caution as write permissions.

Chapter 22: Seeing the Unseen — Visualizing IAM Permission Boundaries and Cross-Account Trust Chains

Quick Skim Checklist

- Are **permission boundaries** applied to any roles or users?

- Are **cross-account role assumptions** failing or behaving unexpectedly?

- Have you reviewed **trust policies and session policies**?

- Are you using tools like **IAM Access Analyzer**, **AWS Policy Simulator**, or **CloudTrail**?

- Have you tried **IAM roles visualizer** or **third-party graphing tools** to map relationships?

How This Happens in the Real World

A developer sets up an IAM role in Account A that allows `s3:PutObject`. That role is then assumed from Account B. But when the action is attempted, the call fails with `AccessDenied`. The team double-checks the IAM role policy—it says "Allow."

The culprit? A permission boundary limits the role to `s3:GetObject` only, and no one knew it existed. In another case, a trust policy allowed access from a cross-account role, but the role in the source account had its own permission boundary that quietly neutered the allowed permissions.

These kinds of issues don't show up in the Console until things break. Without the right tooling, mapping all the policies and relationships—especially across accounts—is like solving a jigsaw puzzle blindfolded.

Root Causes

Root Cause	Description
Hidden permission boundaries	Boundaries restrict permissions even if IAM policies allow the action.
Complex trust policies across accounts	Roles can only be assumed if both trust and identity policies align.
No visualization of policy flows	Manual review leads to missed relationships or overlooked conditions.
Session policies limit assumed role capability	Temporary credentials might include restrictive inline session policies.
SCPs silently denying actions	Organizational guardrails override even valid IAM logic.

Compliance & Financial Fallout

- **Access Gaps During Incidents:** Teams lose time debugging instead of resolving the issue.

- **Undetected Escalation Risks:** Without visualizing trust chains, lateral movement across roles can go unnoticed.

- **Audit Confusion:** Inability to show policy scope and boundaries to auditors leads to control failures.

- **Excessive Permissions Creep:** In desperation, developers over-permission IAM entities to "just make it work."

- **Deployment Delays:** Cross-account automation breaks when trust paths or permission scopes are misunderstood.

How Developers Misread the Situation

- "My IAM policy says `Allow`, so it should work."

- "Permission boundaries are just for guardrails, right?"

- "We don't use session policies, so there's nothing extra to check."

- "I don't need to worry about the trust policy—it's someone else's account."

- "Cross-account trust is simple once the role is assumable."

Detection Steps (AWS CLI preferred)

1. Check if a permission boundary is applied:

```
aws iam get-role --role-name MyAppRole
```

Look for:

```
"PermissionsBoundary": {
  "PermissionsBoundaryType": "Policy",
  "PermissionsBoundaryArn":
"arn:aws:iam::123456789012:policy/MyBoundar
y"
}
```

2. Simulate the final permissions (including boundaries):

```
aws iam simulate-principal-policy \
  --policy-source-arn
arn:aws:iam::123456789012:role/MyAppRole \
  --action-names s3:PutObject \
```

```
  --resource-arns
arn:aws:s3:::mybucket/data/file.txt \
  --permissions-boundary-policy
file://boundary.json
```

3. View Access Analyzer findings for trust issues:

```
aws accessanalyzer list-analyzers
aws accessanalyzer list-findings --
analyzer-name MyAnalyzer
```

Filter for:

- Cross-account trust

- Unused access paths

- External resource sharing

4. Investigate trust relationships for roles:

```
aws iam get-role --role-name
CrossAccountRole
```

Look for:

- `Principal` includes trusted AWS account ID

- Action includes `sts:AssumeRole`

- Condition blocks or tag-based restrictions

5. Check session policies from STS AssumeRole calls:

```
aws sts assume-role \
  --role-arn
arn:aws:iam::123456789012:role/CrossAccount
Role \
  --role-session-name test-session \
  --policy file://session-limiter.json
```

Diagram: IAM Trust and Boundary Evaluation Flow

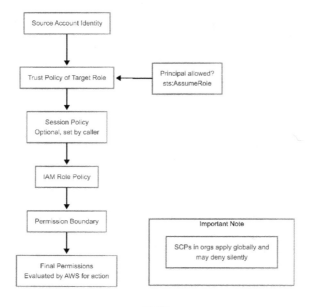

Fix Instructions

Step 1: Use IAM Access Analyzer to identify trust paths

Create an analyzer:

```
aws accessanalyzer create-analyzer \
  --analyzer-name TrustFlowAnalyzer \
  --type ACCOUNT
```

List findings:

```
aws accessanalyzer list-findings --
analyzer-name TrustFlowAnalyzer
```

Step 2: Use Policy Simulator to test assumptions with boundary

```
aws iam simulate-principal-policy \
  --policy-source-arn
arn:aws:iam::111122223333:role/DevRole \
  --action-names ec2:StartInstances \
  --resource-arns arn:aws:ec2:us-east-
1:111122223333:instance/i-0123456789abcdef
\
```

```
--permissions-boundary-policy
file://boundary.json
```

Step 3: Use graphical tools for trust chain visualization

- **Access Analyzer Console**
  (https://console.aws.amazon.com/access-
  analyzer/)

  - ○ Visualizes external access, cross-account
    trust, and overexposed resources

- **Policy Sentry + IAM Data Tracker**

  - ○ Helps generate least-privilege policies and
    understand role lineage

- **Third-party IAM graphing tools**

  - ○ Tools like **CloudMapper**, **PMapper**, and
    Cartography show principal relationships

**Step 4: Reconstruct or adjust trust policies with tags
or conditions**

Example trust policy:

```
{
  "Effect": "Allow",
  "Principal": {
    "AWS": "arn:aws:iam::222233334444:root"
```

```
  },
  "Action": "sts:AssumeRole",
  "Condition": {
    "StringEquals": {
      "aws:PrincipalTag/Team": "DevOps"
    }
  }
}
```

Step 5: Enforce visual guardrails with SCPs and naming conventions

Example:

```
{
  "Effect": "Deny",
  "Action": "*",
  "Resource": "*",
  "Condition": {
    "StringNotLike": {
      "aws:PrincipalArn":
"arn:aws:iam::*:role/Team*"
    }
  }
}
```

What You Probably Missed

- **Session policies override IAM permissions.** They can deny actions even if everything else allows it.

- **Permission boundaries are not visible in most CLI outputs.** You must explicitly request them.

- **Trust chains break without a mutual match.** Both sides must allow the AssumeRole action with matching trust and policy.

- **IAM Access Analyzer can detect unintended trust paths.** Especially for public or cross-account access.

- **Third-party tools often surface what the AWS Console hides.** Graph-based visualizers can reveal indirect relationships or over-permissioned paths.

Chapter 23: The Trust Trap — Why Your Lambda Function Fails to Assume a Role

Quick Skim Checklist

- Is the **Lambda function's execution role** defined and attached?

- Does the **trust policy of the target role** include `lambda.amazonaws.com`?

- Are **required** `sts:AssumeRole` **permissions** granted in the function's policy?

- Did you check for **permission boundaries, SCPs,** or **tag-based conditions**?

- Is **CloudTrail logging enabled** to catch failed AssumeRole attempts?

How This Happens in the Real World

You deploy a Lambda function that needs to assume a secondary role to write to S3, access DynamoDB, or invoke resources in another AWS account. You wire everything up, deploy successfully, but then…

Boom. Every invocation fails with an `AccessDenied` or `Not authorized to perform sts:AssumeRole` error.

What gives?

The IAM policy attached to the Lambda looks fine. The role it's trying to assume also seems open. But you forgot to check the **trust relationship**, which doesn't include `lambda.amazonaws.com`. Or perhaps the trust policy includes the Lambda's role ARN, but a **permissions boundary** or **missing tag condition** blocks the call. These errors can be subtle, and debugging them without knowing the trust evaluation flow is like navigating a maze blindfolded.

Root Causes

Root Cause	Description
Missing `sts:AssumeRole` in Lambda's role	Lambda execution role lacks permission to assume the target role.
Target role trust policy missing Lambda	Trust policy does not include `lambda.amazonaws.com` or the specific Lambda execution role.
Mismatch in role ARN or account ID	The trust relationship specifies the wrong principal ARN or account.
Tag conditions not met	Trust policy includes `aws:PrincipalTag` or `aws:SourceArn` conditions that the Lambda doesn't match.
Session policies or permission boundaries	Temporary credentials from Lambda are restricted further than expected.
SCPs blocking `sts:AssumeRole`	Organization-wide guardrails deny the AssumeRole action even if IAM allows it.

Compliance & Financial Fallout

- **Service Outages:** Lambda functions silently fail if AssumeRole fails mid-invocation.

- **Over-provisioned Fixes:** Teams overcorrect by granting `AdministratorAccess` to get things working.

- **Audit Gaps:** Improper trust setups make it harder to prove least-privilege and cross-account security.

- **Deployment Delays:** Functions meant to automate tasks across environments stall in production.

- **Incident Response Issues:** Lambda can't assume roles to scan, remediate, or alert in time-sensitive scenarios.

How Developers Misread the Situation

- "Lambda has its own permissions; it should just work."

- "The role policy has `Allow: sts:AssumeRole`, so it's fine."

- "It worked in dev—must be a bug in prod."

- "I thought the Lambda function name was enough."

- "Why would I need to touch the trust policy? Isn't that automatic?"

Detection Steps (AWS CLI preferred)

1. Confirm the Lambda function's execution role

```
aws lambda get-function-configuration --
function-name MyFunction
```

Output should include:

```
"Role":
"arn:aws:iam::123456789012:role/MyLambdaExe
cutionRole"
```

2. Verify the Lambda role has permission to assume the target role

```
aws iam get-role-policy \
  --role-name MyLambdaExecutionRole \
  --policy-name AssumeCrossAccountRole
```

Look for:

```
{
  "Effect": "Allow",
  "Action": "sts:AssumeRole",
  "Resource":
"arn:aws:iam::111122223333:role/TargetRole"
}
```

3. Check the trust policy of the target role

```
aws iam get-role --role-name TargetRole
```

Look for this block in `AssumeRolePolicyDocument`:

```
{
  "Effect": "Allow",
  "Principal": {
    "Service": "lambda.amazonaws.com"
  },
  "Action": "sts:AssumeRole"
}
```

Or for cross-account:

```
"Principal": {
  "AWS":
"arn:aws:iam::123456789012:role/MyLambdaExe
cutionRole"
```

```
}
```

4. Look for failed assume events in CloudTrail

```
aws cloudtrail lookup-events \
  --lookup-attributes
AttributeKey=EventName,AttributeValue=Assum
eRole
```

Failed attempts will show:

```
"errorCode": "AccessDenied"
```

5. Validate permissions boundaries or tag conditions

```
aws iam get-role --role-name
MyLambdaExecutionRole
```

Check for:

```
"PermissionsBoundary": {...}
```

And in trust policy:

```
"Condition": {
```

```
  "StringEquals": {
    "aws:PrincipalTag/Team": "Platform"
  }
}
```

Diagram: Lambda AssumeRole Trust Flow

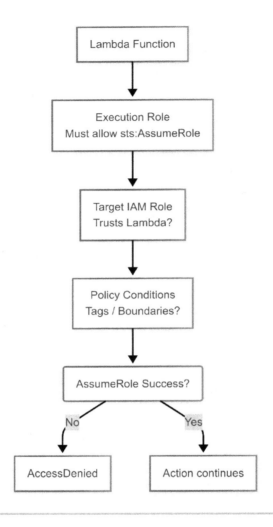

Fix Instructions

Step 1: Grant `sts:AssumeRole` in Lambda execution role

{

```
  "Effect": "Allow",
  "Action": "sts:AssumeRole",
  "Resource":
"arn:aws:iam::111122223333:role/TargetRole"
}
```

Step 2: Update trust policy of target role

```
{
  "Version": "2012-10-17",
  "Statement": [
    {
      "Effect": "Allow",
      "Principal": {
        "AWS":
"arn:aws:iam::123456789012:role/MyLambdaExe
cutionRole"
      },
      "Action": "sts:AssumeRole"
    }
  ]
}
```

Update with CLI:

```
aws iam update-assume-role-policy \
  --role-name TargetRole \
```

```
  --policy-document file://trust-
policy.json
```

Step 3: Add tag-based conditions if using ABAC

```
"Condition": {
  "StringEquals": {
    "aws:PrincipalTag/Project":
"BillingAPI"
  }
}
```

Then tag the Lambda execution role:

```
aws iam tag-role \
  --role-name MyLambdaExecutionRole \
  --tags Key=Project,Value=BillingAPI
```

Step 4: Re-test the Lambda invocation

Re-trigger the function from the console or CLI:

```
aws lambda invoke \
  --function-name MyFunction \
  --payload file://event.json \
  output.json
```

What You Probably Missed

- **IAM roles for Lambda must be explicitly trusted.**
  The trust policy must reference either the service or
  the role ARN.

- **Lambda runs with temporary credentials.** These
  credentials must satisfy any session policy or trust
  condition.

- **Cross-account AssumeRole requires trust *and*
  permissions.** Both accounts need to agree on the
  relationship.

- **SCPs can override everything.** In an org, SCPs
  might block `sts:AssumeRole` and not show up in
  IAM simulation.

- **Lambda console shows no detail**. You must use
  CloudTrail to understand the real cause of
  `AccessDenied`.

Chapter 24: The Forgotten Few — Detecting and Decommissioning Unused IAM Identities

Quick Skim Checklist

- Are there IAM users or roles with **no recent activity** in the past 90 days?

- Have **access keys** or **passwords** gone unused for months?

- Are there **groups** with no attached users or policies?

- Have you reviewed the **last accessed info** for roles and policies?

- Are there **inactive identities** that still have admin or broad permissions?

How This Happens in the Real World

A cloud migration ends. A contractor leaves. A batch job gets deprecated. But their IAM identities live on.

Teams often forget to clean up IAM users, roles, or groups after temporary projects. These lingering identities pose major risks: unused accounts still have credentials, some even with `AdministratorAccess`, waiting to be exploited.

This isn't just bad hygiene—it's a ticking time bomb. Without scheduled reviews and decommissioning policies, your AWS account collects ghost permissions that quietly erode security.

Root Causes

Root Cause	Description
No lifecycle management for IAM identities	Users and roles are created for short-term use but never removed.
Lack of visibility into access history	Teams don't regularly review last accessed timestamps.
Policies attached "just in case"	Permissions remain attached to dormant roles or users.
Forgotten CI/CD or dev environment roles	Orphaned Lambda, EC2, or ECS roles from dismantled environments persist.
Unused groups with broad permissions	IAM groups stay in place even after all users leave.

Compliance & Financial Fallout

- **Security Breaches:** Unused credentials with excessive permissions can be exploited in lateral attacks.

- **Audit Failures:** IAM sprawl violates least-privilege and identity lifecycle standards in SOC 2, ISO 27001, and PCI.

- **Operational Complexity:** Increased IAM policy surface makes debugging and permission audits harder.

- **Billing Anomalies:** Roles tied to metered services may still trigger charges (e.g., Lambda functions left behind).

- **Over-permissioned Failures:** Risk of privilege escalation increases through neglected access pathways.

How Developers Misread the Situation

- "Nobody's using that account, but we might need it later."

- "That role was created for testing, so it's harmless."

- "It's just a group—what's the risk if it's empty?"

- "We can audit IAM later during a security review."

- "I don't think AWS charges for idle users or roles, right?"

Detection Steps (AWS CLI preferred)

1. Generate a credential report (CSV):

```
aws iam generate-credential-report
```

Then download it:

```
aws iam get-credential-report --query
'Content' --output text | base64 --decode >
credential-report.csv
```

Open the file and check:

- `password_last_used`

- `access_key_1_last_used_date`

- `access_key_2_last_used_date`

Look for N/A or timestamps older than 90 days.

---

2. Use IAM access advisor to detect unused roles and policies:

List all roles:

```
aws iam list-roles --query
'Roles[*].RoleName'
```

Then for each role:

```
aws iam get-role --role-name MyRole
aws iam generate-service-last-accessed-
details --arn
arn:aws:iam::123456789012:role/MyRole
```

Get the report details:

```
aws iam get-service-last-accessed-details \
  --job-id <job-id>
```

Check for:

- `"LastAuthenticated"`: `null` or older than 90 days

- No services listed in usage summary

---

3. Identify unused groups:

```
aws iam list-groups
```

Then for each group:

```
aws iam get-group --group-name MyGroup
```

If the `Users` list is empty **and** the group has no attached policies, it's likely safe to remove.

Diagram: IAM Identity Usage Monitoring and Decommissioning

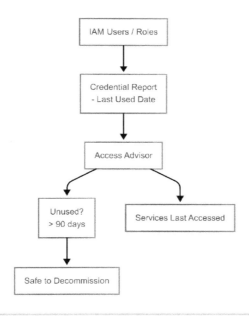

Fix Instructions

Step 1: Tag identities with ownership and expiration metadata

```
aws iam tag-user \
  --user-name temp-deploy-user \
```

```
  --tags Key=Owner,Value=ci-team
Key=TTL,Value=30d
```

Step 2: Remove access keys or deactivate unused credentials

```
aws iam update-access-key \
  --user-name old-user \
  --access-key-id AKIAEXAMPLE123 \
  --status Inactive
```

Or remove entirely:

```
aws iam delete-access-key \
  --user-name old-user \
  --access-key-id AKIAEXAMPLE123
```

Step 3: Delete unused users

```
aws iam delete-user --user-name old-user
```

Step 4: Detach and delete unused roles

```
aws iam detach-role-policy \
  --role-name old-test-role \
```

```
--policy-arn
arn:aws:iam::aws:policy/AdministratorAccess

aws iam delete-role --role-name old-test-
role
```

Step 5: Remove empty groups with no policies

```
aws iam list-attached-group-policies --
group-name OldGroup
aws iam delete-group --group-name OldGroup
```

What You Probably Missed

- **Console-created users often go unused.**
  Accounts created for testing the Console UI are
  rarely cleaned up.

- **Access keys may still be active even after user
  offboarding.** Unless revoked explicitly, they remain
  valid.

- **IAM roles tied to Lambda or EC2 may survive
  deletion.** These orphaned roles can drift
  undetected.

- **Groups with no users still affect audit scope.**
  Auditors will question any identity linked to wide
  policies.

- **You can use Config or CloudTrail to alert on stale identities.** Automate alerts when identities go unused for 60+ days.

Chapter 25: The Invisible Delay — Understanding IAM's Eventual Consistency and Propagation Lag

Quick Skim Checklist

- Did you just create or modify an IAM policy or role?

- Are new permissions not taking effect right away?

- Did a Lambda, EC2 instance, or IAM user fail immediately after a permission change?

- Are `AccessDenied` errors showing up despite correct-looking configurations?

- Did you wait 5–30 seconds before retrying a failed action?

How This Happens in the Real World

You attach a new policy to a role. You immediately run a deployment script or invoke a Lambda function that depends on that permission. It fails with `AccessDenied`. You double-check the IAM policy—it's correct.

You try again a minute later—and it works perfectly.

What just happened?

This is the classic AWS **eventual consistency** scenario. IAM is a globally distributed service, and changes to permissions, policies, and trust relationships don't always propagate instantly across the infrastructure. This propagation lag can be confusing, especially during rapid-fire CI/CD deployments or just-in-time provisioning.

Root Causes

Root Cause	Description
IAM propagation delay (eventual consistency)	Changes to roles, policies, or trust relationships take seconds to minutes to fully propagate.
Role or policy created and used too quickly	Resource attempts to use an IAM role before permissions are fully available.
Lambda or EC2 attached role not recognized yet	Instances or functions fail on first call due to IAM role not being fully registered.
Rapid AssumeRole attempts post-creation	STS calls may fail immediately after the role becomes available.
Automation scripts not accounting for lag	Terraform, CloudFormation, or CLI scripts deploy resources assuming instant IAM readiness.

Compliance & Financial Fallout

- **Deployment Failures:** Rollbacks or failed automation due to premature `AccessDenied` errors.

- **Misdiagnosed Permissions:** Engineers waste time debugging correct policies, assuming they're broken.

- **Security Misconfigurations:** Inconsistent behavior might mask over-permissioned setups (i.e., it "starts working" later).

- **Increased Support Load:** Junior developers file tickets or escalate because changes "don't work."

- **Delayed Rollouts:** Mission-critical code halts due to inconsistent role assumption or Lambda invocation.

How Developers Misread the Situation

- "The policy is there—why isn't it working?"

- "AWS must be broken or buggy today."

- "It failed, so the permission must be wrong."

- "Retrying shouldn't make a difference if it's misconfigured."

- "I'll just give it admin to bypass the issue."

Detection Steps (AWS CLI preferred)

1. Validate that the policy change succeeded:

```
aws iam get-role-policy \
  --role-name MyRole \
  --policy-name MyPolicy
```

Make sure the new policy appears as expected.

2. Simulate permission as a sanity check:

```
aws iam simulate-principal-policy \
  --policy-source-arn
arn:aws:iam::123456789012:role/MyRole \
  --action-names s3:PutObject \
  --resource-arns
arn:aws:s3:::mybucket/newfile.txt
```

If the simulation says `"allowed"` but the real request fails, you're likely hitting propagation delay.

3. Check CloudTrail for AccessDenied events after recent IAM changes:

```
aws cloudtrail lookup-events \
  --lookup-attributes
AttributeKey=EventName,AttributeValue=Assum
eRole
```

Look for failures immediately following a role creation or trust policy update.

4. Retry after a delay to confirm consistency issue:

Wait 30–60 seconds and retry the same request or action.

Diagram: IAM Change Propagation Flow

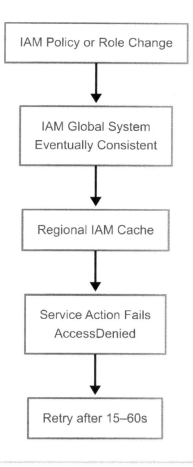

Fix Instructions

Step 1: Build wait steps into automation

If your automation chain includes IAM changes, insert a delay or polling step before proceeding:

```
sleep 30  # Bash
```

Or, poll until the role is ready:

```
aws iam get-role --role-name MyNewRole
```

Step 2: Use AWS SDK exponential backoff for retries

If you're making AssumeRole or resource calls programmatically, leverage the AWS SDK's built-in retry mechanism with jitter:

```
import boto3
from botocore.exceptions import ClientError
import time

client = boto3.client('sts')

for attempt in range(5):
    try:
        response = client.assume_role(
```

```
RoleArn='arn:aws:iam::123456789012:role/MyR
ole',
            RoleSessionName='debug-session'
        )
        break
    except ClientError as e:
        print(f"Retrying... {e}")
        time.sleep((2 ** attempt) + 1)
```

Step 3: Use `depends_on` and `wait_condition` in Terraform or CloudFormation

Terraform example:

```
resource "aws_lambda_function" "example" {
  depends_on = [aws_iam_role.lambda_exec]
}
```

Step 4: Document propagation delays in team runbooks

Make sure engineers know to wait 1–2 minutes after IAM changes before testing access. It avoids unnecessary troubleshooting.

What You Probably Missed

- **IAM is globally scoped, but AWS services are regional.** Caching discrepancies between regions can cause behavior mismatches.

- **New Lambda executions or EC2 startups may fail once, then succeed.** Retry patterns are essential.

- **Trust policies are just as prone to lag as permission policies.** Especially important in cross-account roles.

- **AssumeRole failures post-create are almost always propagation-related.**

- **Over-permissioning as a workaround is dangerous.** Some teams panic and apply `AdministratorAccess` when the issue is just time delay.

Chapter 26: Conditions Matter — Enforcing IAM Security with IP, Time, and MFA-Based Controls

Quick Skim Checklist

- Are IAM policies using the `Condition` block to enforce access constraints?

- Have you specified `aws:SourceIp`, `aws:MultiFactorAuthPresent`, or `aws:CurrentTime`?

- Do your policies fail when accessed from outside expected IPs or without MFA?

- Are users bypassing MFA or accessing from unknown networks?

- Are scheduled access windows (e.g., business hours only) configured?

How This Happens in the Real World

Your team wants to allow administrative actions only during business hours, from your corporate IP range, and only if the user has authenticated with MFA. You try to enforce it with a custom IAM policy, but it doesn't work. Some actions are still allowed after hours or from personal laptops. Others are blocked unexpectedly.

Why? Because IAM `Condition` logic wasn't used—or it was misapplied.

IAM Conditions are the most overlooked but powerful part of AWS access control. They let you enforce fine-grained security constraints without hardcoding logic into your application. But misusing or omitting conditions opens the door to privilege escalation, credential theft, and unmonitored access from anywhere, anytime.

Root Causes

Root Cause	Description
Missing or incorrect `Condition` block	Policies grant access without IP, time, or MFA constraints.
Improper syntax or operators	Using `StringEquals` where `Bool` or `DateGreaterThan` is required.
IP restriction applied at wrong level	Applied only to identity-based policies, not resource policies where needed.
No fallback Deny policy	Users may still have overlapping permissions outside the intended scope.
MFA checked, but not enforced everywhere	Partial enforcement leaves some actions unguarded.

Compliance & Financial Fallout

- **Data Breach via Lost or Stolen Credentials:** Access from non-MFA logins or public IPs may lead to unauthorized actions.

- **Regulatory Violations (e.g., HIPAA, PCI DSS):** Policies requiring restricted access times or MFA may not be provably enforced.

- **Privilege Escalation:** Users schedule jobs or API calls outside approved hours or bypass MFA-protected actions.

- **Cost Overruns from Automation Gone Rogue:** Scripts run from unintended IPs or times, provisioning resources or data egress.

- **Security Review Failures:** Lack of conditions is flagged during audits, particularly in financial or healthcare sectors.

How Developers Misread the Situation

- "The policy grants access, so why does the time of day matter?"

- "We turned on MFA in the Console—shouldn't that be enough?"

- "IP restrictions only work on VPCs, right?"

- "Conditions are optional extras, not a core part of access control."

- "I didn't know you could restrict IAM access by time."

Detection Steps (AWS CLI preferred)

1. Inspect IAM policies for missing or incorrect Condition blocks:

```
aws iam get-user-policy \
  --user-name dev-user \
  --policy-name SensitiveAccessPolicy
```

Check if there's a Condition block like:

```
"Condition": {
  "Bool": {
    "aws:MultiFactorAuthPresent": "true"
  }
}
```

Or IP-based:

```
"Condition": {
  "IpAddress": {
    "aws:SourceIp": "203.0.113.0/24"
  }
}
```

2. Simulate access with and without conditions met:

244

```
aws iam simulate-principal-policy \
  --policy-source-arn
arn:aws:iam::123456789012:user/dev-user \
  --action-names s3:ListBucket \
  --resource-arns arn:aws:s3:::mybucket \
  --context-entries
key=aws:SourceIp,value=198.51.100.45,type=i
p
```

Expected Output:

- `"decision": "allowed"` or `"decision": "explicitDeny"`

3. Validate time-based condition logic:

```
aws iam simulate-principal-policy \
  --context-entries
key=aws:CurrentTime,value=2025-04-
08T03:00:00Z,type=datetime
```

Confirm the action is denied if outside the window.

Diagram: IAM Condition Evaluation Layers

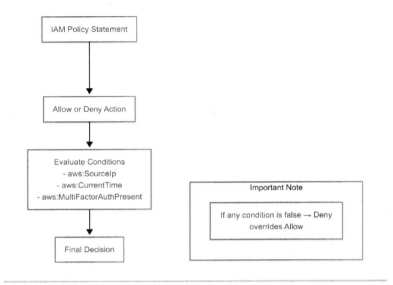

Fix Instructions

Step 1: Require MFA for all privileged actions

Add this block to your policy:

```
"Condition": {
  "BoolIfExists": {
    "aws:MultiFactorAuthPresent": "true"
  }
}
```

Use `BoolIfExists` to allow service accounts that can't use MFA (e.g., roles).

Step 2: Restrict access to corporate IP range

```
"Condition": {
  "IpAddress": {
    "aws:SourceIp": "198.51.100.0/24"
  }
}
```

Step 3: Limit access to specific time windows

```
"Condition": {
  "DateGreaterThan": {
    "aws:CurrentTime": "2025-04-
08T08:00:00Z"
  },
  "DateLessThan": {
    "aws:CurrentTime": "2025-04-
08T18:00:00Z"
  }
}
```

For working hours in UTC.

Step 4: Apply all three together for secure access

```
{
  "Effect": "Allow",
  "Action": [
    "s3:GetObject",
```

```
      "s3:ListBucket"
    ],
    "Resource": "*",
    "Condition": {
      "Bool": {
        "aws:MultiFactorAuthPresent": "true"
      },
      "IpAddress": {
        "aws:SourceIp": "203.0.113.0/24"
      },
      "DateGreaterThan": {
        "aws:CurrentTime": "2025-04-
08T09:00:00Z"
      },
      "DateLessThan": {
        "aws:CurrentTime": "2025-04-
08T17:00:00Z"
      }
    }
}
```

What You Probably Missed

- `BoolIfExists` **avoids breaking non-MFA roles.**
  Use it to apply MFA enforcement only when MFA is
  available.

- **IP address must match the *external* source IP.**
  Proxies or NAT gateways can cause mismatches.

- **Date conditions are in ISO 8601 UTC.** Local timezones must be manually adjusted.

- **Condition evaluation is *AND* by default.** All subconditions must be true unless explicitly grouped differently.

- **Service control policies (SCPs) can use similar conditions.** Don't assume IAM policies are your only control layer.

Part 3: Scaling and Securing EC2 Instances

Chapter 27: The Open Door You Forgot to Close — Securing EC2 from Open Ports and Obsolete AMIs

---

🔍 Quick Skim Checklist

- ☑ Security groups with **0.0.0.0/0** access on ports other than **80** or **443**

- ☑ SSH (**22**) or RDP (**3389**) exposed to the internet

- ☑ Instances launched from AMIs older than 90 days

- ☑ No Systems Manager patching or compliance enforcement

- ☑ AMIs not tagged or versioned according to org policy

- ☑ Lack of network ACLs to enforce port-level control

How This Happens in the Real World

Scenario 1: Open for Debugging, Forgotten Forever
A dev team opens port **22** to **0.0.0.0/0** for "just 15 minutes" during a CI/CD issue. Two months later, it's still exposed — and gets picked up by a bot scanning AWS IP ranges.

Scenario 2: Custom AMI Gone Stale
Your org builds golden AMIs once a quarter. But a project launches using one that's six months old. The base image hasn't been patched, and the included web server has multiple CVEs.

Scenario 3: Marketplace Mirage
A developer launches a workload using a third-party Marketplace AMI for Redis. The AMI is two years old, contains no auto-update script, and the vendor has discontinued support.

Root Causes

- **Wide-open security groups**
  Misconfigured rules with **0.0.0.0/0** allow inbound traffic from any source.

- **No AMI version lifecycle management**
  Teams use outdated AMIs because there's no process to deprecate or flag them.

- **Missing patch automation**
  No AWS Systems Manager (SSM) Patch Manager policies applied.

- **Custom AMIs without compliance checks**
  Internal AMIs lack CIS benchmarking or software

bill of materials (SBOM) validation.

- **Improper tagging**
  No metadata tagging to identify AMI age or
  security posture.

✳ Compliance & Financial Fallout

- **✗ PCI-DSS 1.1.6 & 2.2.4** – Open ports and
  outdated software violate segmentation and
  hardening standards

- **✗ GDPR Article 32** – Failure to ensure "integrity
  and confidentiality of systems"

- **✗ CIS AWS Foundations 4.1–4.5** – Security
  group hygiene and AMI control benchmarks failed

- **✗ SOC 2 Trust Services Criteria** – Poor
  configuration management impacts audit readiness

- **⚠ CloudTrail audit gaps** – Open ports bypass
  centralized control, leading to undetected access
  violations

- **◈ Cost of Incident Response** – Unpatched AMIs
  are often initial access points for breaches

- **◈ Cryptojacking Risk** – Open ports make EC2s
  an easy target for mining malware

How Developers Misread the Situation

- "It's just a dev box — nobody will find it."

- "The AMI worked last time, so it should still be fine."

- "AWS handles security, right?"

- "Security groups are isolated inside the VPC — no risk."

- "We'll fix it later, we just need to meet the release deadline."

🦴 Detection Steps (AWS CLI preferred)

1. List All Security Groups with Inbound Rules

```
aws ec2 describe-security-groups \
  --query
"SecurityGroups[*].{GroupName:GroupName,
Inbound:IpPermissions}" \
  --output table
```

2. Identify Security Groups with Open Ports to 0.0.0.0/0

```
aws ec2 describe-security-groups \
```

```
   --query
"SecurityGroups[?IpPermissions[?contains(Ip
Ranges[].CidrIp,
'0.0.0.0/0')]].{ID:GroupId,Name:GroupName}"
\
   --output table
```

3. List EC2 Instances and Their AMIs

```
aws ec2 describe-instances \
  --query
"Reservations[].Instances[].{InstanceId:Ins
tanceId,ImageId:ImageId,LaunchTime:LaunchTi
me}" \
  --output json
```

Example Output:

```
[
  {
    "InstanceId": "i-0abc1234",
    "ImageId": "ami-098765",
    "LaunchTime": "2023-12-01T12:34:56Z"
  }
]
```

4. Check Patch Compliance (if using Systems Manager)

```
aws ssm describe-instance-patch-states \
  --query
"InstancePatchStates[*].{InstanceId:Instanc
eId,Missing:MissingCount}" \
  --output table
```

Diagram

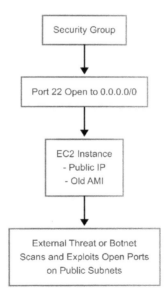

✂ Fix Instructions

1. Restrict Security Groups to Known IPs

```
aws ec2 revoke-security-group-ingress \
  --group-id sg-0123456789abcdef0 \
  --protocol tcp --port 22 \
  --cidr 0.0.0.0/0
```

Then explicitly allow only trusted IPs:

```
aws ec2 authorize-security-group-ingress \
  --group-id sg-0123456789abcdef0 \
  --protocol tcp --port 22 \
  --cidr 203.0.113.0/32
```

2. Replace Outdated AMIs

Use SSM Parameter Store to fetch latest AMI:

```
aws ssm get-parameters-by-path \
  --path /aws/service/ami-amazon-linux-
latest \
  --query
"Parameters[?Name=='/aws/service/ami-
amazon-linux-latest/amzn2-ami-hvm-x86_64-
gp2'].Value"
```

3. Enable Patch Management via SSM

```
aws ssm create-patch-baseline \
  --name "LinuxBaseline" \
  --operating-system AMAZON_LINUX_2 \
  --approval-rules
"PatchRules=[{ApproveAfterDays=7,Compliance
Level=CRITICAL}]"
```

4. Consider AWS Config Automation

Use these managed AWS Config rules:

- `INCOMING_SSH_DISABLED` — Flags security groups that allow SSH from **0.0.0.0/0**

- `APPROVED_AMIS_BY_ID` — Ensures only approved AMIs are used for launching EC2 instances

---

What You Probably Missed

- **Marketplace AMIs** can be abandoned or unpatched silently

- **Stopped instances** retain old security groups that reopen once started

- **Launch templates** may point to deprecated AMIs

- **Default security groups** allow all outbound traffic by default

- **Insecure NAT exposure** expands the attack surface if not locked down

---

Chapter 28: The EC2 Money Leak — Finding Hidden Cost Spikes from Misconfigured or Idle Instances

🔍 Quick Skim Checklist

- ☑ EC2 instances running 24/7 with low CPU/network usage

- ☑ Instances in "running" state with no active connections

- ☑ Overprovisioned instance types (e.g., `m5.4xlarge` for small workloads)

- ☑ Old **EBS** volumes unattached but still billed

- ☑ **Load balancers** or **Auto Scaling Groups** launching excessive instances

- ☑ Stale **Reserved Instances** not being utilized

- ☑ Idle **Elastic IPs** or **NAT gateways** still incurring charges

---

How This Happens in the Real World

Scenario 1: "We Left That Running?"
A dev spun up an EC2 instance for a load test and forgot

to stop it. It sat idle for 45 days, quietly racking up hundreds in on-demand charges—until the monthly AWS bill arrived.

Scenario 2: Staging Environment Scale-Out Storm
An **Auto Scaling Group** was misconfigured with a minimum size of 10 for a staging environment. When load testing hit, it scaled out to 30 and never scaled back in. The team didn't notice until the **AWS Budget** alert triggered a panic.

Scenario 3: Old Instance Types, New Bills
A legacy machine running `r4.8xlarge` was never rightsized. The memory-intensive workload it once supported is gone, but the instance type remains—costing thousands each month without justification.

Root Causes

- **Idle or unused EC2 instances**
  Instances left running without real traffic or tasks consuming resources.

- **Overprovisioned instance types**
  Choosing larger-than-necessary instance types for workloads.

- **Forgotten staging/dev/test environments**
  Environments left running after testing or QA cycles.

- **Auto Scaling misconfiguration**
  Minimum instance counts too high or no scale-in

policies in place.

- **Unattached EBS volumes or orphaned snapshots**
  Storage remnants that accumulate costs unnoticed.

- **Unused Elastic IPs or NAT gateways
  Resources billed by the hour even when unused.

- **Unutilized Reserved Instances or Savings Plans**
  Commitments made but not matched with actual usage patterns.

✴ Compliance & Financial Fallout

- 🔹 **Unexpected budget overruns** — Minor misconfigurations compound into major expenses

- 🔹 **Wasted Reserved Instance coverage** — Paying upfront for capacity no one's using

- 🔹 **Inefficient scaling costs** — Auto Scaling Groups deploying more instances than needed

- ⚠ **SOX reporting risks** — Financial controls require cost tracking and reporting accuracy

- ⚠ **Internal audit flags** — Missed cleanup of test/staging environments can lead to findings

- ⚠ **CloudTrail logs + Cost Explorer** — Help trace when unexpected resources were launched and by whom

---

How Developers Misread the Situation

- "It's only one small instance, what's the harm?"

- "**Auto Scaling** will take care of the rest."

- "We need those bigger instance types 'just in case'."

- "If it's stopped, AWS doesn't charge, right?" *(Not true for **EBS** volumes or **Elastic IPs**.)*

- "Someone else is managing that environment—I think?"

🔧 **Detection Steps (AWS CLI preferred)**

1. Find Idle Instances Based on CPU Usage (via CloudWatch)

```
aws cloudwatch get-metric-statistics \
```

```
  --namespace AWS/EC2 \
  --metric-name CPUUtilization \
  --dimensions Name=InstanceId,Value=i-
0123456789abcdef0 \
  --statistics Average \
  --start-time $(date -d '-7 days' --utc
+%FT%TZ) \
  --end-time $(date --utc +%FT%TZ) \
  --period 3600
```

Look for average CPU < **5%** over a 7-day period.

---

2. List Running EC2 Instances with Launch Times

```
aws ec2 describe-instances \
  --query
"Reservations[].Instances[?State.Name=='run
ning'].{Instance:InstanceId,Type:InstanceTy
pe,LaunchTime:LaunchTime}" \
  --output table
```

Helps identify long-running or forgotten instances.

---

3. Identify Unattached EBS Volumes

```
aws ec2 describe-volumes \
  --filters Name=status,Values=available \
  --query
"Volumes[*].{ID:VolumeId,Size:Size}" \
  --output table
```

These unattached **EBS** volumes still incur charges.

---

4. Detect Overprovisioned Instances with Compute Optimizer

First, summarize:

```
aws compute-optimizer get-recommendation-
summaries \
  --query
"recommendationSummaries[*].{InstanceType:c
urrentInstanceType,Finding:finding}" \
  --output table
```

Then get **full details** for actionable insights:

```
aws compute-optimizer get-ec2-instance-
recommendations \
  --query
"instanceRecommendations[*].{InstanceId:ins
tanceId,Current:instanceType,CPU:utilizatio
```

```
nMetrics[?name=='Cpu'].value,Recommendation
:recommendationOptions[0].instanceType}" \
  --output table
```

The detailed view includes CPU, memory, and IOPS
utilization.

---

5. List Reserved Instances (and Cross-Reference)

```
aws ec2 describe-reserved-instances \
  --filters Name=state,Values=active \
  --query
"ReservedInstances[*].{InstanceType:Instanc
eType,Count:InstanceCount}" \
  --output table
```

◆ **Reminder**: Cross-reference with `describe-`
`instances` output to identify **Reserved Instances** that
aren't being matched by current workloads.

Diagram

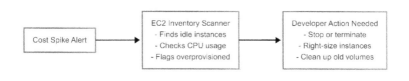

🛠 Fix Instructions

1. Stop or Terminate Idle Instances

```
aws ec2 stop-instances --instance-ids i-
0123456789abcdef0
```

For unused, deprecated machines:

```
aws ec2 terminate-instances --instance-ids
i-0123456789abcdef0
```

---

2. Delete Unattached EBS Volumes

```
aws ec2 delete-volume --volume-id vol-
0123456789abcdef0
```

---

3. Right-Size with Compute Optimizer

```
aws compute-optimizer get-ec2-instance-
recommendations \
  --query
"instanceRecommendations[*].{InstanceId:ins
tanceId,Recommendation:recommendationOption
s[0].instanceType}" \
```

```
--output table
```

Then stop and modify instance type accordingly.

---

4. Automate with AWS Budgets, Trusted Advisor, and Config

- Set **AWS Budgets** to trigger when monthly usage exceeds forecast

- Use **Trusted Advisor** to identify underutilized EC2 and **EBS** volumes

- Enable **AWS Config** rules for cost-draining patterns (e.g., **EBS** volumes in "available" state)

What You Probably Missed

- **Elastic IPs** still charge you when not attached to a running instance

- **NAT gateways** incur hourly charges—even when idle

- **Old AMIs** stored in your account can accumulate **EBS** snapshot charges

- **Stopped instances** still incur **EBS** costs for root and attached volumes

- **Launch templates** may continue spawning large instances unless updated

Chapter 29: When the Terminal Won't Talk — Troubleshooting EC2 SSH Failures

🔍 Quick Skim Checklist

- ☑ Instance is in a **running** state with a **public IP or Elastic IP** assigned

- ☑ Security group allows **inbound port 22** (SSH) from your IP

- ☑ Correct **key pair (.pem file)** used when connecting

- ☑ You're using **ec2-user**, **ubuntu**, or the correct default username

- ☑ **NACLs** and **route tables** don't block traffic

- ☑ **SSM Agent** isn't available as a fallback (when SSH fails)

How This Happens in the Real World

Scenario 1: Security Group Forgot the Invite
A developer launches a new EC2 instance and tries to connect from their laptop. The SSH request times out. Turns out the security group allows SSH—but only from the office IP range, not their current home IP.

269

Scenario 2: Wrong Key, Right Idea

An engineer copies the connection string from an old README. The `.pem` file referenced isn't associated with the running instance. Despite all other settings being correct, authentication fails.

Scenario 3: User Error, Literally

You're using `ubuntu@` to connect to an Amazon Linux 2 instance instead of `ec2-user@`. The key matches, the instance is reachable, but SSH says "Permission denied".

Root Causes

- **Security group misconfiguration**
  Port **22** isn't open to the current IP, or traffic is blocked altogether.

- **Wrong key pair**
  The private key being used doesn't match the key pair associated with the instance.

- **Incorrect username**
  Default usernames vary by AMI (e.g., `ec2-user`, `ubuntu`, `admin`, etc.)

- **Missing public IP or misconfigured networking**
  Instance has no route to the internet or no public IP.

- **NACL or route table blocks**
  Network ACLs or routes block inbound/outbound

access.

- **SSH service not running**
  Instance boot script or user-data stopped or misconfigured sshd.

- **Host key mismatch in known_hosts**
  Your SSH client detects a host key change and blocks the connection.

✵ Compliance & Financial Fallout

- ⚠ **Blocked access to production** — Causes downtime during incidents

- ⚠ **Missed SLA or RTO** — Incidents take longer due to unreachable systems

- ⚠ **Audit trail gaps** — No access means no way to validate compliance fixes

- ⚠ **Improper key management** — Untracked .pem files can violate **SOC 2**, **ISO 27001**, or **PCI-DSS**

- ⚠ **CloudTrail + VPC Flow Logs** — When enabled, these help identify brute-force attempts, blocked port scans, and unauthorized access patterns

How Developers Misread the Situation

- "The instance is running—so it *should* work."

- "I used the same key last week—it must be fine."

- "I can ping the public IP, so SSH isn't blocked."

- "Security groups and NACLs do the same thing, right?"

- "I'm using ubuntu@ for all servers—it always works." *(Spoiler: It doesn't.)*

🔧 Detection Steps (AWS CLI preferred)

1. Confirm Instance State and Public IP

```
aws ec2 describe-instances \
  --instance-ids i-0123456789abcdef0 \
  --query
"Reservations[*].Instances[*].{State:State.
Name,PublicIP:PublicIpAddress,KeyName:KeyNa
me}" \
  --output table
```

2. Check Associated Key Pair

Make sure the KeyName matches the .pem file you're using.

---

3. Verify Security Group Inbound Rule for SSH (port 22)

```
aws ec2 describe-security-groups \
  --group-ids sg-0123456789abcdef0 \
  --query
"SecurityGroups[*].IpPermissions[?FromPort=
=`22`]" \
  --output table
```

---

4. Confirm VPC Networking and Route Table

```
aws ec2 describe-route-tables \
  --filters Name=association.subnet-
id,Values=subnet-abcdef12 \
  --query "RouteTables[*].Routes" \
  --output table
```

Ensure that **0.0.0.0/0** is routed to an **Internet Gateway**.

---

5. Inspect Network ACLs

```
aws ec2 describe-network-acls \
  --filters Name=association.subnet-
id,Values=subnet-abcdef12 \
  --output table
```

Check for overly restrictive inbound or outbound rules.

Diagram

⚒ Fix Instructions

1. Allow SSH from Your IP in the Security Group

```
aws ec2 authorize-security-group-ingress \
  --group-id sg-0123456789abcdef0 \
  --protocol tcp --port 22 --cidr
203.0.113.0/32
```

---

2. Attach an Elastic IP if Needed

```
aws ec2 associate-address \
  --instance-id i-0123456789abcdef0 \
  --allocation-id eipalloc-0123abcd
```

3. Use the Correct SSH Username

AMI Type	Default Username
Amazon Linux	`ec2-user`
Ubuntu	`ubuntu`
RHEL	`ec2-user`
Debian	`admin`
SUSE	`ec2-user`
Bitnami/Marketplace AMIs	`bitnami` or `admin` (check docs)

4. Use EC2 Instance Connect (Web SSH) as a fallback

```
aws ec2-instance-connect send-ssh-public-
key \
  --instance-id i-0123456789abcdef0 \
  --availability-zone us-east-1a \
  --instance-os-user ec2-user \
  --ssh-public-key file://~/.ssh/id_rsa.pub
```

5. Full EC2 Instance Recovery Workflow (When SSH is Broken or Key is Lost)

- **Step 1:** Stop the instance

- **Step 2:** Detach the root EBS volume

- **Step 3:** Attach it to another EC2 instance as a secondary volume

- **Step 4:** Mount and edit `/home/ec2-user/.ssh/authorized_keys`

- **Step 5:** Reattach volume to the original instance and restart

This method recovers access without destroying the instance or data.

What You Probably Missed

- **EC2 instances in private subnets** won't have public IPs

- **SSH service (sshd) might not be running** if the instance booted incorrectly

- **User-data scripts** can overwrite firewall or user settings

- **Host key mismatches** in your `~/.ssh/known_hosts` can block access

- **.pem file permissions** must be `chmod 400` or stricter for OpenSSH to accept

- **CloudTrail + VPC Flow Logs + GuardDuty** can correlate failed SSH attempts, brute-force scans, and anomalous traffic if enabled

Chapter 30: Right-Sizing the Beast — Selecting the Optimal EC2 Instance for Your Workload

🔍 Quick Skim Checklist

- ☑ Workload classified as **CPU-bound, memory-bound, storage-heavy**, or **network-intensive**

- ☑ Familiar with EC2 **instance families**: General Purpose, Compute, Memory, Storage, Accelerated

- ☑ Reviewed **vCPU**, **RAM**, **network throughput**, and **EBS performance** per instance type

- ☑ Compared **on-demand vs. spot vs. reserved pricing** for cost impact

- ☑ Tested with **AWS Compute Optimizer** or **benchmark tools**

- ☑ Checked for **burstable performance** limitations (e.g., T-series CPU credits)

How This Happens in the Real World

Scenario 1: Compute-Hungry, Memory-Starved
A machine learning pipeline uses a `c5.large` instance expecting fast training. However, the process frequently

crashes. Why? The model fits in CPU, but not in the 4 GiB of RAM. Memory pressure kills performance—and the job.

Scenario 2: Paying for Power You Don't Need
A small web app runs on an `r5.4xlarge` with 128 GiB of RAM, even though it only uses 2 GiB. The dev team picked it thinking "more is better." Result: thousands in wasted EC2 costs monthly.

Scenario 3: Latency Hits the Logs
A logging system writes terabytes to disk per day. It runs on an `m5.xlarge` with standard EBS. Write latency skyrockets. The fix? Move to an `i4i` instance with local NVMe instance store—built for IOPS-heavy tasks.

Root Causes

- **Misunderstanding workload characteristics**
  Choosing compute-optimized for memory-heavy tasks (or vice versa).

- **Wrong storage assumptions**
  Ignoring disk IOPS/throughput requirements; using EBS where instance store excels.

- **Lack of benchmarking**
  No load testing or profiling prior to instance selection.

- **Defaulting to general-purpose**
  Developers pick `t` or `m` types "just to get started" but never revisit for production.

279

- **Ignoring network performance**
  Underestimating data transfer needs for analytics or media workloads.

- **Burstable CPU confusion**
  T-series instances perform well... until the CPU credits run out.

✳ Compliance & Financial Fallout

- ◈ **Overprovisioned resources** — Inflated bills from choosing oversized instances

- ◈ **Underprovisioned systems** — Application crashes lead to availability risks

- ⚠ **Failure to meet SLAs** — Misaligned infrastructure causes slow responses or downtime

- ⚠ **Inefficient reserved instance planning** — Wrong instance family = unused commitments

- ⚠ **Audit red flags (e.g., SOC 2)** — Inability to justify cost controls or architecture decisions

---

How Developers Misread the Situation

- "Just give me the biggest one—it'll handle anything."

- "If it runs on my laptop, it'll run on a t2.micro."

- "All EC2s are the same—just different sizes."

- "I don't need to test first, we'll monitor later."

- "I/O won't be a problem—we're on SSD." *(SSD ≠ low latency under all loads.)*

🔧 Detection Steps (AWS CLI preferred)

1. List All EC2 Instance Families and Specs

Use the EC2 Instance Type Info page or AWS CLI:

```
aws ec2 describe-instance-types \
  --query
'InstanceTypes[*].{Type:InstanceType,Family
:InstanceFamily,vCPU:VCpuInfo.DefaultVCpus,
Memory:MemoryInfo.SizeInMiB}' \
  --output table
```

---

2. Use AWS Compute Optimizer to Get Recommendations

```
aws compute-optimizer get-ec2-instance-
recommendations \
  --query
'instanceRecommendations[*].{InstanceId:ins
tanceId,Current:instanceType,Recommended:re
commendationOptions[0].instanceType,Reason:
finding}' \
  --output table
```

---

3. Monitor Actual Usage with CloudWatch Metrics

```
aws cloudwatch get-metric-statistics \
  --metric-name CPUUtilization \
  --namespace AWS/EC2 \
  --statistics Average \
  --dimensions Name=InstanceId,Value=i-
0123456789abcdef0 \
  --start-time $(date -d '-7 days' --utc
+%FT%TZ) \
  --end-time $(date --utc +%FT%TZ) \
  --period 3600
```

Also check:

- DiskWriteOps, DiskReadOps

- `NetworkIn`, `NetworkOut`

- `StatusCheckFailed` for hardware/network issues

Diagram

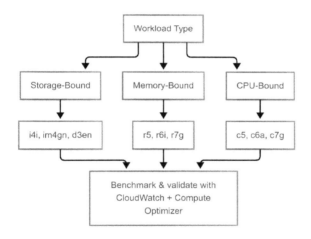

🛠 Fix Instructions

1. Profile Your Workload First

Use local or cloud-based benchmarks (e.g., `stress-ng`, `fio`, `sysbench`) to determine needs.

2. Choose Instance by Primary Resource Dependency

Workload Type	Recommended Families
Web servers	`t3`, `t4g`, `m6g`, `m7i`

Compute-heavy	c5, c6a, c7g, hpc7a
Memory-intensive	r6g, r7i, x2idn
Storage/I/O	i4i, im4gn, d3en
ML/AI	p4, trn1, inf2
GPU	g5, g6, p5
Containers/Fargate	m6a, c6g, t4g

3. Use Compute Optimizer for Ongoing Adjustments

Run regularly to detect over- or under-provisioning.

What You Probably Missed

- **ARM-based instances (Graviton2/3)** offer 40% price-performance gain—but require compatibility testing

- **EBS performance is tied to instance type —** some limit throughput or IOPS

- **Not all families support hibernation, Nitro, or ENA networking**

- **Auto Scaling launch templates may still use old instance types**

- **T-series instances throttle without CPU credits** — monitor with CPUCreditBalance

---

Chapter 31: Scaling Smart — How to Auto-Scale Without Overprovisioning or Lag

🔍 Quick Skim Checklist

- ☑ Auto Scaling group has **right-sized instance types**

- ☑ **Scaling policies** are based on meaningful metrics (e.g., CPU, memory, queue depth)

- ☑ **Cooldown periods** and **instance warm-up** are set appropriately

- ☑ **Target tracking or step scaling** is used instead of basic thresholds

- ☑ Minimum and maximum capacity limits are clearly defined

- ☑ Launch templates use **latest AMIs** and **optimized networking**

- ☑ **Lifecycle hooks** are used for boot-time readiness where needed

How This Happens in the Real World

Scenario 1: The Avalanche of Idle EC2s
 A dev team configures an Auto Scaling Group with CPU threshold-based scaling. When load briefly spikes, it adds 10 instances. But due to high cooldown timers and no scale-in logic, all instances remain idle—burning through the budget for hours.

Scenario 2: The Cold Start Disaster
 A media streaming app sees spikes in traffic, but scaling is based on CPU thresholds alone. When traffic increases, new instances are launched—but they take 3 minutes to boot. Users experience lag and buffering during those crucial moments.

Scenario 3: Always-On by Accident
 An eCommerce app sets a min size of 6 instances just in case. But the app rarely gets more than a few hundred visitors. Scaling never kicks in—because it's overprovisioned from the start.

Root Causes

- **High cooldown or warm-up settings**
  Prevent timely scale-in or cause delays in responding to demand.

- **Poor metric selection**
  Using CPU alone for I/O-bound or queue-based workloads (e.g., SQS, ALB request count).

- **Lack of predictive scaling**
  Reacting to usage instead of forecasting it based

on trends.

- **Static min/max configurations**
  Fixed instance counts that don't match real usage patterns.

- **Improper step sizes**
  Adding or removing too many instances at once, causing whiplash behavior.

- **Old AMIs and launch templates**
  Instances take longer to boot due to unnecessary services or updates.

✳ Compliance & Financial Fallout

- ◇ **Cost overruns** — Overprovisioned groups run unused instances 24/7

- ◇ **Lost revenue** — Under-scaled applications time out or fail during traffic spikes

- ⚠ **Service Availability SLAs** — Performance issues lead to downtime or degraded user experience

- ⚠ **PCI-DSS 6.5.5** — Improper session handling during scale-in can expose in-flight data

- ⚠ **SOC 2 Availability Principle** — Poor scaling undermines high availability commitments

---

How Developers Misread the Situation

- "Auto Scaling = set it and forget it."

- "CPU is enough—we're not that complex."

- "We need a buffer, so let's start with 5 or 6 minimum."

- "We'll just manually scale during peak seasons."

- "Predictive scaling is overkill for us."

🔧 Detection Steps (AWS CLI preferred)

1. Check Current Auto Scaling Group Configuration

```
aws autoscaling describe-auto-scaling-
groups \
  --query
"AutoScalingGroups[*].{GroupName:AutoScalin
gGroupName,Min:MinSize,Max:MaxSize,Desired:
DesiredCapacity}" \
  --output table
```

2. Review Scaling Policies in Use

```
aws autoscaling describe-policies \
  --auto-scaling-group-name my-asg-name \
  --output table
```

Look for TargetTrackingScaling, StepScaling, or SimpleScaling.

3. Review Metrics Associated with Policies

```
aws cloudwatch describe-alarms \
  --query
"MetricAlarms[?Namespace=='AWS/EC2'].{Name:
AlarmName,Metric:MetricName,Threshold:Thres
hold}" \
  --output table
```

Identify whether metrics like **CPUUtilization**, **RequestCountPerTarget**, or **ApproximateNumberOfMessages** are in use.

4. Evaluate Instance Warm-Up and Cooldown Settings

```
aws autoscaling describe-auto-scaling-
groups \
  --query
"AutoScalingGroups[*].{GroupName:AutoScalin
gGroupName,DefaultCooldown:DefaultCooldown}
" \
  --output table
```

Also check `EstimatedInstanceWarmup` on target
tracking policies.

Diagram

⚒ Fix Instructions

1. Use Target Tracking for Simpler, Smarter Scaling

```
aws autoscaling put-scaling-policy \
  --auto-scaling-group-name my-asg-name \
  --policy-name cpu-tracking-policy \
  --policy-type TargetTrackingScaling \
  --target-tracking-configuration
file://cpu-tracking-config.json
```

Example cpu-tracking-config.json:

```
{
  "PredefinedMetricSpecification": {
    "PredefinedMetricType":
"ASGAverageCPUUtilization"
  },
  "TargetValue": 50.0,
  "EstimatedInstanceWarmup": 120
}
```

---

2. Add Step Scaling for Queue-Backed or Traffic Spikes

```
aws autoscaling put-scaling-policy \
  --policy-name queue-scale-up \
  --auto-scaling-group-name my-asg-name \
  --policy-type StepScaling \
  --adjustment-type ChangeInCapacity \
```

```
  --step-adjustments
'[{"MetricIntervalLowerBound": 0,
"ScalingAdjustment": 2}]' \
  --cooldown 60
```

3. Optimize Instance Warm-Up Settings

Use estimated boot time based on startup scripts and instance type:

```
aws autoscaling update-auto-scaling-group \
  --auto-scaling-group-name my-asg-name \
  --default-cooldown 120
```

4. Use Lifecycle Hooks for Boot-Time Initialization

Register a lifecycle hook:

```
aws autoscaling put-lifecycle-hook \
  --lifecycle-hook-name WaitForAppInit \
  --auto-scaling-group-name my-asg-name \
  --lifecycle-transition
autoscaling:EC2_INSTANCE_LAUNCHING \
  --default-result CONTINUE \
  --heartbeat-timeout 300
```

Have your app signal when ready using:

```
aws autoscaling complete-lifecycle-action \
  --lifecycle-hook-name WaitForAppInit \
  --auto-scaling-group-name my-asg-name \
  --lifecycle-action-result CONTINUE \
  --instance-id i-0123456789abcdef0
```

What You Probably Missed

- **Use ALB request count**, not CPU, for scaling web traffic

- **SQS-based scaling** should use `ApproximateNumberOfMessages` as a metric

- **Instance warm-up ≠ cooldown** — both must be tuned independently

- **Launch templates with old AMIs** can make boot times longer than expected

- **Predictive scaling** (for EC2 + Application Load Balancer) can anticipate patterns—use it if traffic is regular

Chapter 32: The Missing Link — Enabling SSM on EC2 Instances After Launch

---

🔍 Quick Skim Checklist

- ☑ EC2 instance has **SSM Agent** installed and running

- ☑ Instance is in a **supported VPC with outbound internet** or a **VPC endpoint for SSM**

- ☑ IAM role with **AmazonSSMManagedInstanceCore** is attached

- ☑ Port **443** is open to AWS SSM endpoints (via NAT Gateway, SSM VPC endpoint, or internet gateway)

- ☑ Instance uses **Amazon Linux, Ubuntu, Windows**, or another SSM-compatible OS

- ☑ Instance metadata service (IMDS) is enabled

How This Happens in the Real World

Scenario 1: Launched Too Quickly
A developer spins up several EC2 instances using an old launch template that doesn't assign an IAM role.

Everything looks fine—until they try to use Session Manager and it silently fails.

Scenario 2: Private Subnet, No NAT

A security-conscious team runs all EC2s in a private subnet with no internet access. They try to use SSM but forget to create VPC endpoints for Systems Manager and EC2 Messages.

Scenario 3: SSM Agent Is MIA

An older Ubuntu AMI is used to launch an instance. It boots fine, but SSM Agent isn't installed. Attempts to use `send-command` or `session-manager` produce a "not managed" error in the SSM console.

Root Causes

- **No IAM role attached to instance**
  Without `AmazonSSMManagedInstanceCore`, the instance cannot register with SSM.

- **SSM Agent not installed or running**
  Older or custom AMIs may not include the agent by default.

- **Network misconfiguration**
  No route to the internet or missing VPC endpoints to reach SSM services.

- **Metadata service disabled or misconfigured**
  SSM Agent relies on EC2 metadata for instance identity.

- **SSM Agent version incompatible or corrupted**
  Some Linux distros may have outdated or broken packages.

✳ Compliance & Financial Fallout

- ⚠ **No secure remote access** — Without SSM, teams fall back to SSH/RDP, increasing exposure

- ⚠ **Audit and incident gaps** — SSM logs actions; without it, session trails disappear

- ⚠ **Missed patch compliance** — Systems Manager Patch Manager cannot apply updates

- ⚠ **SOC 2 / ISO 27001 violations** — Security control automation (access, remediation) may be unachievable

- ◈ **Increased cost** — Teams must maintain bastion hosts or VPNs for manual instance access

---

How Developers Misread the Situation

- "The instance is reachable, so SSM should just work."

- "I thought all Amazon AMIs came with the agent."

- "It's in a private subnet for security—why would it need internet?"

- "We added the policy to the user, that should be enough." *(Spoiler: it needs to be on the **instance role**.)*

- "The SSM console doesn't show the instance, must be a bug."

🔧 Detection Steps (AWS CLI preferred)

1. Check If Instance Is Managed by SSM

```
aws ssm describe-instance-information \
  --query
"InstanceInformationList[*].{InstanceId:Ins
tanceId,Status:PingStatus}" \
  --output table
```

Expected output:

```
+---------------------+-----------+
|     InstanceId      | PingStatus |
+---------------------+-----------+
|  i-0123456789abcde0 |   Online   |
```

297

```
+---------------------+-----------+
```

If the instance is missing or shows `Inactive`, it is **not properly configured**.

---

2. Confirm IAM Role Is Attached

```
aws ec2 describe-instances \
  --instance-ids i-0123456789abcde0 \
  --query
"Reservations[].Instances[].IamInstanceProf
ile.Arn"
```

No output = no role. You'll need to attach one.

---

3. Check Agent Logs (Optional, via SSH)

```
cat /var/log/amazon/ssm/amazon-ssm-
agent.log
```

Look for entries like:

```
Failed to register instance with Systems
Manager
```

Diagram

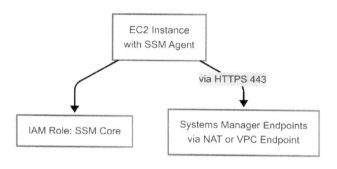

⚒ Fix Instructions

Step 1: Attach IAM Role with SSM Permissions

Create IAM role (if not done already):

```
aws iam create-instance-profile --instance-
profile-name SSMInstanceProfile
aws iam add-role-to-instance-profile \
  --instance-profile-name
SSMInstanceProfile \
  --role-name
YourSSMRoleWithAmazonSSMManagedInstanceCore
```

Attach to EC2 instance:

```
aws ec2 associate-iam-instance-profile \
  --instance-id i-0123456789abcde0 \
  --iam-instance-profile
Name=SSMInstanceProfile
```

Step 2: Install the SSM Agent (Linux example)

```
sudo snap install amazon-ssm-agent --
classic
sudo systemctl enable amazon-ssm-agent
sudo systemctl start amazon-ssm-agent
```

For Amazon Linux:

```
sudo yum install -y amazon-ssm-agent
sudo systemctl start amazon-ssm-agent
```

For Ubuntu DEB:

```
wget https://s3.amazonaws.com/amazon-ssm-
us-east-1/latest/debian_amd64/amazon-ssm-
agent.deb
sudo dpkg -i amazon-ssm-agent.deb
sudo systemctl start amazon-ssm-agent
```

Step 3: Provide Network Access to SSM

Option 1: Public Subnet with Internet Gateway

Ensure route to `0.0.0.0/0` via Internet Gateway.

Option 2: Private Subnet with VPC Endpoints

Create endpoints for:

- `com.amazonaws.region.ssm`

- `com.amazonaws.region.ec2messages`

- `com.amazonaws.region.ssmmessages`

Example:

```
aws ec2 create-vpc-endpoint \
  --vpc-id vpc-12345678 \
  --service-name com.amazonaws.us-east-
1.ssm \
  --vpc-endpoint-type Interface \
  --subnet-ids subnet-abc12345 \
  --security-group-ids sg-0abc12345def
```

Step 4: Verify Connection

```
aws ssm describe-instance-information \
```

```
--query
"InstanceInformationList[?InstanceId=='i-
0123456789abcde0'].PingStatus"
```

What You Probably Missed

- **Bastion alternatives** — Once enabled, you can **disable SSH completely** and use SSM exclusively

- **Patch automation, Run Command, Inventory, Session Manager** — All require SSM to be functional

- **Older AMIs** may include SSM Agent, but disabled by default

- **SSM agent logs** may indicate certificate or token issues with expired IMDS sessions

- **Multi-Region endpoints** — SSM is region-specific; cross-region agents don't register

Chapter 33: Bringing It Back — Recovering Data from a Terminated or Lost EC2 Instance

🔍 Quick Skim Checklist

- ☑ **EBS-backed instance** was terminated (vs. instance-store)

- ☑ **Termination protection** was not enabled

- ☑ **Root or additional EBS volumes** were not encrypted with lost KMS keys

- ☑ You have access to **snapshots**, **backups**, or **CloudTrail logs**

- ☑ IAM permissions allow access to EC2, EBS, and snapshots

- ☑ You know the **instance ID**, **volume ID**, or **snapshot ID** for recovery

How This Happens in the Real World

Scenario 1: "Oops, wrong instance."
An engineer intends to terminate a dev instance, but the CLI command includes the wrong instance ID—and a production EC2 instance disappears. No backups, no protection, and panic ensues.

Scenario 2: Script Gone Rogue
A faulty cleanup script in the CI/CD pipeline auto-terminates unused instances. It tags EC2s as "idle" and terminates them, but one was mid-deployment. The EBS volume went with it—and took key logs and configs along.

Scenario 3: Volume Was Encrypted... and the KMS Key Is Gone
An EC2 was terminated, but its attached volume had server-side encryption using a custom KMS key. That key was deleted as part of a security cleanup, and now the snapshot can't be decrypted—even though it exists.

Root Causes

- **Termination protection disabled**
  Instances were vulnerable to manual or automated deletion.

- **EBS volumes deleted with instance**
  Default EC2 launch settings delete the root volume on termination.

- **No backup automation in place**
  Lack of scheduled snapshots or AWS Backup usage.

- **Misuse of instance-store volumes**
  Data stored on ephemeral disks was lost at termination.

- **Encrypted volumes tied to deleted KMS keys**
  Once the key is gone, encrypted volumes or

snapshots are unusable.

- **Missing tagging or inventory**
  Hard to find snapshots or volumes without proper tags or naming.

✹ Compliance & Financial Fallout

- ◈ **Data loss incidents** — Lack of recoverability can breach SLAs and result in service disruption

- ⚠ **GDPR Article 5(1)(f)** — Failure to ensure integrity and availability of systems

- ⚠ **PCI-DSS 3.6.6** — Lost encrypted data with missing KMS key violates key management controls

- ✗ **ISO 27001 A.12.3.1** — Improper backup and recovery procedures

- ✗ **SOX & SOC 2 controls** — Failure to implement disaster recovery readiness

---

How Developers Misread the Situation

- "We'll just re-launch it if anything happens."

- "EBS volumes don't get deleted by default... right?"

- "Snapshots take care of themselves."

- "I thought that script only removed **stopped** instances."

- "KMS keys can't break recovery unless the data's encrypted... oh wait."

🔧 Detection Steps (AWS CLI preferred)

1. List Recent Snapshots by Owner

```
aws ec2 describe-snapshots \
  --owner-ids self \
  --query
"Snapshots[*].{ID:SnapshotId,Time:StartTime
,VolumeSize:VolumeSize,Desc:Description}" \
  --output table
```

---

2. Find Snapshots by Volume or Instance Tag

```
aws ec2 describe-snapshots \
  --filters
Name=tag:Name,Values="ProdServer" \
```

```
 --query
"Snapshots[*].{ID:SnapshotId,Time:StartTime
}" \
 --output table
```

3. Check If Volumes Still Exist

```
aws ec2 describe-volumes \
 --query
"Volumes[*].{ID:VolumeId,State:State,Size:S
ize,AZ:AvailabilityZone}" \
 --output table
```

4. Use CloudTrail to Find Termination Events

```
aws cloudtrail lookup-events \
 --lookup-attributes
AttributeKey=EventName,AttributeValue=Termi
nateInstances \
 --max-results 10
```

This can help identify when and **who** terminated the
instance.

Diagram

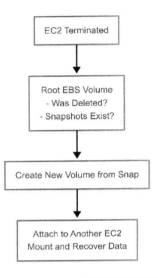

🛠 Fix Instructions

Step 1: Identify and Restore from Snapshot

```
aws ec2 create-volume \
  --availability-zone us-east-1a \
  --snapshot-id snap-0123456789abcdef0 \
  --volume-type gp3 \
  --tag-specifications
'ResourceType=volume,Tags=[{Key=Name,Value=
RecoveredVolume}]'
```

Step 2: Attach the Volume to Another Instance

```
aws ec2 attach-volume \
  --volume-id vol-0123456789abcdef0 \
  --instance-id i-0abcdef1234567890 \
  --device /dev/xvdf
```

Step 3: Mount and Recover Data (Linux)

```
sudo mkdir /mnt/recovery
sudo mount /dev/xvdf1 /mnt/recovery
```

Use `lsblk` or `file -s` to identify partitions if needed.

Step 4: Prevent Future Loss

- **Enable termination protection**:

```
aws ec2 modify-instance-attribute \
  --instance-id i-0abcdef1234567890 \
  --no-disable-api-termination
```

- **Automate EBS snapshots** using AWS Backup or custom Lambda scripts

- **Tag snapshots with purpose and instance info**

- **Use AWS Config** to detect unprotected resources

- **Retain KMS keys** used for encryption as long as backups exist

---

What You Probably Missed

- **Instance-store EC2s** cannot be recovered— data is gone forever

- **Default behavior deletes root volumes** unless overridden

- **Snapshots of encrypted volumes require KMS key access**—don't delete keys blindly

- **Multi-volume recovery** requires recreating all data disks in correct mount order

- **Orphaned snapshots** can be invisible without proper tags—use cost allocation reports to find them

---

Chapter 34: The Bottleneck Below — Diagnosing and Fixing EBS Volume Performance Issues

🔍 **Quick Skim Checklist**

- ☑ EBS volume type matches your workload (e.g., gp3, io1, st1)

- ☑ Instance supports EBS-optimized throughput

- ☑ Volume size is sufficient to unlock performance thresholds

- ☑ IOPS or throughput limits aren't being hit (check CloudWatch metrics)

- ☑ No burst balance depletion (for gp2 or t-type instances)

- ☑ Network bandwidth isn't throttling volume performance

- ☑ Mount options and file system tuning aren't degrading speed

How This Happens in the Real World

Scenario 1: The Misleading "SSD" Assumption

A developer provisions a `gp2` EBS volume for a logging server expecting SSD-level performance. As logs flood in, IOPS tank. Turns out the volume is only 100 GiB—so it's capped at 300 IOPS with minimal burst capacity.

Scenario 2: Throughput vs. IOPS Confusion

An analytics team runs a data-intensive workload on `io1` with 5,000 provisioned IOPS—but throughput flatlines at 250 MB/s. The culprit? They didn't account for the instance's EBS throughput ceiling.

Scenario 3: Great Volume, Wrong Instance

An `io2` volume is mounted to a `t3.medium` instance for a production workload. Despite the premium storage, performance is throttled by the instance's network and burstable limits.

Root Causes

- **Inappropriate volume type**
  `gp2` and `gp3` are general-purpose SSDs—not suitable for sustained high IOPS workloads.

- **Undersized volume**
  Performance on `gp2` and `gp3` scales with size; small volumes = limited baseline IOPS/throughput.

- **Instance type limitations**
  Each EC2 type has max EBS bandwidth and IOPS caps—these are often lower than the attached

volume's specs.

- **Depleted burst balance**

  gp2 and t3/t4 instances rely on burst credits—
  once exhausted, performance drops sharply.

- **File system or OS bottlenecks**

  Poor mount options, single-threaded workloads, or
  small I/O block sizes reduce EBS utilization.

- **Shared network channel contention**

  EBS traffic shares bandwidth with other network
  interfaces unless using dedicated EBS-optimized
  instances.

✷ Compliance & Financial Fallout

- ◌ **Performance degradation** — Application
  slowdowns can impact SLA adherence

- ◌ **Overprovisioned volumes or IOPS** — Paying
  for performance you can't reach

- ⚠ **GDPR Article 32** — Unavailable or degraded
  services risk compliance around data availability

- ⚠ **PCI-DSS 10.3.6** — Inadequate log storage
  performance may lead to loss of audit data

- ✕ **SOC 2 (Availability Principle)** — Volumes
  throttling under load can violate uptime

expectations

How Developers Misread the Situation

- "It's an SSD volume—it should be fast."

- "The volume is provisioned for 5,000 IOPS, so we'll always get that."

- "My instance type doesn't affect EBS—I only care about CPU and RAM."

- "We're not hitting limits, so something else must be broken."

- "gp2 and gp3 are interchangeable, right?" *(Not quite.)*

🦴 Detection Steps (AWS CLI preferred)

1. Get EBS Volume Details and Type

```
aws ec2 describe-volumes \
  --volume-ids vol-0123456789abcdef0 \
  --query
"Volumes[*].{ID:VolumeId,Type:VolumeType,Size:Size,IOPS:Iops,Throughput:Throughput}" \
```

```
  --output table
```

---

2. Check Instance's EBS Bandwidth Limits

Use instance documentation or:

```
aws ec2 describe-instance-types \
  --instance-types m5.large \
  --query
"InstanceTypes[*].EbsInfo.EbsOptimizedInfo.
{Bandwidth:EbsThroughput,MaxIOPS:EbsOptimiz
edIops}" \
  --output table
```

---

3. Monitor Volume Metrics via CloudWatch

```
aws cloudwatch get-metric-statistics \
  --namespace AWS/EBS \
  --metric-name VolumeReadOps \
  --dimensions Name=VolumeId,Value=vol-
0123456789abcdef0 \
  --statistics Average \
  --start-time $(date -d '-1 hour' --utc
+%FT%TZ) \
  --end-time $(date --utc +%FT%TZ) \
  --period 300
```

Repeat for:

- `VolumeWriteOps`

- `VolumeReadBytes` / `VolumeWriteBytes`

- `BurstBalance` (for gp2)

Diagram

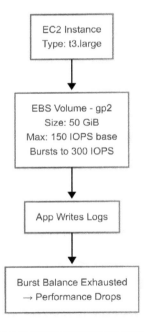

⚒ Fix Instructions

Option 1: Switch to gp3 and Tune IOPS/Throughput

```
aws ec2 modify-volume \
  --volume-id vol-0123456789abcdef0 \
  --volume-type gp3 \
  --iops 6000 \
  --throughput 250
```

Note: gp3 gives **baseline IOPS and throughput**
independent of volume size.

Option 2: Use io1 or io2 for Predictable Performance

```
aws ec2 modify-volume \
  --volume-id vol-0123456789abcdef0 \
  --volume-type io2 \
  --iops 10000
```

Pair with an instance that supports provisioned IOPS levels
(e.g., `m5.4xlarge`, `r5b.2xlarge`, etc.)

Option 3: Match EC2 Type to Volume Needs

```
aws ec2 describe-instance-types \
  --instance-types r5b.large \
```

```
  --query
"InstanceTypes[*].EbsInfo.EbsOptimizedInfo"
\
  --output table
```

Select an instance with matching or greater **EBS bandwidth** and **IOPS capacity**.

Option 4: Monitor and Resize Volume

```
aws ec2 modify-volume \
  --volume-id vol-0123456789abcdef0 \
  --size 200
```

Increasing size on gp2 = more baseline IOPS and burst capacity.

What You Probably Missed

- **gp2 scales IOPS with size**, up to 3,000 IOPS at 1 TiB

- **gp3 decouples size from performance**—ideal for tuning without waste

- **BurstBalance metric drops to 0** = IOPS throttling for gp2 volumes

- **Network traffic and EBS throughput share the same pipe**—especially on smaller instances

- **File system block size and mount options** (e.g., `noatime`, `deadline scheduler`) can significantly affect write performance

Chapter 35: Sluggish from the Start — Diagnosing and Fixing EC2 Boot Time Delays

🔍 Quick Skim Checklist

- ☑ **EC2 launch time** is noticeably longer than expected (> 2–3 minutes)

- ☑ Long-running or complex **user-data scripts** are used at launch

- ☑ Instance relies on **outdated AMIs** with bloated or legacy software

- ☑ **SSM Agent** or initialization services take time to register

- ☑ Network delays (e.g., in pulling files or updates) are observed

- ☑ **Cloud-init** or `systemd` logs show long waits during boot

How This Happens in the Real World

Scenario 1: The "One Script to Rule Them All" Problem
A monolithic user-data script installs dependencies, pulls code from Git, provisions the app, and runs DB

migrations—all on first boot. The instance takes over 10 minutes to become usable, delaying auto scaling and causing health check failures.

Scenario 2: Zombie AMIs
A team uses an AMI built 18 months ago. It still works… mostly. But outdated packages require lengthy updates, and deprecated init scripts block startup. Boot times slowly balloon to 5+ minutes.

Scenario 3: Silent Timeouts
User-data scripts rely on a private S3 bucket, but the instance has no access to it (wrong IAM role). The script hangs silently for 300 seconds trying to pull a file before failing and continuing—resulting in a frustrating black-box delay.

Root Causes

- **Heavy or synchronous user-data scripts**
  Long operations (e.g., installs, updates) block the EC2 boot sequence.

- **No timeout or backgrounding in user-data logic**
  Commands run sequentially with no fallbacks or retries.

- **Stale or bloated AMIs**
  Older AMIs often require updates that delay readiness.

- **I/O blocking**
  Package installs or data fetches are slow due to

EBS performance or networking issues.

- **Missing IAM permissions**
  EC2 startup relies on S3, Parameter Store, or Secrets Manager—failing quietly without access.

- **Cloud-init hangs**
  Initialization services (cloud-init, systemd) wait for unreachable resources.

✵ **Compliance & Financial Fallout**

- 🔄 **Slow auto scaling reactions** — Boot delays lead to performance degradation during traffic spikes

- ⚠ **Health check failures** — Load balancers mark instances as unhealthy if startup lags

- ⚠ **Delayed security agent registration** — SSM/CloudWatch agents may not start in time

- ✕ **SOC 2, ISO 27001 gaps** — Systems not "readily available" on launch may violate availability and recovery policies

- ⚠ **Cost waste** — Instances launch and burn billable minutes before doing anything productive

---

How Developers Misread the Situation

- "User-data scripts run in the background, right?" *(Nope, they run blocking by default.)*

- "This AMI worked six months ago—still fine!"

- "A little extra setup at launch won't hurt."

- "Let's just `yum update -y` every time—can't hurt."

- "If the script fails, it fails quickly." *(Often false— scripts may hang on DNS, S3, etc.)*

🔧 Detection Steps (AWS CLI preferred)

1. Review EC2 Launch Time and Lifecycle Hooks

```
aws ec2 describe-instances \
  --query
"Reservations[*].Instances[*].{ID:InstanceI
d,LaunchTime:LaunchTime,State:State.Name}"
\
  --output table
```

---

2. Check System Log for Boot Delays

```
aws ec2 get-console-output --instance-id i-
0123456789abcdef0
```

Look for lines that show hangups or delays in:

- cloud-init stages

- `systemd` service waits

- user-data execution

---

3. Review SSM Logs (if enabled)

```
aws ssm describe-instance-information \
  --query
"InstanceInformationList[*].{InstanceId:Ins
tanceId,Status:PingStatus,PlatformType:Plat
formType}" \
  --output table
```

If SSM reports `Inactive`, startup agents may not have loaded yet.

---

4. Inspect CloudWatch Boot Metrics

```
aws cloudwatch get-metric-statistics \
  --namespace AWS/EC2 \
  --metric-name StatusCheckFailed \
  --dimensions Name=InstanceId,Value=i-
0123456789abcdef0 \
  --statistics Maximum \
  --start-time $(date -d '-15 minutes' --
utc +%FT%TZ) \
  --end-time $(date --utc +%FT%TZ) \
  --period 60
```

Diagram

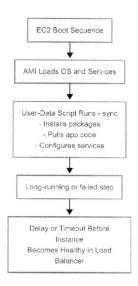

🛠 Fix Instructions

1. Background Non-Essential User-Data Tasks

In your user-data script:

```bash
#!/bin/bash
yum update -y &
/usr/bin/setup-my-app.sh &
```

Use & to parallelize non-critical startup work.

---

2. Add Logging to CloudWatch or Local Disk

```bash
#!/bin/bash
exec > >(tee /var/log/user-data.log|logger
-t user-data -s 2>/dev/console) 2>&1
```

This helps you debug hangs and unexpected behavior.

---

3. Use Prebaked AMIs for Repetitive Setup

Instead of re-running the same setup steps:

- Build a **golden AMI** using EC2 Image Builder or Packer

- Pre-install software, packages, and base configs

- Use `cloud-init` only for dynamic config at boot

---

4. Use Cloud-Init "Final Message" to Time Startup

Append this to user-data:

```
echo "EC2 BOOT COMPLETE" | systemd-cat -t
ec2-boot
```

Then search for this in CloudWatch logs to measure boot time.

---

5. Validate IAM Role Access for Boot-Time Resources

Ensure your instance profile includes access to:

- S3 buckets used in startup

- Parameter Store or Secrets Manager

- Any APIs queried during initialization

Example:

```
aws iam attach-role-policy \
  --role-name EC2StartupRole \
```

```
--policy-arn
arn:aws:iam::aws:policy/AmazonSSMManagedIns
tanceCore
```

What You Probably Missed

- **EC2 Auto Scaling treats instance as "InService" only after health checks pass**

- **cloud-init logs live at** `/var/log/cloud-init.log` **and** `/var/log/cloud-init-output.log`

- **AMIs can be version-controlled and updated monthly using EC2 Image Builder**

- **OS-level service dependencies (e.g.,** `NetworkManager-wait-online.service`**) can add silent 30–60s delays**

- **DNS resolution failures** (e.g., on `apt` or `yum`) during boot can add long timeouts—use `--timeout` flags

---

Chapter 36: Set It, Seal It, Ship It — Building Immutable EC2 Infrastructure with AMI Pipelines

🔍 Quick Skim Checklist

- ☑ You're using **prebaked AMIs** instead of long user-data scripts

- ☑ AMIs are versioned, tested, and stored centrally

- ☑ EC2 instances are **replaced**, not patched in place

- ☑ You've configured **EC2 Image Builder** or CI/CD-backed image automation

- ☑ Instances launched from AMIs are **stateless or ephemeral**

- ☑ No manual configuration is done on running instances post-launch

How This Happens in the Real World

Scenario 1: Patch Tuesday Panic
A security team flags a critical vulnerability in a base package. The dev team manually SSHs into 30 EC2s to patch them. One server is missed, leading to inconsistent

behavior in production. If they had used immutable AMIs, redeployment would've been fast, consistent, and secure.

Scenario 2: User-Data Drift
A developer modifies a user-data script, but forgets to update the script in version control. The next EC2 launches with old logic. The app fails to initialize, and the bug isn't caught for hours. Immutable AMIs would've locked the environment and minimized config drift.

Scenario 3: Downtime by Patch
A system administrator updates a running instance with new software. It breaks the app—and rolling it back isn't straightforward. With immutable images, the fix would have been a simple rollback to the last known-good AMI.

Root Causes

- **Mutable infrastructure mindset**
  Teams rely on long-lived EC2 instances and manual patches instead of rebuilds.

- **Overuse of user-data scripts**
  Complex provisioning logic during boot makes behavior unpredictable.

- **Lack of versioned AMIs**
  No structured way to trace what changed between deployments.

- **Manual configuration drift**
  SSH access and "hotfixing" introduce stateful

differences across instances.

- **No automated image creation pipeline**
  AMIs are built manually and inconsistently.

✸ Compliance & Financial Fallout

- ⚠ **Unpatched vulnerabilities** — Manually updated instances often miss updates

- ⚠ **SOX and SOC 2 violations** — Inability to reproduce system state exactly

- ⚠ **PCI-DSS 11.5.2** — Systems must be monitored for unauthorized changes, harder with mutable infra

- ◈ **Time wasted in troubleshooting drift** — Debugging "it works on one box" scenarios

- ⚠ **Lack of auditability** — No single source of truth for what was deployed

---

How Developers Misread the Situation

- "It's faster to SSH and fix it directly."

- "We'll patch it later—this is a temporary environment."

- "Immutable infra is only for big companies with Kubernetes."

- "Building AMIs takes too long."

- "EC2 Image Builder is overkill for our team."

🔧 Detection Steps (AWS CLI preferred)

1. List All AMIs You Own (Filter by Tag or Pipeline)

```
aws ec2 describe-images \
  --owners self \
  --query
"Images[*].{ID:ImageId,Name:Name,Creation:C
reationDate}" \
  --output table
```

---

2. Check Launch Template or Auto Scaling Group to Verify AMI Usage

```
aws ec2 describe-launch-template-versions \
  --launch-template-name my-template \
  --versions 1 \
```

```
--query
"LaunchTemplateVersions[*].LaunchTemplateDa
ta.ImageId"
```

---

3. Review EC2 Image Builder Pipelines

```
aws imagebuilder list-image-pipelines \
  --query
"imagePipelineList[*].{Name:name,Status:sta
tus,ARN:arn}" \
  --output table
```

---

4. Get Last Built AMIs From Pipeline

```
aws imagebuilder list-image-builds \
  --query
"imageSummaryList[*].{Name:name,Version:ver
sion,State:state}" \
  --output table
```

Diagram

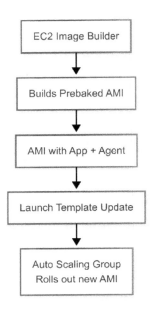

```
EC2 Image Builder
        ↓
Builds Prebaked AMI
        ↓
AMI with App + Agent
        ↓
Launch Template Update
        ↓
Auto Scaling Group
Rolls out new AMI
```

⚒ Fix Instructions

Step 1: Restrict SSH Access

Only allow SSH from your office or VPN IP:

```
aws ec2 authorize-security-group-ingress \
  --group-id sg-0abc1234567890def \
  --protocol tcp --port 22 \
  --cidr 203.0.113.0/32
```

☑ Also limit **SSM access** via IAM policies:

```
{
```

```
  "Effect": "Allow",
  "Action": [
    "ssm:StartSession",
    "ssm:SendCommand"
  ],
  "Resource": [
    "arn:aws:ec2:region:account-
id:instance/instance-id"
  ]
}
```

> ⚠ Avoid wildcard permissions like `ssm:*`
> across all resources.

Step 2: Harden SSH Configuration

Edit the file:

```
sudo vi /etc/ssh/sshd_config
```

Set or ensure the following:

```
PermitRootLogin no
PasswordAuthentication no
AllowUsers ec2-user youradminuser
```

☑ Validate the config:

```
sudo sshd -t
```

Restart SSH:

```
sudo systemctl restart sshd
```

Step 3: Install and Fully Enable SELinux (Amazon Linux 2)

Amazon Linux 2 ships with SELinux in *permissive* or *disabled* mode by default.

Install (if needed):

```
sudo yum install -y policycoreutils
selinux-policy-targeted
```

Edit the config:

```
sudo vi /etc/selinux/config
# Change to:
SELINUX=enforcing
```

⚠ A reboot is required to fully activate SELinux on Amazon Linux 2.

```
sudo reboot
```

Verify after reboot:

```
sestatus
```

Step 4: Enable Automatic Security Updates

For Amazon Linux:

```
sudo yum install -y yum-cron
sudo systemctl enable yum-cron
sudo systemctl start yum-cron
```

For Ubuntu:

```
sudo apt install -y unattended-upgrades
sudo dpkg-reconfigure --priority=low
unattended-upgrades
```

Step 5: Use a Minimal AMI and Remove Unneeded Packages

Audit and prune:

```
sudo yum list installed
sudo yum remove ftp telnet httpd samba nfs-
utils -y
```

Step 6: Enable File Integrity Monitoring with auditd

Install and start `auditd`:

```
sudo yum install -y audit
sudo systemctl enable auditd
sudo systemctl start auditd
```

Check status:

```
sudo auditctl -s
```

> ☑ Use `auditctl` or
> `/etc/audit/rules.d/` to add custom file
> monitoring rules.

What You Probably Missed

- **SSM Agent access** gives shell access without SSH—ensure IAM policies are scoped

- **cron jobs and** `/tmp` **permissions** can be exploited if world-writable

- **Disabling IPv6** can reduce some attack surface if unused

- **Auditd** logs critical file and process events— helpful for forensics

- **Immutable infrastructure** (see Chapter 36) minimizes attack surface from the start

Chapter 38: Metadata Mayhem — Securing EC2 Against SSRF and Credential Theft

---

🔍 Quick Skim Checklist

- ☑ Instance metadata access is limited using **IMDSv2**

- ☑ Applications do **not** fetch metadata from `http://169.254.169.254` directly

- ☑ Web apps are protected against **SSRF injection**

- ☑ No hardcoded calls to instance metadata from user-supplied input

- ☑ IAM roles assigned to instances follow **least privilege**

- ☑ Application-layer firewalls or reverse proxies are hardened

---

How This Happens in the Real World

Scenario 1: SSRF Opens the Metadata Door
A web app lets users enter URLs to fetch preview

340

thumbnails. An attacker inputs
`http://169.254.169.254/latest/meta-data/iam/security-credentials/`. The app fetches it, unknowingly leaking temporary IAM credentials back to the attacker, who uses them to exfiltrate S3 data.

Scenario 2: IMDSv1 Left Enabled
An EC2 instance has both IMDSv1 and IMDSv2 enabled. An attacker compromises a vulnerable internal service and makes a server-side request to retrieve credentials via IMDSv1, which doesn't require a token—credentials are immediately exposed.

Scenario 3: Too Much Privilege
A misconfigured application runs on an EC2 instance with an overprivileged IAM role. Through SSRF or local compromise, an attacker gets temporary credentials and finds they can list buckets, modify Lambda functions, and more.

Root Causes

- **IMDSv1 still enabled**
  Version 1 of the Instance Metadata Service allows unauthenticated access from within the instance.

- **No SSRF protection in apps**
  Apps fetch arbitrary URLs based on user input without validation or sanitization.

- **Over-permissioned IAM roles**
  EC2 instances are granted wildcard permissions or

admin-level access.

- **Unmonitored metadata calls**
  Lack of logging or alerting on internal access to metadata endpoints.

- **No web application firewall (WAF)**
  External requests are not filtered or inspected for SSRF-style attacks.

✳ Compliance & Financial Fallout

- ✖ **SOC 2 CC6.6 / CC7.1** — Sensitive metadata exposed due to insecure defaults

- ✖ **PCI-DSS 3.3.3** — Failure to protect credentials used in system authentication

- ✖ **GDPR Article 32** — Inadequate protection of identity credentials or PII

- ◈ **IAM key leakage = cost explosion** — Compromised credentials used for crypto mining

- ⚠ **Audit trail gaps** — Metadata access isn't logged unless explicitly monitored

- ◈ **Data exfiltration risk** — Attackers can query IAM, S3, and Lambda APIs with stolen credentials

How Developers Misread the Situation

- "Metadata access is only internal—what's the risk?"

- "Our app doesn't use that IP, so we're safe."

- "IMDSv1 is just the default; it's fine for now."

- "The role only has read-only access. That's safe, right?"

- "If someone gets inside the instance, we're already compromised anyway." *(But you can reduce damage.)*

🔧 Detection Steps (AWS CLI preferred)

1. Identify EC2 Instances With IMDSv1 Enabled

```
aws ec2 describe-instances \
  --query
"Reservations[*].Instances[*].{ID:InstanceI
d,IMDS:MetadataOptions.HttpTokens}" \
  --output table
```

Expected secure value: required (IMDSv2 only).

2. Review IAM Role Permissions for Attached Instance Profiles

```
aws iam list-attached-role-policies \
  --role-name EC2AppRole
```

Then inspect each policy:

```
aws iam get-policy-version \
  --policy-arn
arn:aws:iam::123456789012:policy/EC2AccessP
olicy \
  --version-id v1
```

Look for overbroad permissions like `iam:*`, `s3:*`, or `AdministratorAccess`.

---

3. Use VPC Flow Logs to Detect Metadata Access

Enable flow logs and inspect logs with Athena, CloudWatch Logs, or GuardDuty.

```
aws ec2 describe-flow-logs
```

---

4. Use GuardDuty to Detect Metadata Theft Attempts

List recent findings:

```
aws guardduty list-findings \
  --detector-id <your-detector-id> \
  --query "FindingIds"
```

Then fetch full details:

```
aws guardduty get-findings \
  --detector-id <your-detector-id> \
  --finding-ids <comma-separated-list>
```

Look for:

- UnauthorizedAccess:EC2/InstanceMetadata

- Recon:EC2/PortProbeUnprotectedPort

Diagram

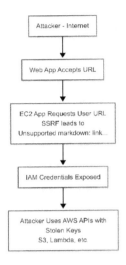

⚒ Fix Instructions

Step 1: Enforce IMDSv2 Only

```
aws ec2 modify-instance-metadata-
options \

  --instance-id i-
0123456789abcdef0 \

  --http-tokens required \

  --http-endpoint enabled
```

☑ New instances should also be launched with these settings via **launch templates**.

Step 2: Harden IAM Roles

Use tightly scoped IAM policies. Avoid wildcards and overly permissive roles.

```
{

  "Effect": "Allow",

  "Action": ["s3:GetObject"],

  "Resource": ["arn:aws:s3:::my-
  secure-bucket/*"]

}
```

Step 3: Sanitize URLs and Enforce SSRF Protections

- Block internal IPs in application logic

- Use allowlists for domains

- Validate input before fetching any external URLs

Step 4: Harden NGINX and Proxy Layers

Block direct access to metadata endpoints:

```
# Block metadata endpoint in NGINX
reverse proxy

location ~* ^/169\.254\.169\.254 {

    return 403;

}
```

Step 5: Enable GuardDuty and Flow Logs

```
aws guardduty create-detector --
enable
```


```
aws ec2 create-flow-logs \

  --resource-type VPC \

  --resource-ids vpc-abc123 \

  --traffic-type ALL \
```

```
--log-group-name VPCFlowLogGroup
\

--deliver-logs-permission-arn
arn:aws:iam::123456789012:role/VPC
FlowLogRole
```

What You Probably Missed

- **IMDSv2 must be explicitly enabled in launch templates** — even new EC2s may default to IMDSv1 unless overridden

- **Launch templates may default to IMDSv1 unless explicitly overridden** — always validate via CLI or console

- **SSRF payloads** can be embedded in innocuous-looking parameters like `img=https://169.254.169.254`

- **Reverse proxies like NGINX** can unintentionally forward internal metadata requests if not filtered

- **Scan source code** for hardcoded metadata URLs or insecure fetch logic (`curl`, `requests.get()`, etc.)

Chapter 39: Silent Failures — Using CloudWatch to Catch EC2 Memory Leaks and Resource Starvation Early

🔍 Quick Skim Checklist

- ☑ CloudWatch agent is installed and configured to collect memory and disk metrics

- ☑ EC2 dashboards include swap usage, memory utilization, and disk inodes

- ☑ Alarms are set for sustained memory growth, not just CPU

- ☑ Application logs and system logs are shipped to CloudWatch for deeper context

- ☑ Metrics are visualized over days or weeks, not just hourly snapshots

- ☑ EC2 roles have the correct IAM permissions to push custom metrics

How This Happens in the Real World

Scenario 1: Memory Leak in Production
A Node.js app runs fine for days but suddenly crashes without warning. CPU looks fine in CloudWatch. Later, the

team discovers the app had a memory leak. Because default CloudWatch metrics didn't include memory, the problem went unnoticed until it broke the app.

Scenario 2: Swap Storm
An underprovisioned EC2 instance starts swapping due to high memory pressure. Performance tanks. No alarms triggered because swap and memory metrics weren't being collected. If CloudWatch alarms had been set on swap usage, the issue would've been caught days earlier.

Scenario 3: "It Works on My Dashboard"
CPU and disk space looked fine in the CloudWatch console, so devs dismissed user complaints of slowness. Later, analysis showed inode exhaustion was preventing new file creation—an invisible issue in the default metrics set.

Root Causes

- **Memory metrics not enabled**
  CloudWatch does not collect memory usage by default; the agent must be installed and configured.

- **Overreliance on CPU-based alerts**
  CPUUtilization can stay low even when memory leaks or disk inodes cause issues.

- **Lack of swap monitoring**
  Swap usage is a strong signal of resource stress but is often unmonitored.

- **Short observation windows**
  Issues like memory leaks unfold over hours or days—not visible in 1-hour charts.

- **Missing alarm thresholds**
  Teams fail to define what "bad" looks like for memory and file system saturation.

✳ Compliance & Financial Fallout

- ⚠ **SLA breaches** — Apps crash due to resource starvation, causing unplanned downtime

- ⚠ **SOX/SOC 2 Audit Risks** — Inability to detect service degradation proactively

- ✘ **PCI-DSS 10.5.5** — Missing logging of critical performance issues

- ◇ **Increased support cost** — Debugging postmortems on memory exhaustion is time-consuming

- ◇ **Overprovisioning** — Teams may scale up unnecessarily instead of fixing a leak

---

How Developers Misread the Situation

- "If CPU is low, the instance must be healthy."

- "CloudWatch already monitors everything, right?"

- "We don't need memory metrics—it's Linux, it'll manage itself."

- "Memory leaks show up in logs, we'll catch it there." *(But only if you're collecting them.)*

- "Swap usage isn't a problem unless it crashes." *(It's a warning sign, not just a consequence.)*

🔧 Detection Steps (AWS CLI preferred)

1. Check if CloudWatch Agent Is Running

```
ps aux | grep amazon-cloudwatch-agent
```

You should see an active process. If not, install and configure the agent.

---

2. Verify Memory and Swap Metrics Are Being Sent

```
aws cloudwatch list-metrics \
  --namespace CWAgent \
  --metric-name mem_used_percent
```

Repeat for:

- `mem_available_percent`

- `swap_used_percent`

- `disk_inodes_free`

---

3. Create a Dashboard to Visualize Memory Usage

```
aws cloudwatch put-dashboard \
  --dashboard-name EC2-Memory-Health \
  --dashboard-body file://dashboard.json
```

Sample `dashboard.json` (snippet):

```
{
  "widgets": [
    {
      "type": "metric",
      "x": 0,
      "y": 0,
      "width": 12,
      "height": 6,
      "properties": {
```

```
        "metrics": [
          [ "CWAgent", "mem_used_percent",
"InstanceId", "i-0123456789abcdef0" ]
        ],
        "period": 300,
        "stat": "Average",
        "title": "Memory Usage (%)"
      }
    }
  ]
}
```

4. List Alarms Related to Memory or Swap (if any)

```
aws cloudwatch describe-alarms \
  --query
"MetricAlarms[?contains(MetricName, 'mem')
|| contains(MetricName,
'swap')].[AlarmName,StateValue]" \
  --output table
```

Diagram

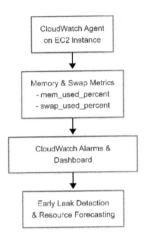

🛠️ Fix Instructions

Step 1: Install the CloudWatch Agent

For Amazon Linux 2:

```
sudo yum install amazon-cloudwatch-agent -y
```

For Ubuntu:

```
sudo apt install amazon-cloudwatch-agent -y
```

> ☑ Make sure the EC2 instance role has the CloudWatchAgentServerPolicy IAM policy attached to allow metric publishing.

Step 2: Create a Config File to Include Memory & Swap Metrics

```
{
  "metrics": {
    "metrics_collected": {
      "mem": {
        "measurement": [
          "mem_used_percent",
          "mem_available_percent"
        ]
      },
      "swap": {
        "measurement": [
          "swap_used_percent"
        ]
      },
      "disk": {
        "measurement": [
          "inodes_free"
        ],
        "resources": ["/"]
      }
    }
  }
}
```

Save as `/opt/aws/amazon-cloudwatch-agent/etc/amazon-cloudwatch-agent.json`

Step 3: Start the CloudWatch Agent

```
sudo /opt/aws/amazon-cloudwatch-agent/bin/amazon-cloudwatch-agent-ctl \
  -a fetch-config \
  -m ec2 \
  -c file:/opt/aws/amazon-cloudwatch-agent/etc/amazon-cloudwatch-agent.json \
  -s
```

Step 4: Create Memory and Swap Alarms

Memory usage:

```
aws cloudwatch put-metric-alarm \
  --alarm-name HighMemoryUsage \
  --metric-name mem_used_percent \
  --namespace CWAgent \
  --statistic Average \
  --period 300 \
  --threshold 80 \
  --comparison-operator GreaterThanThreshold \
  --evaluation-periods 2 \
```

```
  --alarm-actions arn:aws:sns:us-east-
1:123456789012:NotifyMe
```

Swap usage:

```
aws cloudwatch put-metric-alarm \
  --alarm-name HighSwapUsage \
  --metric-name swap_used_percent \
  --namespace CWAgent \
  --statistic Average \
  --period 300 \
  --threshold 30 \
  --comparison-operator
GreaterThanThreshold \
  --evaluation-periods 2 \
  --alarm-actions arn:aws:sns:us-east-
1:123456789012:NotifyMe
```

Inode exhaustion:

```
aws cloudwatch put-metric-alarm \
  --alarm-name LowInodes \
  --metric-name disk_inodes_free \
  --namespace CWAgent \
  --statistic Average \
  --period 300 \
  --threshold 10000 \
  --comparison-operator LessThanThreshold \
```

```
--evaluation-periods 2 \
--alarm-actions arn:aws:sns:us-east-
1:123456789012:NotifyMe
```

What You Probably Missed

- **CloudWatch doesn't collect memory metrics by default** — you must install and configure the agent

- **Slow memory leaks evade short-term monitoring** — use 1- and 7-day views to see gradual creep

- **Inodes can run out even if disk space is fine** — especially in log-heavy apps

- **Inodes exhaustion won't show up in** `df -h` — use `df -i` to check inode availability and monitor `disk_inodes_free` for alerting

- **Swap growth is an early distress signal** — not just a postmortem metric

- **IAM roles must have** `cloudwatch:PutMetricData` to push memory stats

Part 4: Optimizing Serverless with AWS Lambda

Chapter 40: The IAM Trap—How Lambda Permissions Break and What to Do About It

🔍 **Quick Skim Checklist — Practical checks for the reader**

- ☑ Confirm that the Lambda execution role includes all required `Action` + `Resource` permissions.

- ☑ Use `list-attached-role-policies` to identify both inline and managed IAM policies.

- ☑ Check if the *caller* service (S3, SQS, etc.) is allowed in the Lambda's **resource-based policy**.

- ☑ Validate IAM condition keys like `aws:SourceArn` and `aws:SourceAccount`.

- ☑ Confirm network path to services if Lambda runs in a VPC (e.g., NAT or endpoints for S3/DynamoDB).

- ☑ Inspect CloudWatch logs for silent `AccessDenied` errors or failed event trigger mappings.

Quick Rule:

- **Lambda calling something?** →
  Needs execution role permission

- **Something calling Lambda?** → That
  service needs to be listed in Lambda's
  resource policy

How This Happens in the Real World — 2–3 real scenarios

1. **S3 Trigger That Never Fires**
   A photo-processing app sets up an S3 trigger to
   invoke a Lambda on upload. The S3 bucket is
   correctly configured, and Lambda permissions
   seem fine—but no events come through. The
   culprit? The Lambda lacks a **resource policy**
   allowing s3.amazonaws.com to invoke it.

2. **DynamoDB Streams Trigger Ignored**
   A retail inventory system enables a Lambda to
   process stream records from DynamoDB. Despite
   enabling the trigger, no invocations occur. Later it's
   discovered the Lambda's execution role lacks
   dynamodb:GetRecords, so event source
   mapping fails silently.

3. **Cross-Region SNS Publishing Fails Silently**
   A Lambda function publishes to an SNS topic in a
   different AWS region. Permissions *look* right, but
   the publish action is blocked. The issue:

`aws:SourceArn` in the SNS topic's resource policy expected a different region than where Lambda runs.

Root Causes

- ◆ **Missing Execution Role Permissions**
  Lambda execution role lacks fine-grained access (e.g., `sqs:SendMessage`, `dynamodb:PutItem`).

- ◆ **No Resource-Based Policy on Target Service**
  Services like S3, SNS, SQS must explicitly allow Lambda to access them.

- ◆ **Condition Keys Mismatch**
  Policies using `aws:SourceArn` or `aws:SourceAccount` fail when values don't match precisely—**including region differences**.

- ◆ **VPC Isolation**
  A Lambda inside a private subnet without internet access (or interface endpoints) can't reach public AWS services, leading to confusing permission errors.

✳ Compliance & Financial Fallout

- 🛡 **GDPR**: Missed audit logs from failed CloudWatch or S3 writes.

- 💳 **PCI-DSS**: Over-permissive roles used as quick fixes violate least privilege.

- 💠 **Hidden CloudWatch Charges**: Endless retries on broken permissions generate excess logs.

- 🪓 **Business Impact**: Broken triggers in event-driven systems result in silent operational outages.

How Developers Misread the Situation — Wrong assumptions

- "My role has $*:*$, so what's the issue?" — Resource policies can still block the invocation.

- "I tested with the console and it worked." — But live triggers (e.g., from S3 or SNS) use different trust paths.

- "I copied a permission statement from another region and it worked there." — But `aws:SourceArn` region mismatch caused silent denial.

🔧 Detection Steps (AWS CLI preferred) — Commands and flags

```
# Check attached managed and inline
policies for the Lambda role
aws iam list-attached-role-policies --role-
name MyLambdaRole
aws iam list-role-policies --role-name
MyLambdaRole

# Retrieve and inspect a specific managed
policy
aws iam get-policy --policy-arn
arn:aws:iam::aws:policy/MyManagedPolicy
aws iam get-policy-version \
  --policy-arn
arn:aws:iam::aws:policy/MyManagedPolicy \
  --version-id v1

# Simulate IAM access for specific actions
aws iam simulate-principal-policy \
  --policy-source-arn
arn:aws:iam::123456789012:role/MyLambdaRole
\
  --action-names s3:GetObject \
  --resource-arns arn:aws:s3:::my-
bucket/data.json

# Check if Lambda allows the service to
invoke it
```

```
aws lambda get-policy --function-name
MyFunction

# Check if S3 bucket has a relevant policy
aws s3api get-bucket-policy --bucket my-
source-bucket

# Review CloudWatch logs for permission-
related errors
aws logs describe-log-streams --log-group-
name /aws/lambda/MyFunction
```

Diagram — ASCII block for visual clarity

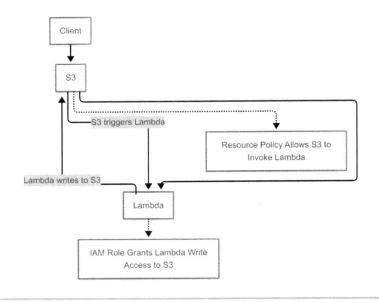

🔧 Fix Instructions — Step-by-step code and config fixes

1. **Attach IAM Permissions to Lambda's Execution Role**

```json
{
  "Version": "2012-10-17",
  "Statement": [
    {
      "Effect": "Allow",
      "Action": ["s3:GetObject"],
      "Resource": "arn:aws:s3:::my-bucket/*"
    }
  ]
}
```

2. **Grant S3 Permission to Invoke Lambda**

```
aws lambda add-permission \
  --function-name MyFunction \
  --statement-id S3Invoke \
  --action lambda:InvokeFunction \
  --principal s3.amazonaws.com \
  --source-arn arn:aws:s3:::my-bucket
```

3. Add IAM Role Trust to Resource (if Lambda writes to S3)

```json
{
  "Version": "2012-10-17",
  "Statement": [
    {
      "Sid": "AllowLambdaWrites",
      "Effect": "Allow",
      "Principal": {
        "AWS":
"arn:aws:iam::123456789012:role/MyLambdaRol
e"
      },
      "Action": "s3:PutObject",
      "Resource": "arn:aws:s3:::my-output-
bucket/*"
    }
  ]
}
```

What You Probably Missed — Lesser-known edge cases, hidden pitfalls

- 🧠 **Lambda Layers Need Permissions Too**
  If your layer uses the AWS SDK or calls other services, make sure your execution role grants it

permissions too.

- 🕵️ **Silent Failures from Condition Key Mismatches**
  Cross-account or cross-region mismatches in
  `aws:SourceArn` or `aws:SourceAccount` can
  silently block invocations.

- `simulate-principal-policy` **Is Not the Whole Story**
  It simulates only **identity-based policies**, not
  resource-based ones. Always check both.

- ⚠️ **Function URLs Introduce a Separate IAM Path**
  Function URLs require either IAM auth or `NONE` +
  CORS headers. Missing this leads to access issues
  masked as runtime errors.

Chapter 41: Cold Starts, Hot Pain — Demystifying Lambda Latency and Runtime Readiness

---

🔍 Quick Skim Checklist — Practical checks for the reader

- ☑ Identify whether your function uses a **VPC**, and if so, whether it has **NAT gateway** or **VPC endpoints** configured.

- ☑ Check your **Lambda runtime**—some have longer cold starts (Java, .NET) than others (Node.js, Python).

- ☑ Use **provisioned concurrency** for latency-sensitive or steady workloads.

- ☑ Enable **SnapStart** (for Java 11 only) where available.

- ☑ Minimize initialization code outside the handler (`/global scope`) to speed up init phase—unless using provisioned concurrency.

- ☑ Monitor `InitDuration` metric in **CloudWatch (Enhanced Monitoring)** for cold start trends.

How This Happens in the Real World — 2–3 real scenarios

1. **The API That Sleeps on You**
   A fintech startup deploys a Python-based Lambda API behind API Gateway. During low-traffic hours, the first request takes nearly 2 seconds. Cold starts strike because the function had been idle for over 15 minutes and had no provisioned concurrency.

2. **Java Makes You Wait**
   A Java Lambda function used for image processing performs great in load tests—but sporadic user reports show long latency spikes. Logs reveal 3–5 second cold start times due to JVM warm-up and class loading in the init phase.

3. **VPC Without a Plan**
   A healthcare Lambda app in a VPC talks to RDS but experiences random latency spikes. Each cold start includes an Elastic Network Interface (ENI) attachment process, increasing cold start duration up to 10+ seconds.

Root Causes

- ◆ **Lambda Initialization Lifecycle**
  Cold starts happen when AWS has to set up a new **execution environment** for your Lambda—especially if there's no idle container to reuse.

- ◆ **Heavy Runtimes**
  JVM-based runtimes (Java, .NET, custom) have longer startup times due to bytecode loading, dependency injection, and JIT compilation.

- ◆ **VPC Attachments**
  If your Lambda function is VPC-attached, each cold start must allocate an ENI, which can take 3–10 seconds if not optimized.

- ◆ **Code in Global Scope**
  Long-running initializations (e.g., DB connection, ML model loading) outside the handler prolong the init phase.

- ◆ **Lack of Provisioned Concurrency**
  Without provisioned concurrency, functions scale reactively—leading to fresh cold starts under unpredictable traffic surges.

✳ Compliance & Financial Fallout — List of risks

- **HIPAA / PCI-DSS**: Latency SLAs may be violated if patient/transactional data pipelines are delayed.

- **Missed Alarms**: Alerting and event-driven systems may misfire or timeout due to long cold starts.

- 🔄 **Customer Churn**: Sluggish first-response latency in web/mobile apps causes abandonment and brand erosion.
- 📉 **Inaccurate Billing Metrics**: Cold starts inflate reported durations, especially when billed by millisecond.

How Developers Misread the Situation — Wrong assumptions

- "We're not scaling yet, so cold starts don't matter." — Cold starts hit **even with a single user** after inactivity.
- "Python/Node are immune to cold starts." — They're faster, not immune. Global scope bloat or VPC config still hurts.
- "Provisioned concurrency is too expensive." — Not necessarily. It can reduce invocation duration and cost in latency-critical apps.
- "All cold starts are the same." — Actually, Java and .NET functions suffer far more without SnapStart or tuning.

🔧 Detection Steps (AWS CLI preferred) — Commands and flags

```
# Get recent logs with cold start durations
aws logs filter-log-events \
  --log-group-name /aws/lambda/my-function \
  --filter-pattern '"Init Duration"' \
  --limit 10

# Use CloudWatch Insights to find worst offenders
aws logs start-query \
  --log-group-name /aws/lambda/my-function \
  --start-time $(date -d '15 minutes ago' +%s) \
  --end-time $(date +%s) \
  --query-string "fields @timestamp, @message | filter @message like /Init Duration/ | sort @timestamp desc"

# Check function concurrency configuration
aws lambda get-function-concurrency --function-name my-function

# Check if SnapStart is enabled (Java only)
aws lambda get-function-configuration --function-name my-java-fn \
  --query 'SnapStart'
```

`InitDuration` is emitted as a separate CloudWatch metric only with **Enhanced Monitoring**. Use it to graph cold start frequency across functions or versions.

Diagram — ASCII block for visual clarity

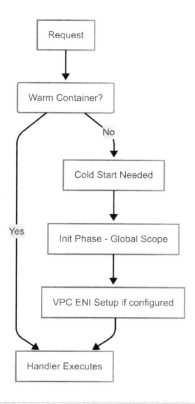

🛠 Fix Instructions — Step-by-step code and config fixes

1. Reduce Init Code in Global Scope (Python Example)

```
# ✖ Slow global setup
client = boto3.client('dynamodb')
model = load_big_ml_model()

def handler(event, context):
    ...

# ☑ Fast init: lazy loading
client = None
model = None

def handler(event, context):
    global client, model
    if not client:
        client = boto3.client('dynamodb')
    if not model:
        model = load_big_ml_model()
    ...
```

💡 For **provisioned concurrency** or **long-running jobs**, initializing in global scope can be fine—it avoids redoing setup each time.

---

2. Enable Provisioned Concurrency (for steady workloads)

```
aws lambda put-provisioned-concurrency-
config \
  --function-name my-function \
  --qualifier "prod" \
  --provisioned-concurrent-executions 5
```

3. Enable SnapStart for Java 11 Functions

```
aws lambda update-function-configuration \
  --function-name my-java-fn \
  --snap-start ApplyOn=PublishedVersions
```

⚠ SnapStart is available **only** for Java 11 runtimes (as of 2024). Java 17 support is in preview.

---

4. Optimize VPC Setup

- Prefer public Lambda (no VPC) when accessing public AWS services.

- If VPC is necessary:

- Use **VPC endpoints** for S3/DynamoDB

- Ensure **ENIs are reused** (keep functions warm or use provisioned concurrency)

- Minimize number of subnets/security groups attached

What You Probably Missed — Lesser-known edge cases, hidden pitfalls

- 🧠 **Lambda@Edge cold starts are region-specific and more frequent** due to globally distributed infrastructure.

- ⚠ **Provisioned Concurrency must be applied to a published version or alias—not** $LATEST.

- 🍪 **Dependencies can introduce bloat.** Avoid bundling large libraries or redundant SDKs already available in the runtime.

- 🍪 **Custom runtimes or Docker images** often have longer cold starts due to larger bootstraps and more complex initialization logic.

Chapter 42: Lean, Mean, Lambda Machine — Optimizing Memory, Timeout, and Size

🔍 Quick Skim Checklist — Practical checks for the reader

- ☑ Is memory allocation too low (causing slow execution) or too high (wasting cost)?

- ☑ Have you reviewed `Duration` **vs** `MaxMemoryUsed` metrics in CloudWatch?

- ☑ Are timeouts long enough for reliable execution, but not too long for runaway cost?

- ☑ Is your deployment package within the 250MB unzipped size limit?

- ☑ Are you bundling unnecessary dependencies (e.g., entire SDKs already available in the runtime)?
- ☑ Use Lambda Layers for shared dependencies — but avoid layering large monoliths; keep them under 50MB zipped for speed.

- ☑ Have you tested multiple memory settings using AWS Lambda Power Tuning?

How This Happens in the Real World — 2–3 real scenarios

1. **The Slow Python Function**
   A Lambda function written in Python processes S3 objects and takes over 8 seconds to run. With 128MB of memory, CPU is throttled. After bumping memory to 512MB, the same job completes in under 2 seconds—with lower cost due to shorter duration.

2. **The Oversized Deployment**
   A Java Lambda app bundles its entire `lib/` folder with unused Apache Commons libraries and AWS SDKs already included in the runtime. The function crosses the 250MB unzipped limit, failing silently during deployment via CI/CD.

3. **The Silent Timeout Killer**
   A Node.js-based function integrates with an external HTTP API. Random invocations fail silently due to a timeout misaligned with the upstream API's latency. Increasing the timeout from 3 to 10 seconds fixed the issue and reduced reprocessing logic in upstream code.

Root Causes

- **Undersized Memory Configurations**
  CPU and network are tied to memory allocation. Under-provisioning results in longer runtimes and potentially higher cost.

- **Over-allocated Timeouts**
  Excessive timeouts can cause runaway executions in error scenarios, increasing cost and hurting downstream systems.

- **Oversized Deployment Packages**
  Lambda limits: 50MB zipped (direct upload), 250MB unzipped (including layers). Large packages delay cold starts and may hit hard limits.

- **Lack of Iterative Testing**
  Memory and timeout defaults are rarely revisited after the first deploy, leading to performance degradation over time.

✳ Compliance & Financial Fallout — List of risks

- **Cost Overruns**: Longer execution time or excessive memory allocation bloats your AWS bill.

- **PCI-DSS**: Timeout mismatches can cause failed log shipping or security data drops.

- **Missed SLAs**: Timeouts or memory errors can break real-time pipelines, violating customer-facing SLAs.

- **CI/CD Failures**: Oversized packages may fail in pipeline deploys without clear errors.

How Developers Misread the Situation — Wrong assumptions

- "More memory = more cost." — Not always. More memory = more CPU, often resulting in **lower overall cost** due to faster execution.

- "My function never hits timeout, so it's fine." — Until a third-party API or S3 read delays your function beyond its current setting.

- "The AWS SDK is bundled by default." — It is, for Node.js and Python. But Java or Docker-based runtimes require careful packaging.

- "Cold starts are only about runtime." — Package size plays a significant role in cold start latency, especially for zipped deployments.

🔧 Detection Steps (AWS CLI preferred) — Commands and flags

```
# Get function configuration (memory,
timeout, code size)
aws lambda get-function-configuration \
  --function-name my-function


# Check function metrics: duration, memory
usage
```

```
aws cloudwatch get-metric-statistics \
  --namespace AWS/Lambda \
  --metric-name Duration \
  --dimensions Name=FunctionName,Value=my-
function \
  --start-time $(date -u --iso-8601=seconds
-d '1 hour ago') \
  --end-time $(date -u --iso-8601=seconds)
\
  --period 60 \
  --statistics Average Maximum

aws cloudwatch get-metric-statistics \
  --namespace AWS/Lambda \
  --metric-name MaxMemoryUsed \
  --dimensions Name=FunctionName,Value=my-
function \
  --start-time $(date -u --iso-8601=seconds
-d '1 hour ago') \
  --end-time $(date -u --iso-8601=seconds)
\
  --period 60 \
  --statistics Average Maximum

# List deployment package size
aws lambda get-function \
  --function-name my-function \
  --query 'Configuration.CodeSize'
```

Diagram — ASCII block for visual clarity

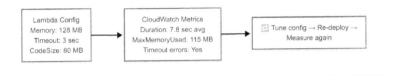

🛠 Fix Instructions — Step-by-step code and config fixes

1. **Use AWS Lambda Power Tuning Tool (via Step Functions)**
   AWS provides a state machine that tests various memory configurations and recommends the optimal setting based on speed and cost trade-offs.
   👉 Tool: https://github.com/alexcasalboni/aws-lambda-power-tuning

2. **Update Memory and Timeout Settings**

```
aws lambda update-function-configuration \
  --function-name my-function \
  --memory-size 512 \
  --timeout 10
```

3. **Minimize Deployment Package Size**

- ☑ Use Lambda Layers for shared dependencies (e.g., boto3, numpy).

- ☑ Use tools like Webpack (Node.js) or `pip --no-deps` (Python) to avoid bundling excess.

- ☑ Prune unused code/libs before zipping.

4. **Monitor and Set Alerts**

Create CloudWatch alarms for high memory usage:

```
aws cloudwatch put-metric-alarm \
  --alarm-name "HighMemoryUsage" \
  --metric-name MaxMemoryUsed \
  --namespace AWS/Lambda \
  --statistic Maximum \
  --period 300 \
  --threshold 90 \
  --comparison-operator
GreaterThanThreshold \
  --evaluation-periods 1 \
  --dimensions Name=FunctionName,Value=my-
function \
  --alarm-actions
arn:aws:sns:region:account-id:notify-topic
```

What You Probably Missed — Lesser-known edge cases, hidden pitfalls

- **Memory increase also boosts CPU & network** — a 1024MB config has 2x the CPU of 512MB, which can drastically reduce duration.

- **Timeout settings must account for retries** — AWS retries some events (e.g., SQS, EventBridge) upon timeout.

- **Docker images still follow size limits** — Though the 10GB limit is generous, bloated images mean slower cold starts.

- **Lambda Insights (optional)** gives granular metrics including memory, init duration, and per-invocation traces.

Chapter 43: The Silent Fail — Troubleshooting Lambda Functions That Hang or Vanish Without Logs

🔍 **Quick Skim Checklist — Practical checks for the reader**

- ☑ Does your function have a **timeout setting** that's too high or too low?

- ☑ Is your Lambda attached to a **VPC** without proper network access (e.g., NAT, VPC endpoints)?

- ☑ Are you using **async SDK methods** without `await` or proper callbacks?

- ☑ Have you checked **CloudWatch log group retention and existence**?

- ☑ Is your **handler function returning or exiting properly**?

- ☑ Are **Lambda destinations or DLQs** configured to capture failed invocations?

How This Happens in the Real World — 2–3 real scenarios

1. **The Ghost Function**
   A Node.js Lambda is invoked via API Gateway, but no logs appear in CloudWatch. Eventually, API Gateway times out. The function hangs because an `await` was accidentally left off an async S3 `putObject` call, preventing the handler from completing.

2. **The Black Hole Timeout**
   A Python Lambda, running inside a VPC, tries to reach an external HTTP endpoint. No internet access is available due to missing NAT Gateway. The function hits its 15-second timeout silently—no logs are emitted because the `requests.get()` call never returns.

3. **The Logless Crash**
   A Java Lambda initializes a heavy dependency in global scope, which throws an exception before the logger is initialized. Because the exception occurs before the `Handler` is invoked, CloudWatch logs never capture the failure.

Root Causes

- ◆ **Missing or incorrect async handling**
  Forgetting `await` (Node.js, Python) or using callback patterns incorrectly prevents the Lambda from exiting or triggers an early return.

- ◆ **Silent network failures inside VPCs**
  Lambda functions inside private subnets require a
  NAT Gateway or interface VPC endpoints to reach
  public services like S3, STS, or external APIs.

- ◆ **Unhandled exceptions before handler start**
  Crashes during init phase or global scope may not
  reach CloudWatch if they occur before the
  execution context is ready.

- ◆ **Insufficient IAM permissions for logging**
  If the Lambda execution role lacks
  `logs:CreateLogStream` or
  `logs:PutLogEvents`, no logs are emitted—even
  on errors.

- ◆ **Timeout with no logging before exit**
  Long-running operations like HTTP requests or DB
  calls may consume all runtime without logging
  anything, ending in a hard timeout.

✳ Compliance & Financial Fallout

- **Undetected service outages**: Failed
  invocations with no logs hinder observability,
  breaking SLA tracking and alerting.

- **Audit trail gaps**: Lack of logs violates
  compliance requirements (e.g., **GDPR**, **HIPAA**,

SOX) for data access and failure tracking.

- ◈ **Wasted execution time**: Functions that hang due to silent network or logic bugs waste time and cost without delivering results.

- ⚠ **Downstream data loss**: Events may be dropped or fail silently without retry mechanisms like DLQ or destinations.

How Developers Misread the Situation — Wrong assumptions

- "If it failed, there would be logs." — Not true if it never reached the handler or if logging permissions were missing.

- "My function times out, but that's expected." — A timeout is a symptom; root cause is often poor async handling or network blocking.

- "I set the timeout high to be safe." — Higher timeouts just delay detection of problems and increase cost.

- "It works locally, so it's not my code." — Local tests don't replicate VPC config, IAM permissions, or the AWS Lambda runtime environment.

🔧 Detection Steps (AWS CLI preferred) — Commands and flags

```
# Check Lambda function configuration
(timeout, memory, VPC config)
aws lambda get-function-configuration \
  --function-name my-function

# Check CloudWatch logs group existence
aws logs describe-log-groups \
  --log-group-name-prefix /aws/lambda/my-
function

# Check for recent log streams
aws logs describe-log-streams \
  --log-group-name /aws/lambda/my-function
\
  --order-by LastEventTime \
  --descending
```

🔧 **Tip**: get-role-policy only reveals **inline** IAM policies. If none are attached, check managed permissions with:

```
aws iam list-attached-role-policies --role-
name LambdaExecutionRole
aws iam get-policy --policy-arn <policy-
arn>
```

```
aws iam get-policy-version --policy-arn
<policy-arn> --version-id <id>


# List VPC subnets and verify they have NAT
or endpoints
aws ec2 describe-subnets \
  --filters Name=vpc-id,Values=vpc-abc123


# If using destinations, check their config
aws lambda get-function-event-invoke-config
\
  --function-name my-function
```

Diagram — ASCII block for visual clarity

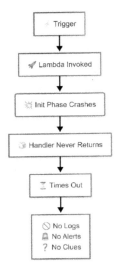

🛠 Fix Instructions — Step-by-step code and config fixes

1. **Add logging early and often in global scope + handler**

```python
import logging
logger = logging.getLogger()
logger.setLevel(logging.INFO)

logger.info("Global init starting")  # Will show on cold start

def handler(event, context):
    logger.info("Handler invoked")
    ...
```

2. **Ensure proper async handling (Node.js example)**

```javascript
// ✖ Missing await
exports.handler = async (event) => {
  s3.putObject({ Bucket, Key, Body }); // doesn't wait!
  return { status: "ok" };
};
```

```
// ☑ Proper async
exports.handler = async (event) => {
  await s3.putObject({ Bucket, Key, Body
}).promise();
  return { status: "ok" };
};
```

3. **Check and fix IAM permissions for CloudWatch logging**

```
{
  "Effect": "Allow",
  "Action": [
    "logs:CreateLogGroup",
    "logs:CreateLogStream",
    "logs:PutLogEvents"
  ],
  "Resource": "*"
}
```

4. **Add a Dead Letter Queue or Lambda destination for post-failure capture**

```
aws lambda update-function-configuration \
  --function-name my-function \
```

```
--dead-letter-config
TargetArn=arn:aws:sqs:us-east-
1:123456789012:my-dlq
```

5. **Timeout sanity check**

```
aws lambda update-function-configuration \
  --function-name my-function \
  --timeout 10
```

6. **If in a VPC, ensure NAT gateway or interface endpoints exist**

- For internet access, ensure the subnet routes to a **NAT Gateway**

- For AWS services, add **VPC endpoints** for:

    ○ `com.amazonaws.region.s3`

    ○ `com.amazonaws.region.logs`

    ○ `com.amazonaws.region.sts`

What You Probably Missed — Lesser-known edge cases, hidden pitfalls

- 🔍 **Init errors don't always generate logs**, especially if the runtime crashes before the first logging call.

- 💡 **Tip**: Cold start failures during the **init phase** (e.g., global scope crashes) might not emit any logs—especially in compiled runtimes like Java or custom bootstraps. This connects directly to the Lambda cold start lifecycle described in Chapter 41.

- **CloudWatch log group might not exist** if this is the first cold start and your role can't create it.

- 💬 **Function URLs and ALB targets won't retry** failed invocations—DLQ is not an option unless you configure destinations.

- ⚠ **Custom runtimes** or poorly implemented bootstraps can break silently if the invocation doesn't return an expected payload.

Chapter 44: The VPC Trap — Solving Timeouts in Lambda Networking

🔍 Quick Skim Checklist — Practical checks for the reader

- ☑ Is your Lambda function configured to connect to a **VPC**?

- ☑ Are the subnets assigned to the Lambda **public or private**?

- ☑ If Lambda needs to access the **internet**, is there a **NAT Gateway** attached?

- ☑ If Lambda only needs to access AWS services (like S3, DynamoDB), are **VPC endpoints** configured?

- ☑ Do the subnets span **multiple Availability Zones** for resilience?

- ☑ Are **security groups and NACLs** allowing the required outbound traffic?

How This Happens in the Real World — 2–3 real scenarios

1. **The Silent Internet Failure**
   A Lambda function attempts to call an external payments API. It's attached to a private subnet with no NAT Gateway. Every call hangs until the Lambda timeout hits. There are **no logs**, because the HTTP call never completes.

2. **The Mysterious S3 Denial**
   A Lambda in a VPC tries to fetch configuration data from an S3 bucket. There's no internet route, and no **S3 VPC endpoint** is configured. Logs show timeouts and `GetObject` retries, confusing devs into blaming IAM.

3. **The ALB Redirect Loop**
   A Lambda behind an Application Load Balancer is deployed in a VPC. Requests intermittently fail because the function's security group doesn't allow **egress**, blocking calls to the ALB health check and internal AWS APIs.

Root Causes — Markdown bullet list with explanation

- ◆ **No NAT Gateway in Private Subnets**
  Without a NAT Gateway, Lambda functions in private subnets can't access the public internet— even if outbound access seems configured.

- ◆ **Missing VPC Endpoints**
  AWS services like S3, DynamoDB, and Secrets Manager are not reachable from a VPC by default.

398

You need to explicitly attach **interface or gateway endpoints**.

- ◆ **Misconfigured Route Tables**
  Subnets might be marked public but routed only to local or NAT-less paths, blocking outbound requests silently.

- ◆ **Over-restrictive Security Groups or NACLs**
  Outbound rules on Lambda's security group or subnet-level NACLs can block traffic, even within the VPC.

- ◆ **Unbalanced AZ Coverage**
  If subnets don't span at least **two Availability Zones**, Lambda may have no compute in certain AZs, leading to invocation failures.

✷ Compliance & Financial Fallout

- **HIPAA / PCI-DSS**: Inability to reach audit/logging services like CloudTrail, or fail to fetch secrets securely.

- **SLA Breaches**: Missed backend calls or unavailable services due to timeout can degrade API performance.

- **Excessive Retries**: Timeout issues cause retries and longer invocation durations, ballooning

Lambda and data transfer costs.

- 🔔 **Monitoring Blindness**: Lambda unable to reach X-Ray, CloudWatch, or Secrets Manager due to VPC misconfig can leave teams blind to failure.

How Developers Misread the Situation — Wrong assumptions

- "It worked outside the VPC, so the problem isn't networking." — VPC mode has **entirely different** egress behavior.

- "The subnet is public, so outbound traffic should work." — Not without a **NAT Gateway** or properly configured route table.

- "IAM looks good, so access to S3 must be fine." — IAM alone won't help if **network routes don't reach S3**.

- "The Lambda is in a VPC for 'security'—so it must be better." — Without the right setup, it's just isolated and broken.

🔧 Detection Steps (AWS CLI preferred) — Commands and flags

```
# Check VPC config for the function
```

```
aws lambda get-function-configuration \
  --function-name my-vpc-function \
  --query 'VpcConfig'

# Inspect subnet routing
aws ec2 describe-route-tables \
  --filters "Name=association.subnet-
id,Values=subnet-abc123"

# Describe security groups associated with
the function
aws ec2 describe-security-groups \
  --group-ids sg-12345678

# Check if a VPC endpoint for S3 or
DynamoDB exists
aws ec2 describe-vpc-endpoints \
  --filters "Name=service-
name,Values=com.amazonaws.us-east-1.s3"

# Check NAT Gateway presence
aws ec2 describe-nat-gateways \
  --filter "Name=vpc-id,Values=vpc-abc123"

# Confirm subnet AZ coverage
aws ec2 describe-subnets \
  --filters Name=vpc-id,Values=vpc-abc123 \
  --query 'Subnets[*].AvailabilityZone'
```

Diagram — ASCII block for visual clarity

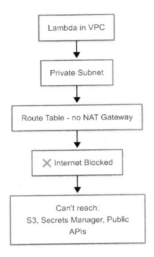

⚒ Fix Instructions — Step-by-step code and config fixes

1. **If Lambda needs public internet access, attach a NAT Gateway**

- Ensure your Lambda is in **private subnets**

- Add a NAT Gateway in a **public subnet**

- Update the **private subnet's route table** to send `0.0.0.0/0` through the NAT GW

```
aws ec2 create-route \
```

```
--route-table-id rtb-abc123 \
--destination-cidr-block 0.0.0.0/0 \
--nat-gateway-id nat-1234567890abcdef0
```

2. **If Lambda only needs AWS service access, attach VPC Endpoints**

```
aws ec2 create-vpc-endpoint \
  --vpc-id vpc-abc123 \
  --service-name com.amazonaws.us-east-1.s3 \
  --vpc-endpoint-type Gateway \
  --route-table-ids rtb-abc123
```

For interface endpoints (e.g., Secrets Manager):

```
aws ec2 create-vpc-endpoint \
  --vpc-id vpc-abc123 \
  --service-name com.amazonaws.us-east-1.secretsmanager \
  --vpc-endpoint-type Interface \
  --subnet-ids subnet-123,subnet-456 \
  --security-group-ids sg-789
```

3. **Verify Lambda has at least two subnets in different AZs**

```
aws lambda update-function-configuration \
  --function-name my-vpc-function \
  --vpc-config SubnetIds=subnet-az1,subnet-
az2 \
                SecurityGroupIds=sg-12345678
```

4. Ensure Security Groups allow outbound traffic

```
aws ec2 authorize-security-group-egress \
  --group-id sg-12345678 \
  --protocol -1 \
  --cidr 0.0.0.0/0
```

What You Probably Missed — Lesser-known edge cases, hidden pitfalls

- **Public subnets don't help Lambda** unless you're using a NAT Gateway. Lambda ENIs are still created in private IP space.

- **Cold start latency increases** in VPCs due to ENI creation unless you use **provisioned concurrency** or **SnapStart**.

- **VPC endpoints don't automatically enable DNS resolution** for some services. You might need to manually adjust DNS settings in certain environments.

- ⚠ **Timeout symptoms can mimic permission errors**, misleading developers into debugging IAM when the issue is networking.

Chapter 45: Secrets Without Scars — Securely Injecting and Rotating Secrets in Lambda

🔍 **Quick Skim Checklist — Practical checks for the reader**

- ☑ Are secrets stored in **AWS Secrets Manager** or **Parameter Store (SSM)** with encryption?

- ☑ Does the Lambda **execution role** have *least-privilege* access to read only the necessary secrets?

- ☑ Are secrets **fetched at runtime**, not hardcoded in code or environment variables?

- ☑ Are logs scrubbed or controlled to avoid exposing secrets (e.g., no raw payload dumps)?

- ☑ Is secret **rotation automated** and supported by downstream code?

- ☑ Are CloudWatch log groups properly permissioned to **prevent unauthorized access**?

How This Happens in the Real World — 2–3 real scenarios

1. **The Hardcoded Password**

   A Lambda function connects to RDS using a database password hardcoded in a `.env` file and committed to Git. After a security audit, the team discovers the secret has been publicly visible for months and rotates it manually across environments.

2. **The Log Exposure Incident**

   A developer adds a debug line `console.log(JSON.stringify(event))`. A secret passed in the payload accidentally ends up in CloudWatch Logs. The team doesn't notice for days, until another dev replays logs during testing and sees sensitive info.

3. **The Silent Expiry**

   A Lambda uses a secret pulled from Secrets Manager—**once**, during cold start. When the secret is rotated automatically 30 days later, the Lambda keeps using the old value during warm invocations. This results in failed logins and retries until the function is redeployed.

Root Causes — Markdown bullet list with explanation

- ◆ **Secrets stored in plaintext or hardcoded**
  Using `.env` files or inline values in source code exposes secrets to version control and human error.

- ◆ **Improper logging of inputs**
  Logging event objects or errors without filtering can accidentally expose secrets in CloudWatch or third-party observability tools.

- ◆ **Secrets fetched only during init phase**
  When secrets are retrieved in the global scope, they don't refresh during warm executions—leading to failures after rotation.

- ◆ **Lack of automated secret rotation**
  Not enabling rotation or not updating the consumer logic leads to drift between credential values and actual secrets.

- ◆ **Over-permissive IAM roles**
  Granting Lambda access to all secrets (`secretsmanager:*`) increases blast radius if the function is compromised.

✳ Compliance & Financial Fallout

- **GDPR / HIPAA / SOC 2**: Leaked secrets in logs may constitute a data breach, requiring disclosure and audit trails.

- **PCI-DSS**: Insecure key management or unrotated secrets violate control 3.5 (Protecting stored cardholder data).

- 🔥 **Security Incident Response**: Hardcoded or untraceable secrets increase MTTR and reduce forensic visibility.

- 💠 **Service Downtime**: Expired secrets used in warm Lambda containers lead to sudden authentication failures and retried requests.

How Developers Misread the Situation — Wrong assumptions

- "Secrets in environment variables are encrypted by AWS, so it's fine." — True at rest, but **they're plaintext in memory** and easily exposed through logs or crash reports.

- "If the secret rotates, the function will pick it up automatically." — Not if it was loaded once at cold start; warm containers won't refresh.

- "We don't log secrets directly." — But you might log the whole payload, stack trace, or accidentally log variables holding secrets.

- "The function needs access to *all* secrets." — Rarely true. You should scope IAM permissions narrowly to the required ARN.

🔧 Detection Steps (AWS CLI preferred) — Commands and flags

```
# Check if environment variables contain
secrets
aws lambda get-function-configuration \
  --function-name my-function \
  --query 'Environment'

# List secrets and check if rotation is
enabled
aws secretsmanager list-secrets \
  --query 'SecretList[*].{Name:Name,
RotationEnabled:RotationEnabled}'

# Get secret value (only for testing in
secure terminal)
aws secretsmanager get-secret-value \
  --secret-id my-db-password

# Check IAM policy for overly broad
permissions
aws iam get-role-policy \
  --role-name MyLambdaRole \
  --policy-name LambdaSecretsPolicy

# Inspect CloudWatch log groups for
overexposure
aws logs describe-log-groups \
```

```
--log-group-name-prefix /aws/lambda/my-
function

# Find any logs that may have leaked
secrets (pattern matching)
aws logs filter-log-events \
  --log-group-name /aws/lambda/my-function
\
  --filter-pattern '"password" || "secret"'
```

Diagram — ASCII block for visual clarity

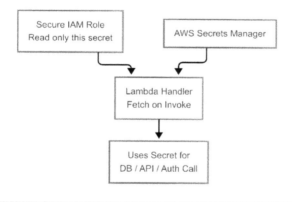

🛠 Fix Instructions — Step-by-step code and config fixes

1. **Move secrets out of environment variables**

```
# ✖ Avoid this:
export DB_PASSWORD='SuperSecret123'

# ☑ Instead, fetch at runtime
```

2. **Fetch secrets securely at invocation time (Python example)**

```python
import boto3
import os

def get_secret(secret_name):
    client = boto3.client('secretsmanager')
    response =
client.get_secret_value(SecretId=secret_nam
e)
    return response['SecretString']

def handler(event, context):
    db_pass =
get_secret("prod/db/password")
    # Use db_pass securely...
```

3. **Enable automatic rotation in Secrets Manager**

```
aws secretsmanager rotate-secret \
```

```
--secret-id prod/db/password
```

4. Limit IAM permissions to specific secrets

```json
{
  "Effect": "Allow",
  "Action": [
    "secretsmanager:GetSecretValue"
  ],
  "Resource": "arn:aws:secretsmanager:us-
east-
1:123456789012:secret:prod/db/password-123"
}
```

5. Scrub logs and avoid logging full objects or secrets

```javascript
// ✖ Bad practice
console.log("Payload:",
JSON.stringify(event));

// ☑ Good practice
console.log("Invoked with record count:",
event.records.length);
```

6. **Rotate secrets safely across warm containers**

If using global scope:

- Add logic to **cache and refresh** secrets periodically.

- Or shift fetching **inside the handler**.

What You Probably Missed — Lesser-known edge cases, hidden pitfalls

- Secrets fetched during **global scope init won't refresh** during warm invocations—leading to stale credentials after rotation.

- **Boto3 and SDK clients can cache credentials**, so reinitializing the client after rotation is necessary.

- **Secrets Manager rotation requires a Lambda hook**—ensure the rotation Lambda has sufficient access and handles multi-step rotation flows.

- **Secrets can be logged indirectly** if used in error messages (e.g., DB exceptions including connection strings).

- 🧠 Parameter Store can also be used, but for **rotating secrets**, Secrets Manager is the better fit.

Chapter 46: The Trigger That Never Fired — Debugging Lambda with S3 and EventBridge

---

🔍 **Quick Skim Checklist — Practical checks for the reader**

- ☑ Does the **event source (S3 or EventBridge)** have the right configuration pointing to your Lambda?

- ☑ Has your Lambda function been granted **permission to be invoked** by the event source via `lambda:InvokeFunction`?

- ☑ Are **resource-based policies** correctly defined for the Lambda?

- ☑ Is your event source emitting events as expected (check S3 PUTs, EventBridge rules, or filters)?

- ☑ Have you reviewed **CloudWatch Logs** and **delivery failures** from EventBridge?

- ☑ Are any **event filters** silently excluding events before invocation?

How This Happens in the Real World — 2–3 real scenarios

1. **The Quiet S3 Upload**
   A dev uploads files to an S3 bucket configured to trigger a Lambda on `ObjectCreated`. Nothing happens. The bucket is configured, but the Lambda has **no resource-based policy allowing** `s3.amazonaws.com` to invoke it.

2. **The Invisible EventBridge Rule**
   A function is subscribed to an EventBridge rule that filters by a specific `detail-type`. Events are flowing, but none match the rule's filter. The rule silently drops all events, and the function is never invoked.

3. **The Cross-Account Trap**
   A Lambda in account A is supposed to be triggered by an EventBridge rule in account B. The rule is configured correctly, but **no permission exists in the Lambda's resource policy** to allow invocation from EventBridge in account B.

Root Causes — Markdown bullet list with explanation

- ◆ **Missing resource-based policy on Lambda**
  Lambda must explicitly allow services like S3 or EventBridge to invoke it using `lambda:InvokeFunction`.

- ◆ **Improper event source configuration**
  The S3 bucket or EventBridge rule is not

configured to send events to the Lambda target.

- ◆ **Misconfigured or overly strict event filtering**
  EventBridge filters by default. If the pattern doesn't
  match incoming events, they are dropped silently.

- ◆ **Cross-account invocation not permitted**
  Cross-account S3 or EventBridge requires both the
  event source and Lambda to trust each other via
  explicit policy.

- ◆ **Wrong Lambda version or alias targeted**
  A trigger may be pointing to $LATEST, while the
  function deployed under a specific alias isn't
  receiving the event.

✵ Compliance & Financial Fallout

- ◈ **Data pipeline disruptions**: Missed events lead
  to loss of critical business workflows.

- ◈ **GDPR**: Failure to process deletion or access
  events may violate user data rights.

- ▬ **PCI-DSS**: Failure to trigger fraud detection logic
  on transaction events due to broken EventBridge
  rules.

- ◇ **Silent cost leaks**: You pay for upstream event producers even when events are never processed.

How Developers Misread the Situation — Wrong assumptions

- "S3 has a trigger, so it should work." — Not unless **Lambda grants S3 permission** via add-permission.

- "The Lambda works when tested manually." — But **event source mappings** or permissions are missing in production.

- "CloudWatch Logs are empty, so it didn't run." — True, but the problem is likely *upstream* (the event was never delivered).

- "The EventBridge rule looks right." — But filters are **case-sensitive**, and even subtle mismatches prevent invocation.

🔧 Detection Steps (AWS CLI preferred) — Commands and flags

```
# Check Lambda's resource-based policy
aws lambda get-policy \
  --function-name my-function
```

```
# List EventBridge rules
aws events list-rules \
  --name-prefix my-rule

# Check targets of an EventBridge rule
aws events list-targets-by-rule \
  --rule my-rule

# Validate event pattern (use with care)
aws events test-event-pattern \
  --event-pattern file://event-pattern.json
\
  --event file://test-event.json

# Review S3 bucket notification config
aws s3api get-bucket-notification-
configuration \
  --bucket my-bucket

# Confirm if the event made it to
EventBridge (via metrics or DLQs)
aws events describe-rule \
  --name my-rule
```

Diagram — ASCII block for visual clarity

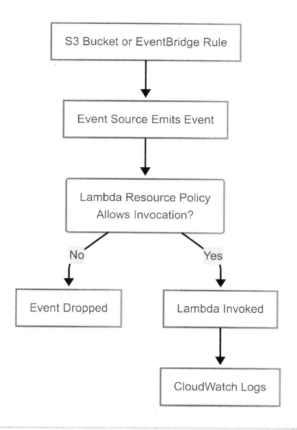

🛠️ Fix Instructions — Step-by-step code and config fixes

1. **Add permission to allow S3 or EventBridge to invoke Lambda**

```
aws lambda add-permission \
  --function-name my-function \
  --statement-id S3Invoke \
```

```
--action lambda:InvokeFunction \
--principal s3.amazonaws.com \
--source-arn arn:aws:s3:::my-bucket
```

For EventBridge (same account):

```
aws lambda add-permission \
  --function-name my-function \
  --statement-id EventBridgeInvoke \
  --action lambda:InvokeFunction \
  --principal events.amazonaws.com \
  --source-arn arn:aws:events:us-east-
1:123456789012:rule/my-rule
```

2. **Check and fix S3 bucket notification config**

```
{
  "LambdaFunctionConfigurations": [
    {
      "LambdaFunctionArn":
"arn:aws:lambda:us-east-
1:123456789012:function:my-function",
      "Events": ["s3:ObjectCreated:*"]
    }
  ]
}
```

Apply it:

```
aws s3api put-bucket-notification-
configuration \
  --bucket my-bucket \
  --notification-configuration file://s3-
config.json
```

3. Validate and correct EventBridge rule filter

```
{
  "source": ["my.service"],
  "detail-type": ["TransactionCreated"]
}
```

Ensure it matches incoming event case and structure.

4. Use DLQ or EventBridge archive for debugging

Enable DLQ:

```
aws events put-targets \
  --rule my-rule \
  --targets
"Id"="1","Arn"="arn:aws:lambda:...",
```

```
"DeadLetterConfig"={"Arn":"arn:aws:sqs:..."
}
```

Or enable archiving:

```
aws events create-archive \
  --name event-archive \
  --source-arn arn:aws:events:us-east-
1:123456789012:event-bus/default
```

What You Probably Missed — Lesser-known edge cases, hidden pitfalls

- ⚠ **S3 triggers only support the $LATEST version** unless you explicitly configure a qualified alias.

- **Lambda versions and aliases matter**—if your EventBridge rule points to an alias, make sure it's the active one.

- **EventBridge rule filters are case-sensitive** and fail silently if values don't match exactly.

- **In cross-account scenarios**, the Lambda **must allow the source account ARN** via resource policy—EventBridge alone can't authorize itself.

- 🔒 **CloudWatch Logs might not exist** if Lambda never runs, so their absence is a *symptom*, not a cause.

Chapter 47: Slim It to Win It — Optimizing Cold Starts with Heavy Lambda Dependencies

🔍 Quick Skim Checklist — Practical checks for the reader

- ☑ Is `boto3`, `botocore`, or AWS SDK bundled unnecessarily? (Already included in the Lambda runtime)

- ☑ Are you importing large libraries (e.g., TensorFlow, pandas, NumPy) only when needed?

- ☑ Are you loading ML models or large assets during the **global scope** instead of at invoke time?

- ☑ Have you considered **Lambda Layers** to separate reusable, versioned packages?

- ☑ Are you compressing deployment artifacts and staying under the 250MB unzipped limit?

- ☑ Have you tried **provisioned concurrency** or **SnapStart (Java)** for latency-critical functions?

How This Happens in the Real World — 2–3 real scenarios

1. **The Data Science Sledgehammer**
   A Lambda function is deployed with a 200MB zipped package including pandas, NumPy, and TensorFlow—most of which aren't used in 90% of invocations. Cold starts are 5–6 seconds. End users experience API timeouts even with low traffic.

2. **The Duplicate Boto3 Trap**
   A developer uses `pip install boto3 -t .` during packaging, not realizing that `boto3` is already included in the AWS runtime. The result? A bloated deployment, longer cold starts, and wasted build time in CI/CD.

3. **The Global Load Bottleneck**
   An ML team loads a 400MB model in the global scope of their Python Lambda. Cold starts spike to 8–10 seconds. Moving the model loading inside the handler, gated by a cache, cuts cold starts by 70% for low-concurrency use cases.

Root Causes — Markdown bullet list with explanation

- ◆ **Bundling unnecessary libraries like boto3**
  Including libraries already provided by the Lambda runtime adds size and delay with no benefit.

- ◆ **Loading ML models in global scope**
  Global initialization increases cold start latency—especially for large files loaded into memory.

- ◈ **Uncompressed or unoptimized packages**
  Packaging tools that include test files, caches, or compiled binaries can inflate deployment size.

- ◈ **Lack of Layer usage**
  Not separating dependencies into Layers leads to code duplication and makes versioning and sharing difficult.

- ◈ **Underutilized runtime features**
  SnapStart for Java or provisioned concurrency for Python/Node can reduce cold start impact but are often overlooked.

✵ Compliance & Financial Fallout

- **SLA violations**: High latency during cold starts breaks real-time guarantees for APIs and event-driven pipelines.

- **Increased costs**: Longer durations (especially from repeated cold starts) inflate Lambda charges.

- **ML pipeline drift**: Improper packaging can lead to model version mismatches across environments.

- **Missed alerts and user interactions**: Functions that fail or timeout due to init latency may drop critical events.

How Developers Misread the Situation — Wrong assumptions

- "Cold starts are just runtime-related." — Nope. **Package size and init code** are just as impactful.

- "boto3 isn't working, I'll add it manually." — It's **already included** in Python runtimes. Bundling it hurts more than helps.

- "Global scope is faster because it's reused." — True for warm starts, but cold starts pay the full price *once*—and it's costly.

- "Provisioned concurrency is overkill." — Not if you have bursty traffic or SLAs under 500ms.

🔧 Detection Steps (AWS CLI preferred) — Commands and flags

```
# Check function configuration (memory,
timeout, size)
aws lambda get-function-configuration \
  --function-name my-function

# Inspect deployment package size
aws lambda get-function \
  --function-name my-function \
```

```
  --query 'Configuration.CodeSize'

# Search CloudWatch logs for cold start
durations
aws logs filter-log-events \
  --log-group-name /aws/lambda/my-function
\
  --filter-pattern '"Init Duration"'

# Use Enhanced Monitoring (CloudWatch
metrics)
aws cloudwatch get-metric-statistics \
  --namespace AWS/Lambda \
  --metric-name InitDuration \
  --start-time $(date -u -d '15 minutes
ago' +%Y-%m-%dT%H:%M:%SZ) \
  --end-time $(date -u +%Y-%m-%dT%H:%M:%SZ)
\
  --period 60 \
  --statistics Average \
  --dimensions Name=FunctionName,Value=my-
function
```

Diagram — ASCII block for visual clarity

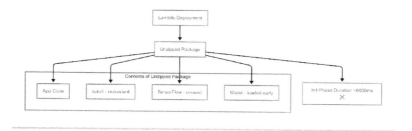

🛠️ Fix Instructions — Step-by-step code and config fixes

1. Avoid bundling boto3 or AWS SDK (Python/Node)

```
# ✖ Don't do this
pip install boto3 -t .

# ☑ Instead, rely on preinstalled version
pip install pandas -t .
```

> 🧠 **Node.js Tip**: Use bundlers like esbuild or webpack with **tree-shaking** to remove unused code and reduce package size.

2. Lazy-load large libraries and ML models inside handler

```
import time
model = None
```

```
# Bonus: Track real-world init time
start = time.time()
# Optional heavy imports here
print(f"Init done in {round(time.time() -
start, 2)}s")

def handler(event, context):
    global model
    if model is None:
        model =
load_model("/tmp/my_model.h5")
    return model.predict(event['input'])
```

💡 For **provisioned concurrency**, global
scope loading is fine. For standard Lambda,
use lazy-load.

3. **Use Lambda Layers to reduce function size**

```
# Create a layer zip containing just the
required packages
mkdir python
pip install pandas -t python/
zip -r pandas-layer.zip python/

# Publish and attach to function
aws lambda publish-layer-version \
```

```
--layer-name pandas-lib \
--zip-file fileb://pandas-layer.zip \
--compatible-runtimes python3.9

aws lambda update-function-configuration \
  --function-name my-function \
  --layers arn:aws:lambda:region:account-
id:layer:pandas-lib:1
```

4. Enable Provisioned Concurrency (for latency-sensitive APIs)

```
aws lambda put-provisioned-concurrency-
config \
  --function-name my-function \
  --qualifier prod \
  --provisioned-concurrent-executions 3
```

5. Use SnapStart (if using Java)

```
aws lambda update-function-configuration \
  --function-name my-java-fn \
  --snap-start ApplyOn=PublishedVersions
```

What You Probably Missed — Lesser-known edge cases, hidden pitfalls

- ⚠ **Lambda Layers count toward the 250MB unzipped limit**—don't assume Layers bypass this.

- 🔖 **Zip files often include unneeded artifacts** (e.g., `__pycache__`, test files). Use `--no-cache-dir` and `.lambdaignore` to exclude them.

- 🔑 **/tmp model caching** can help across invocations, but cold starts still suffer if download/setup is too slow.

- 🔍 Use the **AWS Lambda Power Tuning tool** (via Step Functions) to benchmark memory vs. duration and find your cost-performance sweet spot.

- ⚙ **Amazon Linux 2 environment** may require native dependencies to be compiled within a Docker image mimicking the Lambda runtime.

Chapter 48: Divide and Conquer — Breaking Up Monolithic Lambda Functions the Right Way

---

🔍 Quick Skim Checklist — Practical checks for the reader

- ☑ Is your current Lambda doing **too many unrelated tasks** in one handler?

- ☑ Are different parts of your logic responding to **different types of events** (S3, API Gateway, EventBridge)?

- ☑ Do you struggle to test, monitor, or deploy changes **independently**?

- ☑ Is your Lambda approaching or exceeding size, timeout, or environment limits?

- ☑ Are you trying to implement **shared logic across invocations** or services?

- ☑ Is your retry behavior entangled across multiple flows or side effects?

How This Happens in the Real World — 2–3 real scenarios

1. **The "One Lambda to Rule Them All" Pattern**
   A team builds a serverless app with a single Lambda that handles 10 different API routes, S3 uploads, and a daily cron job—all in one file. Over time, the function grows to 3,000+ lines, becomes painful to test, and fails silently on edge cases that aren't covered by all trigger types.

2. **The Multi-Purpose Monster**
   A Lambda meant to process orders ends up logging metrics, triggering downstream services, doing data enrichment, and sending alerts. When the alert logic fails, it causes the entire order pipeline to back off and retry, even though the order processing succeeded.

3. **The CI/CD Bottleneck**
   Every minor change to a utility method in a single monolithic Lambda triggers a full redeploy and retest. This delays hotfixes and causes cross-team tension as developers step on each other's changes.

Root Causes — Markdown bullet list with explanation

- ◆ **Overloaded function responsibilities**
  A single Lambda is used to handle too many unrelated tasks, violating the Single Responsibility Principle (SRP).

- ◆ **Conflated deployment units**
  All code is deployed together, even when only one subtask changes—slowing delivery and increasing blast radius.

- ◆ **Unclear separation of concerns**
  Logging, transformation, business logic, and error handling are interwoven, making observability and retry logic brittle.

- ◆ **Tightly coupled triggers and logic**
  S3 events, API requests, and scheduled tasks are all routed through conditional branches (`if event.source == ...`), leading to bloated code.

- ◆ **Missing service boundaries**
  Functions aren't split along domain or bounded context lines, leading to friction when trying to scale or evolve independently.

✳ Compliance & Financial Fallout

- ▌ **SOC 2 / ISO 27001**: Complex, entangled codebases make it hard to audit logic paths and enforce least-privilege principles.

- ▦ **Cost amplification from retries**: Failures in one small part of the logic force retries of the entire payload, increasing invocation charges.

- **Testing overhead**: Inability to test microflows individually leads to incomplete coverage and post-deploy bugs.

- **Customer impact**: A small bug in one feature brings down an entire app or pipeline, leading to user dissatisfaction and loss of trust.

How Developers Misread the Situation — Wrong assumptions

- "It's easier to manage one function than five." — Until you have to debug it at 2 a.m.

- "The runtime cost will increase if I split functions." — In reality, **smaller functions are faster and cheaper** because they do less.

- "Everything shares the same IAM role, so it's fine." — Over-permissioned roles break **least-privilege** and increase security risk.

- "I can use conditionals to handle different flows." — That's just a monolith with extra steps—and no separation of concern.

🔧 Detection Steps (AWS CLI preferred) — Commands and flags

```
# Check deployment package size
aws lambda get-function \
  --function-name my-function \
  --query 'Configuration.CodeSize'

# Get CloudWatch logs to assess variability
of events handled
aws logs filter-log-events \
  --log-group-name /aws/lambda/my-function
\
  --limit 50

# Check trigger sources
aws lambda get-function-configuration \
  --function-name my-function \
  --query '{Handler:Handler,
Timeout:Timeout, Memory:MemorySize,
Runtime:Runtime, VpcConfig:VpcConfig}'

# List all event source mappings (for SQS,
DynamoDB, etc.)
aws lambda list-event-source-mappings \
  --function-name my-function

# Review IAM policy scope for over-
permissioned roles
aws iam list-attached-role-policies \
```

439

```
--role-name MyLambdaRole
```

Diagram

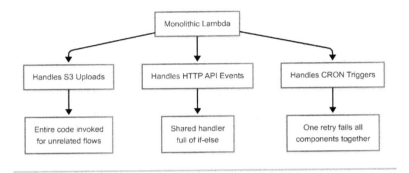

⚒ Fix Instructions — Step-by-step code and config fixes

1. **Identify functional boundaries based on event types or domain logic**

```
From:
  one function = S3 + API Gateway +
EventBridge

To:
  - processS3UploadLambda
  - ordersApiHandler
  - billingCronSummary
```

👑 Naming Guidance

Good function names reflect the trigger or purpose. Try:

- `userUploadProcessor`

- `ordersApiHandler`

- `billingCronSummary`

Avoid vague names like:

- `mainHandler`

- `lambda-1`

- `uploadAndNotifyAndMaybeAPI`

2. **Split code into smaller handlers and deploy separately**

```
# Create new minimal handlers
touch s3_handler.py api_handler.py
cron_handler.py

# Deploy independently via CI/CD or IaC
tooling
```

🔧 **Bonus Tip**: Frameworks like **AWS SAM**, **Serverless Framework**, or **Terraform modules** make it easier to manage multiple smaller functions consistently across environments.

3. **Use small shared libraries or Lambda Layers for common logic**

```
mkdir shared/
echo "def normalize_event(e): return e" >
shared/utils.py
# Reuse in each handler or layer
```

4. **Align IAM roles with least privilege per function**

```
{
  "Effect": "Allow",
  "Action": ["s3:GetObject"],
  "Resource": "arn:aws:s3:::uploads/*"
}
```

5. **Set up separate metrics and alarms per function**

```
aws cloudwatch put-metric-alarm \
  --alarm-name "api-order-errors" \
```

```
--metric-name Errors \
--namespace AWS/Lambda \
--dimensions
Name=FunctionName,Value=apiPostOrderLambda
\
--threshold 1 \
--comparison-operator
GreaterThanThreshold \
--evaluation-periods 1 \
--alarm-actions arn:aws:sns:...
```

What You Probably Missed — Lesser-known edge cases, hidden pitfalls

- ⚠ **Splitting doesn't mean duplicating**—shared logic should go into libraries or Layers, not copied across files.

- ▎ **Monitoring and tracing are cleaner** with separate functions—you get granular visibility without log filtering gymnastics.

- ⸰ **Integration testing is easier**—you can test smaller flows in isolation instead of mocking five unrelated services at once.

- 💬 **Provisioned concurrency becomes easier to tune** when functions are focused and consistent in behavior.

- **Function ownership becomes clearer** across teams—deployments, alerts, and issues are localized to the responsible domain.

Chapter 49: Always Ready — Mastering Provisioned Concurrency for Low-Latency Lambda

🔍 **Quick Skim Checklist — Practical checks for the reader**

- ☑ Does your Lambda function experience **cold start latency spikes**?

- ☑ Is the function triggered by **API Gateway, ALB,** or **user-facing applications**?

- ☑ Are response times critical for **user experience, financial transactions, or SLAs**?

- ☑ Have you measured average and P95+ latency with and without **provisioned concurrency**?

- ☑ Are you using **published versions or aliases** (required for provisioned concurrency)?

- ☑ Is traffic **predictable** (steady or scheduled bursts) to make concurrency pre-warming cost-effective?

How This Happens in the Real World — 2–3 real scenarios

1. **The Customer Checkout Lag**

   An e-commerce platform uses Lambda behind API Gateway to process checkout operations. During peak hours, response times are fine. But during quieter periods, the first request after idle time takes 1.5–2 seconds due to cold starts—impacting conversion rates. Switching to provisioned concurrency eliminated these latency spikes entirely.

2. **The Burst That Broke the App**

   A fintech mobile app leverages Lambda for login and token issuance. During a product launch, 300 users log in within 30 seconds. The function, configured with no concurrency buffer, takes several seconds to scale up. Users see login delays or errors. Pre-warming the function with 100 provisioned concurrency prevented further issues.

3. **The Miscalculated Warm-Up**

   A dev team adds provisioned concurrency to a low-traffic function that processes periodic webhook events. Costs increase, but response time benefits are negligible because the function was rarely cold in practice. A scheduled warm-up call via CloudWatch Events would've achieved the same result at a fraction of the cost.

Root Causes — Markdown bullet list with explanation

- ◆ **Cold starts due to zero idle containers**
  Lambda cold starts occur when no pre-initialized

containers are available, especially after idle periods.

- ◆ **Event sources require fast response**
  API Gateway, ALB, and user-driven invocations expose cold start latency directly to end users.

- ◆ **Lack of traffic predictability tuning**
  Using provisioned concurrency without understanding when spikes happen leads to inefficient (or unnecessary) costs.

- ◆ **Provisioned concurrency not attached to a version/alias**
  $LATEST cannot be used—only published versions and aliases are supported.

- ◆ **Misconception that provisioned concurrency scales automatically**
  Unlike standard concurrency, provisioned concurrency is **pre-allocated** and static unless explicitly updated.

✸ Compliance & Financial Fallout

- ▭ **Lost revenue from latency-sensitive transactions** (e.g., timeouts at checkout)

- ▮ **SLA violations**: APIs with latency guarantees may breach contracts if cold starts occur.

- 🪝 **User churn**: First-time or returning users may abandon workflows when delays exceed thresholds.

- 💠 **Overpaying for underused concurrency**: Without careful tuning, provisioned concurrency can be expensive for idle traffic.

How Developers Misread the Situation — Wrong assumptions

- "Lambda scales instantly, so I don't need prewarming." — Not true; scaling still incurs **cold starts** if no containers are ready.

- "I can just turn it on and forget it." — Provisioned concurrency should be **monitored and adjusted** based on usage patterns.

- "$LATEST is fine." — Provisioned concurrency **requires a version or alias**.

- "It's too expensive." — Not if **used selectively** for user-facing, latency-critical endpoints only.

🔧 Detection Steps (AWS CLI preferred) — Commands and flags

```
# Check which version/alias has provisioned
concurrency enabled
aws lambda get-provisioned-concurrency-
config \
  --function-name my-function \
  --qualifier prod

# Review cold start durations from logs
aws logs filter-log-events \
  --log-group-name /aws/lambda/my-function
\
  --filter-pattern '"Init Duration"' \
  --limit 20

# Monitor latency metrics with and without
provisioned concurrency
aws cloudwatch get-metric-statistics \
  --namespace AWS/Lambda \
  --metric-name Duration \
  --dimensions Name=FunctionName,Value=my-
function \
  --start-time $(date -u -d '1 hour ago'
+%Y-%m-%dT%H:%M:%SZ) \
  --end-time $(date -u +%Y-%m-%dT%H:%M:%SZ)
\
  --period 60 \
  --statistics Maximum
```

Diagram

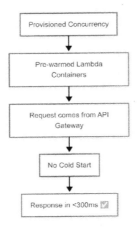

⚒ Fix Instructions — Step-by-step code and config fixes

1. **Publish a Lambda version**

```
aws lambda publish-version \
  --function-name my-function
```

2. **Create an alias to point to the version**

```
aws lambda create-alias \
  --function-name my-function \
  --name prod \
  --function-version 3
```

3. **Enable provisioned concurrency for the alias**

```
aws lambda put-provisioned-concurrency-
config \
  --function-name my-function \
  --qualifier prod \
  --provisioned-concurrent-executions 10
```

4. **Adjust provisioned concurrency dynamically (optional)**
   Use Application Auto Scaling or a scheduler like EventBridge for burst scenarios.

```
# (Optional) Update concurrency during
known busy windows
aws lambda put-provisioned-concurrency-
config \
  --function-name my-function \
  --qualifier prod \
  --provisioned-concurrent-executions 50
```

When in doubt, test it: Use AWS Lambda Power Tuning or CloudWatch metrics to compare cost vs. performance.

Hybrid Strategy Tip
Pair **provisioned concurrency for peak hours** with **scheduled warm-up invocations** during off-peak hours to keep costs predictable without sacrificing latency.

```
# Warm-up example using EventBridge
Scheduler
aws scheduler create-schedule \
  --name warmup-morning \
  --schedule-expression "cron(0 6 * * ? *)" \
  --target Arn=arn:aws:lambda:us-east-1:123456789012:function:my-function
```

📊 **Cost Comparison**
Provisioned concurrency is billed **by the hour per instance**. If your function executes 10 times a day, **scheduled warm-ups may cost 80–90% less** than keeping 5 provisioned containers up 24/7.

What You Probably Missed — Lesser-known edge cases, hidden pitfalls

- ⚠ **Provisioned concurrency is isolated from standard concurrency.** If you don't configure both, scale limits may be hit unexpectedly.

- ◇ **Costs accrue even when idle.** Each provisioned container incurs hourly billing whether invoked or not.

- 🧠 **Warm containers are zone-bound.** Cold starts can still occur during AZ failover unless concurrency is AZ-distributed.

- ▮ **Function URLs and ALB targets expose cold starts more than async triggers**—they benefit most from provisioned concurrency.

- ⬝ **Don't prewarm everything**—use provisioned concurrency **surgically**, on latency-critical, user-facing paths only.

Chapter 50: Abuse-Proofing Your Lambda — Detecting Loops, Surges, and Misuse Before They Drain You

---

🔍 Quick Skim Checklist — Practical checks for the reader

- ☑ Are you tracking **invocation frequency** and **concurrency spikes** in CloudWatch?

- ☑ Have you enabled **Lambda Insights** or **X-Ray** to inspect invocation patterns?

- ☑ Are function triggers from **EventBridge, S3, or SQS** protected from recursive or replay loops?

- ☑ Do you have **CloudTrail** enabled to detect unexpected or unauthorized Lambda invokes?

- ☑ Are there alarms on **invocation count**, **duration**, or **concurrent executions**?

- ☑ Have you configured **reserved and/or account-level concurrency** to protect budget boundaries?

How This Happens in the Real World — 2–3 real scenarios

1. **The Recursive EventBridge Trap**
   A function posts audit logs to an EventBridge bus—but the rule also routes certain logs to the same function. This causes a **loop**: the function invokes itself over and over, eventually hitting concurrency limits and throttling other functions.

2. **The Unthrottled Webhook Flood**
   A public-facing Lambda function connected to a webhook receives an unexpected burst—tens of thousands of invocations in minutes due to a third-party system misbehaving. Without rate limiting or concurrency caps, the team gets a surprise $5,000 Lambda bill overnight.

3. **The Misconfigured Cron Bomb**
   A developer configures a CloudWatch Events rule incorrectly, setting it to trigger every 1 minute instead of once per hour. The function logs look fine—but the number of executions balloons, quietly inflating costs until billing alerts are triggered.

Root Causes — Markdown bullet list with explanation

- ◆ **Unrestricted or misconfigured event sources**
  Loops or floods can result when S3, EventBridge, or DynamoDB triggers re-invoke the same function under certain conditions.

- **Lack of visibility into invocation patterns**
  Without metrics or logs, invocation surges can go unnoticed until billing spikes or throttling occurs.

- **No invocation rate or concurrency guardrails**
  Functions can be called at infinite scale by default unless concurrency is capped.

- **Public triggers with no auth or rate limiting**
  Exposed APIs or function URLs can be hit repeatedly by external users, bots, or misconfigured clients.

- **Improper retry configurations**
  Sources like EventBridge and SQS retry failed invocations automatically, potentially compounding the volume.

✳ Compliance & Financial Fallout

- **Surprise billing from traffic loops**

- **Outage risk from throttled functions**

- **Audit blind spots**: Undetected loops or surges can hide operational or access errors.

- Silent data loss if DLQs aren't used for async events that fail due to abuse or limits.

How Developers Misread the Situation — Wrong assumptions

- "It's just a test event, so it's safe." — One misrouted test can recursively invoke Lambda if routing rules loop.

- "Lambda is infinitely scalable—I don't need to worry." — Yes, until you're **infinitely billed**.

- "CloudWatch will alert me." — Only if you've set **explicit alarms**—most abuse patterns won't trip metrics by default.

- "I'll see it in the logs." — If your function's silent or fails quickly, logs may never be emitted—or will flood too late.

🔧 Detection Steps (AWS CLI preferred) — Commands and flags

```
# Get recent invocation count
aws cloudwatch get-metric-statistics \
  --namespace AWS/Lambda \
  --metric-name Invocations \
```

```
  --dimensions Name=FunctionName,Value=my-
function \
  --start-time $(date -u -d '1 hour ago'
+%Y-%m-%dT%H:%M:%SZ) \
  --end-time $(date -u +%Y-%m-%dT%H:%M:%SZ)
\
  --period 60 \
  --statistics Sum

# Check current concurrency usage
aws cloudwatch get-metric-statistics \
  --namespace AWS/Lambda \
  --metric-name ConcurrentExecutions \
  --start-time $(date -u -d '1 hour ago'
+%Y-%m-%dT%H:%M:%SZ) \
  --end-time $(date -u +%Y-%m-%dT%H:%M:%SZ)
\
  --period 60 \
  --statistics Maximum

# View all function event source mappings
aws lambda list-event-source-mappings \
  --function-name my-function

# Detect invocations via CloudTrail
aws cloudtrail lookup-events \
  --lookup-attributes
AttributeKey=EventName,AttributeValue=Invok
e \
  --max-results 20
```

Diagram

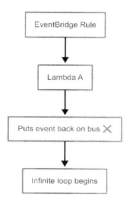

🛠️ Fix Instructions — Step-by-step code and config fixes

1. **Set concurrency caps (per function and optionally global)**

```
# Cap this function
aws lambda put-function-concurrency \
  --function-name my-function \
  --reserved-concurrent-executions 10

# Optional: Set global max concurrency for
cost control
aws lambda put-account-settings \
```

```
--maximum-concurrency 500
```

🔁 If a function uses up its reserved concurrency, it will **spill into unreserved pool**—unless an account-level cap is enforced.

2. **Add EventBridge filtering to prevent reentry**

```
{
  "source": ["my.app"],
  "detail-type": ["trigger.type"]
}
```

```
aws events put-rule \
  --name SafeRule \
  --event-pattern file://pattern.json
```

3. **Create alarms on high invocations or concurrency**

```
aws cloudwatch put-metric-alarm \
  --alarm-name "TooManyInvokes" \
  --metric-name Invocations \
  --namespace AWS/Lambda \
```

```
  --dimensions Name=FunctionName,Value=my-
function \
  --threshold 100 \
  --comparison-operator
GreaterThanThreshold \
  --evaluation-periods 1 \
  --period 60 \
  --alarm-actions arn:aws:sns:...
```

> 📡 **Cost Spike Radar Tip**
> Monitor **ConcurrentExecutions** at the
> **account level** for cross-function surge
> detection:

```
aws cloudwatch put-metric-alarm \
  --alarm-name "AccountConcurrentSpike" \
  --metric-name ConcurrentExecutions \
  --namespace AWS/Lambda \
  --threshold 1000 \
  --comparison-operator
GreaterThanThreshold \
  --evaluation-periods 1 \
  --period 300
```

4. **Set up DLQs for async triggers (S3, EventBridge, etc.)**

```
aws lambda update-function-configuration \
  --function-name my-function \
  --dead-letter-config
TargetArn=arn:aws:sqs:us-east-
1:123456789012:dlq-queue
```

> **Why?** If your function fails due to burst, retries, or abuse, DLQs capture events **instead of dropping them silently**.

5. **Throttle and block abusive traffic (API Gateway)**

```
aws apigateway update-stage \
  --rest-api-id abc123 \
  --stage-name prod \
  --patch-operations
op=replace,path=/*/*/throttling/burstLimit,
value=50
```

> Add AWS WAF to block high-frequency IPs or rate-abusers automatically.

What You Probably Missed — Lesser-known edge cases, hidden pitfalls

- **SQS and EventBridge retries** can simulate abuse even if original traffic was low.

- **Async invokes don't log in CloudTrail** unless traced or monitored explicitly.

- **Lambda URLs** are public by default—use IAM auth or API Gateway to enforce security.

- **Metric averages hide abuse**—watch **P95/P99** latency and spikes, not just mean values.

- **DLQs + account concurrency** is your last line of defense when everything else fails.

Chapter 51: The Log Stream Labyrinth — Unraveling CloudWatch Fragmentation in High-Throughput Lambdas

---

🔍 Quick Skim Checklist — Practical checks for the reader

- ☑ Are you using **multiple concurrent Lambda instances** due to high request volume?

- ☑ Is your logging strategy relying on `console.log`, `print()`, or standard output?

- ☑ Do you expect logs to appear in **chronological order**, but find them scattered across log streams?

- ☑ Are logs missing or out of sync with trace IDs, correlation IDs, or timestamps?

- ☑ Are you using **X-Ray or structured logging** to tie together requests?

- ☑ Have you reviewed **CloudWatch retention and search capabilities** for scalability?

How This Happens in the Real World — 2–3 real scenarios

1. **The API Trace Maze**
   A Lambda fronting an API Gateway sees spikes of 1,000+ requests per minute. Logs are expected to follow request sequence, but developers discover each request's logs are written to different **log streams**, with timestamps out of order due to parallel container invocations. Debugging timeouts and failures becomes guesswork.

2. **The Payment Confusion**
   A payment processor Lambda logs transaction steps (`initiated`, `authorized`, `completed`). Under load, `authorized` logs land in one stream and `completed` in another—making it look like some transactions failed. This fragmented visibility causes false alarms and unnecessary rollbacks.

3. **The "Missing Logs" Myth**
   A developer thinks logs are dropped or lost due to async failure. But in reality, the logs were generated by a **different concurrent container** and landed in a **different log stream** that wasn't immediately visible in the console's default view.

Root Causes — Markdown bullet list with explanation

- ◆ **Concurrency creates separate execution environments**
  Each concurrent Lambda instance writes to its own **unique log stream** under the same log group.

- **CloudWatch doesn't order log streams by timestamp**
  When viewing multiple streams, logs from different containers may appear out of sequence unless explicitly merged.

- **No correlation ID or request ID**
  Without structured logging, it's impossible to associate logs with the request or trace they belong to.

- **Asynchronous or multithreaded logging**
  If your code logs from parallel threads or callbacks (especially in Node.js or Python async), the order may not reflect logical execution.

- **Missing CloudWatch Insights or X-Ray integration**
  Without enhanced tracing, logs are siloed and can't be filtered by trace or invocation metadata.

✴ Compliance & Financial Fallout

- **Audit trail inconsistencies**: In financial or healthcare systems, missing or misordered logs violate traceability requirements (e.g., HIPAA, SOX).

- **Forensic gaps during incident response**: Fragmented logs delay root cause analysis after a breach or system outage.

- ▪ **Inaccurate monitoring alerts**: Log-based alarms on specific strings or sequences may fail due to stream fragmentation.

- $ **Higher costs due to over-retention or duplicated log search operations**.

How Developers Misread the Situation — Wrong assumptions

- "Each invocation logs to the same place." — Nope. **Each concurrent Lambda container writes to its own log stream.**

- "Logs will appear in order." — Only within a single stream. Across streams, CloudWatch doesn't guarantee global order.

- "My logs are missing." — They're probably in **another stream** that isn't loaded in your console or `filter-log-events` scope.

- "I can just grep the logs." — Not easily—**you need correlation IDs** or structured logs to reliably grep across parallel streams.

🔧 Detection Steps (AWS CLI preferred) — Commands and flags

```
# List all log streams in the Lambda's log
group (note different streams)
aws logs describe-log-streams \
  --log-group-name /aws/lambda/my-function
\
  --order-by LastEventTime \
  --descending

# Search for logs across all streams with a
specific correlation ID
aws logs filter-log-events \
  --log-group-name /aws/lambda/my-function
\
  --filter-pattern '"correlationId:abc123"'
\
  --limit 50

# Fetch a specific invocation by request ID
(from CloudWatch Logs or X-Ray)
aws logs filter-log-events \
  --log-group-name /aws/lambda/my-function
\
  --filter-pattern '"RequestId: 1234abcd-
...'"'

# Use Insights for structured queries (if
enabled)
```

```
aws logs start-query \
  --log-group-name /aws/lambda/my-function
\
  --start-time $(date -u -d '15 minutes
ago' +%s) \
  --end-time $(date -u +%s) \
  --query-string 'fields @timestamp,
message | filter message like
/correlationId:abc123/'
```

Diagram

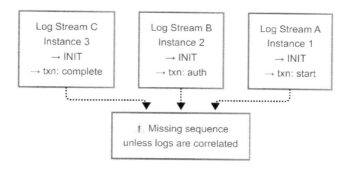

🛠 **Fix Instructions — Step-by-step code and config fixes**

1. **Implement correlation IDs across invocations**

```
import uuid
```

```
def handler(event, context):
    correlation_id =
event.get("correlationId") or
str(uuid.uuid4())
    print(f"correlationId:{correlation_id}
- Processing request...")
```

Pass the same `correlationId` through async queues, APIs, or event buses to connect logs across services.

2. **Use structured logging (JSON or tagged output)**

```
console.log(JSON.stringify({
  level: "info",
  correlationId,
  step: "auth-check",
  timestamp: new Date().toISOString()
}));
```

3. **Enable CloudWatch Logs Insights and use searchable fields**

- Add custom fields (e.g., `correlationId`, `userId`) to logs

- Use `start-query` to filter across streams in a structured way

470

4. Enable X-Ray for request-level tracing

```
aws lambda update-function-configuration \
  --function-name my-function \
  --tracing-config Mode=Active
```

> Use `AWS-X-Ray-Trace-Id` or `segmentId` as part of your log line for automatic correlation.

5. Group logs with common identifiers in Lambda Insights dashboards

- Use custom dimensions (e.g., `function_version`, `region`, `invocation_id`)

- Build widgets in CloudWatch Dashboards based on correlation IDs

---

What You Probably Missed — Lesser-known edge cases, hidden pitfalls

- **High concurrency = high fragmentation.** Each container spins its own stream. At 1,000 TPS, expect 1,000+ active streams/hour.

- **CloudWatch Log Insights won't find your logs unless logs are structured consistently.**

471

JSON helps—regex doesn't scale.

- 🔘 **Retention policies don't apply per stream**, so fragmented logs may linger longer than expected unless grouped or deleted by log group.

- 🔄 **Multiple log statements per invocation can land out of order** if `console.log` is used in async handlers or multithreaded flows.

- 🔧 **Relying only on print/console logs is** insufficient for microservice tracing—structured logs + X-Ray is the gold standard.

Chapter 52: Deploys in the Dark — Debugging Lambda Failures with SAM and Serverless Framework

---

🔍 Quick Skim Checklist — Practical checks for the reader

- ☑ Are you running with `--debug` or verbose logging enabled?

- ☑ Did the deployment fail during **build**, **packaging**, or **CloudFormation stack deployment**?

- ☑ Have you checked the **CloudFormation events** for detailed failure messages?

- ☑ Are your IAM permissions sufficient for the stack operations?

- ☑ Is the function size within Lambda limits (50MB zipped, 250MB unzipped)?

- ☑ Are you cleaning up stale resources (roles, stack remnants) between deploys?

How This Happens in the Real World — 2–3 real scenarios

473

1. **The Disappearing Stack Error**
   A team deploys a new function using AWS SAM, but the terminal logs only show a generic `Deployment failed` message. On closer inspection, CloudFormation failed because the `AWS::Lambda::Function` resource tried to attach to a role that doesn't exist due to a typo in the `RoleName`.

2. **The Oversized Package Mystery**
   A Serverless Framework project suddenly fails deployment with no clear message. The real issue? A recent dependency added to `node_modules` bloated the package to over 250MB unzipped. CloudFormation accepts the stack but the Lambda creation fails silently in the console.

3. **The "Access Denied" at the End**
   Deployment seems to proceed smoothly with SAM, but then errors out near the end with a vague IAM error. The deployer's role lacked `iam:PassRole` permissions, preventing it from assigning the correct role to the Lambda.

Root Causes — Markdown bullet list with explanation

- ◆ **CloudFormation failure hidden in framework CLI output**
  Tools like SAM and Serverless may mask low-level errors unless debug mode is enabled or logs are

retrieved manually.

- ⬧ **IAM permission gaps for stack creation**
The user running the deployment needs rights to create/modify roles, log groups, and other resources.

- ⬧ **Zipped or unzipped package exceeds size limits**
Lambda enforces a 50MB zipped or 250MB unzipped size limit—oversized builds fail silently unless explicitly checked.

- ⬧ **Resource naming conflicts**
Manually deleted or renamed resources (like roles or log groups) can leave stale references in stacks.

- ⬧ **Improperly configured or conflicting stack parameters**
Missing environment variables, misconfigured Layers, or mismatched architecture settings cause runtime deploy failures.

💥 Compliance & Financial Fallout — List of risks (GDPR, PCI-DSS, etc.)

- ⚠ **Deployment delays to production bug fixes**
— Breaks SLA timelines or incident recovery processes.

- 🔷 **Wasted CI/CD compute time** — Repeated deploy retries inflate build pipeline costs.

- ❌ **Untracked configuration drift** — Manual or failed stack changes create compliance audit headaches.

- ⚙ **IAM misconfigurations** — Over-permissioned deploy roles introduced in a rush may violate least-privilege policies (SOC 2, ISO 27001).

How Developers Misread the Situation — Wrong assumptions

- "The framework handles everything." — Not quite. SAM and Serverless use CloudFormation under the hood and errors often originate there.

- "It must be my code if it fails." — Many deployment failures are related to IAM, packaging, or CloudFormation—not function logic.

- "SAM/Serverless would show a detailed error." — Only in --debug mode or by manually inspecting the CloudFormation console.

- "It worked before, so it must be AWS's fault now." — Check for recent changes: role names, region switches, or file size can subtly break things.

✎ Detection Steps (AWS CLI preferred) — Commands and flags

```
# Get CloudFormation stack events to trace
the exact point of failure
aws cloudformation describe-stack-events \
  --stack-name my-lambda-stack

# Check IAM permissions of the deployer
aws iam simulate-principal-policy \
  --policy-source-arn
arn:aws:iam::123456789012:user/my-deployer
\
  --action-names iam:PassRole
cloudformation:CreateStack
logs:CreateLogGroup

# Validate your SAM template locally
sam validate

# Check the size of your packaged artifacts
du -sh .aws-sam/build/*

# Enable debug logs during SAM or
Serverless deploy
sam deploy --debug
sls deploy --verbose
```

Diagram

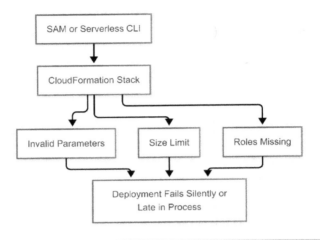

🛠 Fix Instructions — Step-by-step code and config fixes

1. **Enable verbose output during deployment**

```
sam deploy --debug
# or
sls deploy --verbose
```

2. **Check CloudFormation stack events immediately after failure**

```
aws cloudformation describe-stack-events \
```

```
--stack-name my-lambda-stack
```

3. Ensure your deploy role has all required permissions

Include at minimum:

```
{
  "Effect": "Allow",
  "Action": [
    "cloudformation:*",
    "lambda:*",
    "iam:PassRole",
    "logs:*"
  ],
  "Resource": "*"
}
```

4. Validate build output and package size before deploying

```
du -sh .aws-sam/build
du -sh .serverless
```

> If needed, use Lambda Layers to reduce package size or move shared code.

5. **Clear and redeploy failed stacks cleanly**

```
aws cloudformation delete-stack --stack-
name my-lambda-stack
sam delete
sls remove
```

6. **Double-check environment and region variables**

Make sure your AWS CLI, framework config, and resource names are targeting the **same region and environment**.

What You Probably Missed — Lesser-known edge cases, hidden pitfalls

- 💬 **SAM and Serverless silently swallow CloudFormation errors** unless debug mode is enabled.

- ⚠ **Lambda deployment size is unzipped**, even though CLI tools show the zipped size only.

- 🔄 **Reusing a broken stack name** without `--capabilities` or `--force` flags causes partial failures.

- 🔍 **CloudFormation "ROLLBACK_COMPLETE" stacks** must be deleted before re-deploying.

- 🔐 **iam:PassRole** is the #1 hidden permission required for Lambda deployment—but often missed.

Part 5: Building Robust User Authentication with AWS Cognito

Chapter 53: *No Backup Button? Navigating Cognito's Missing Export Feature*

🔍 Quick Skim Checklist

- Know that **Cognito User Pools do not provide native backups**

- Use `ListUsers` + `AdminGetUser` to programmatically extract user data

- Export **custom attributes**, **group memberships**, and **MFA status**

- Automate exports via **AWS Lambda + EventBridge**

- Always **encrypt backups** and **secure IAM permissions**

- Be mindful of **compliance needs (e.g., GDPR portability)**

How This Happens in the Real World

1. **Disaster Recovery Plan Gap**
   A fintech startup building a banking app realizes they can't recover user data after accidentally deleting a test user pool during a Terraform cleanup job. No backup means starting from scratch.

2. **Audit Panic**
   A healthtech company gets a GDPR Subject Access Request (SAR) and needs to export user data fast. But there's no built-in Cognito UI or CLI to download user profiles with all custom attributes.

3. **Migration Blocker**
   A team planning to migrate users to Auth0 discovers too late that Cognito offers no way to bulk-export passwords, and re-verification via email or SMS becomes their only fallback.

Root Causes

- **No native snapshot or export feature:**
  Cognito User Pools lack built-in mechanisms for scheduled backups or on-demand exports.

- **Passwords are never exposed:**
  Due to security and compliance reasons, hashed passwords aren't exportable—even for admins.

- **Scoped API limitations:**
  While the `ListUsers` and `AdminGetUser` APIs allow partial data extraction, they don't include all

security-related metadata in a single call.

- **No CloudFormation drift detection:**
  Resource drift or deletion via IaC can go unnoticed until it's too late.

✴ Compliance & Financial Fallout

- **GDPR Article 20 – Data Portability:**
  You must provide a copy of a user's data in a structured format upon request.

- **HIPAA – Data Retention Obligations:**
  Losing patient account data could violate retention rules.

- **SOC 2 – Availability Principle:**
  Inability to restore user data during an incident affects system reliability ratings.

- **PCI-DSS – Account Management:**
  Poor user data lifecycle management could raise red flags in audits.

How Developers Misread the Situation

- "I'll just export the users from the console." → **You can't. There's no export feature.**

- "The API must include everything, including passwords." → **No, password hashes are never exposed.**

- "The user pool is in CloudFormation, so I can always recreate it." → **Yes, but without the users.**

🦴 Detection Steps (AWS CLI preferred)

```
# List users with pagination
aws cognito-idp list-users \
  --user-pool-id <your_user_pool_id> \
  --limit 60 \
  --query "Users[*].Username"

# Retrieve details about one user
aws cognito-idp admin-get-user \
  --user-pool-id <your_user_pool_id> \
  --username <username>

# Get groups for a user
aws cognito-idp admin-list-groups-for-user \
  --user-pool-id <your_user_pool_id> \
  --username <username>
```

Optional script: Iterate over all users and dump them to a CSV.

Diagram

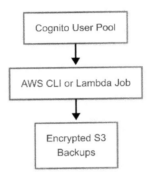

🛠 Fix Instructions

Option 1: Manual Backup Script (Python Example using Boto3)

```python
import boto3, csv

client = boto3.client('cognito-idp')

def export_users(user_pool_id):
    users = []
    paginator =
client.get_paginator('list_users')
    for page in
paginator.paginate(UserPoolId=user_pool_id)
:
        for user in page['Users']:
```

```python
            username = user['Username']
            attrs = {attr['Name']:
attr['Value'] for attr in
user['Attributes']}
            users.append({'Username':
username, **attrs})

    with open('cognito_users.csv', 'w',
newline='') as f:
        writer = csv.DictWriter(f,
fieldnames=users[0].keys())
        writer.writeheader()
        writer.writerows(users)
```

Option 2: Scheduled Automation

1. Create an AWS Lambda function with the logic
   above.

2. Trigger it with **EventBridge** every 24h or weekly.

3. Store the output in **Amazon S3 (with encryption)**.

4. Use **IAM roles** with least-privilege and KMS key
   access control.

What You Probably Missed

- **MFA and verified attributes aren't included by default** in exports—must explicitly fetch with `AdminGetUser`.

- **Users created via federation (Google, SAML)** might have minimal attribute data unless mapped properly.

- **Tokens can't be exported or reused**—access and ID tokens are short-lived and personal to sessions.

- **Backups should include group memberships** (via `admin-list-groups-for-user`) and timestamps if auditing is required.

Chapter 54: *Mind the Gaps — Fixing Cognito's Documentation Deficit for Enterprise Login Flows*

🔍 Quick Skim Checklist

- ☑ Implement Authorization Code Flow with PKCE (not Implicit Flow!)

- ☑ Understand that Cognito's official docs focus on **basic use cases**, not enterprise SSO

- ☑ Enterprise features like **SAML federation**, **OIDC IdPs**, and **custom auth flows** are underdocumented

- ☑ Use **Pre Token Generation** Lambda for dynamic role mapping

- ☑ Validate **redirect URIs**, **token lifetimes**, and **OAuth scopes**

- ☑ Know how to **trace errors in Hosted UI flows** via browser dev tools and logs

---

How This Happens in the Real World

1. **SAML Setup Nightmare**
   A large HR SaaS platform tries integrating Cognito

with Azure AD. Despite following the docs, they hit cryptic errors like `invalid_request` or "token not found" due to vague guidance on SAML attribute mapping and claim transformations.

2. **Broken Production Login**
   An ecommerce platform deploys a Cognito Hosted UI-based login. Everything works in staging, but production fails silently because they missed one callback URL in the app client config—and the doc didn't clearly warn about the mismatch behavior.

3. **Security Audit Blowback**
   A fintech app assumes Cognito enforces PKCE by default. During a pen test, auditors reveal that the client secret is exposed in the frontend due to use of the **Implicit Flow**, which the documentation *doesn't discourage enough*.

Root Causes

- **Vague or Minimal Documentation for Advanced Features**
  Enterprise-level use cases like token customization, multi-provider federation, or OIDC + SAML chaining are mentioned only briefly without examples.

- **Scattered References Across Services**
  Developers must jump between Cognito, IAM, API Gateway, and CloudTrail docs to piece together

secure workflows.

- **Incomplete Coverage of OAuth 2.0 Flows**
  The docs often omit when to use Authorization
  Code with PKCE vs. Implicit Flow—and don't
  emphasize that **Implicit is deprecated** for SPAs.

- **Sparse Error Handling Guidance**
  Many Hosted UI and federation errors (like
  `unauthorized_client` or `invalid_grant`) are
  not mapped to causes or resolutions.

✳ Compliance & Financial Fallout

- **GDPR / CCPA – Unsecure Token Handling**
  Use of Implicit Flow can leak tokens in URLs or
  browser history, violating secure data transmission
  practices.

- **ISO 27001 – Incomplete Audit Logging**
  Without correct logging setup via CloudTrail and
  CloudWatch, user activity tracing is impossible.

- **SOC 2 – Authentication Gaps**
  Weak login flows or exposed client secrets can
  violate Availability and Security Trust Service
  Criteria.

- **Financial Penalties from Data Breaches**
  Federated identity misconfiguration can expose
  internal users or customers to phishing and

unauthorized access.

How Developers Misread the Situation

- "OAuth is secure out of the box in Cognito." → Not unless you **explicitly use Authorization Code + PKCE**.

- "Implicit Flow is fine for SPAs." → Not anymore. **Cognito still allows it** (but it's deprecated by the OAuth spec and a known vulnerability vector for SPAs).

- "Federation errors will show up clearly." → Many are **silent failures** that just redirect back to login.

- "Lambda triggers are optional." → **Lambda triggers are optional for basic login—but essential for custom auth flows** like dynamic role assignment, token claims override, or federated identity linking.

🔧 Detection Steps (AWS CLI preferred)

```
# Check your user pool app client OAuth
flow
aws cognito-idp describe-user-pool-client \
  --user-pool-id <user-pool-id> \
```

```
  --client-id <app-client-id> \
  --query
"UserPoolClient.AllowedOAuthFlows"

# Check allowed callback URLs
aws cognito-idp describe-user-pool-client \
  --user-pool-id <user-pool-id> \
  --client-id <app-client-id> \
  --query "UserPoolClient.CallbackURLs"

# Review Lambda trigger configs
(PreTokenGeneration is key for roles)
aws cognito-idp describe-user-pool \
  --user-pool-id <user-pool-id> \
  --query "UserPool.LambdaConfig"
```

Use browser dev tools to inspect:

- Redirect URIs

- `state` and `code` parameters

- Token expiration (check `exp` in JWT)

Diagram

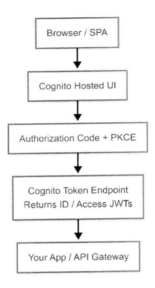

🛠 Fix Instructions

Step 1: Set Up Secure OAuth Flow

- Go to Cognito → App client settings

- Enable **Authorization code grant**

- Disable **Implicit flow**

- Provide **Redirect URIs** and **Logout URIs**

- Set Allowed OAuth Scopes (email, openid, profile)

Step 2: Enable PKCE in Your Frontend

React with AWS Amplify example:

```
import { Auth } from 'aws-amplify';

Auth.federatedSignIn({
  customProvider: 'COGNITO',
  signInOptions: { responseType: 'code' }
// Triggers PKCE flow
});
```

Step 3: Enable Pre Token Lambda Trigger (Optional)

Use `PreTokenGeneration` to inject custom claims or override group-based role assignments:

```
exports.handler = async (event) => {
  event.response.claimsOverrideDetails = {
    claimsToAddOrOverride: {
      'custom:department': 'finance',
    },
    groupOverrideDetails: {
      groupsToOverride: ['finance-admin'],
    }
  };
  return event;
};
```

Step 4: Implement Error Logging and Retry Logic

- Use CloudWatch Logs for Hosted UI Lambda errors.

- Add error intercept logic to frontend to catch and log OAuth failures.

What You Probably Missed

- **Cognito doesn't auto-expire old refresh tokens** across all apps. You need to manage refresh revocation manually.

- **Custom domains used in Hosted UI flows need a valid SSL certificate**—misconfigured certs cause silent redirects.

- **SAML attribute mappings** are case-sensitive and often misaligned unless manually edited.

- **OIDC token audience (aud) mismatch** with client ID will silently break sign-in without error logs.

Chapter 55: *Multi-Factor Mayhem — Avoiding the Top MFA Misconfigurations in Cognito*

🔍 Quick Skim Checklist

- ☑ Confirm MFA is **enabled and enforced** for all users (not just optional)

- ☑ Verify both **SMS and TOTP** are correctly configured with working delivery channels

- ☑ Check **user pool settings allow MFA configuration updates**

- ☑ Ensure **IAM roles and policies** allow MFA-related operations (`SetUserMFAPreference`, etc.)

- ☑ Validate **Lambda triggers** are compatible with MFA flows (especially `DefineAuthChallenge`)

- ☑ Test **MFA challenges in both sign-up and sign-in workflows**

How This Happens in the Real World

1. **The MFA Mirage**
   A healthcare startup believes MFA is protecting their users—but it's only set to "Optional," and no

users are actually enrolled. A security review uncovers that only 2% of accounts ever completed MFA setup.

2. **Broken SMS Flows in Production**
   A dev team sets up SMS-based MFA in staging using personal phone numbers. Once in production, real users can't receive codes— because the SNS region isn't configured, or the Cognito pool isn't linked to an active SES identity for SMS fallback.

3. **TOTP Setup Fails Silently**
   A banking app supports TOTP, but the UI never prompts users for MFA enrollment. The `PreferredMfaSetting` is unset, and `MFAOptions` are blank—leaving users with passwords only, despite expecting MFA protection.

Root Causes

- **MFA Mode Set to Optional Instead of Required**
  Many teams forget to enforce MFA globally; "Optional" means it's up to the user to opt in.

- **SMS Configuration Missing in the Region**
  SNS or SES not set up, or IAM role missing `sns:Publish` permission to send verification codes.

- **TOTP Setup Not Initiated or Stored**
  Developers forget to implement the MFA setup flow that generates the QR code or secret for apps like Google Authenticator.

- **No Default MFA Challenge Lambda Behavior**
  If you're using custom auth flows (via `DefineAuthChallenge`, `CreateAuthChallenge`, etc.), you must handle MFA manually—or it won't work.

- **Client App Doesn't Persist MFA Settings**
  Even if MFA is completed, not saving `PreferredMfaSetting` and `UserMFASettingList` means Cognito won't prompt for it next time.

✳ **Compliance & Financial Fallout**

- **HIPAA — Weak Authentication on PHI Access**
  Failure to enforce MFA for healthcare users accessing Protected Health Information (PHI) is a compliance violation.

- **GDPR — Lack of "Appropriate Security" Controls**
  Weak authentication increases breach risk, especially for European users.

- **SOC 2 & ISO 27001 — Audit Trail Inconsistencies**

MFA-related actions not being logged or enforced can cause failed audits.

- **NIST 800-63 — Inadequate Identity Assurance**
  Optional or broken MFA weakens identity assurance levels required by U.S. government and financial institutions.

How Developers Misread the Situation

- "I turned on MFA in the console, so it's enforced." → If it's **set to 'Optional'**, it's not enforced.

- "SMS works in dev—it'll work in prod too." → SMS can fail in production without proper **SNS/SES verification or IAM permissions**.

- "TOTP will just work once enabled." → You must **initiate setup**, store the preference, and verify it with AssociateSoftwareToken + VerifySoftwareToken.

- "Lambda triggers don't affect MFA." → They **absolutely do**—MFA breaks if DefineAuthChallenge doesn't properly handle it.

🦴 Detection Steps (AWS CLI preferred)

```
# Check if MFA is enabled and enforced on
the user pool
aws cognito-idp describe-user-pool \
  --user-pool-id <user-pool-id> \
  --query "UserPool.MfaConfiguration"

# Check a user's MFA status
aws cognito-idp admin-get-user \
  --user-pool-id <user-pool-id> \
  --username <username> \
  --query "{MFA:UserMFASettingList,
Preferred:PreferredMfaSetting}"

# Test if SMS is set up
aws cognito-idp get-user-attribute-
verification-code \
  --access-token <access-token> \
  --attribute-name phone_number
```

Diagram

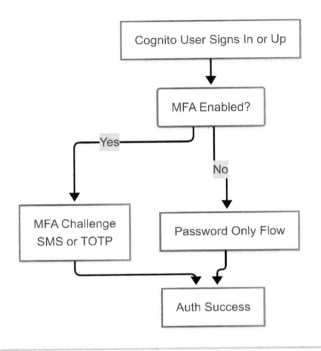

🛠 Fix Instructions

Step 1: Enforce MFA Globally

```
aws cognito-idp set-user-pool-mfa-config \
  --user-pool-id <user-pool-id> \
  --mfa-configuration ON
```

Or via console:

- Go to User Pool → **MFA and verifications**

- Set MFA configuration to **Required**

Step 2: Configure SMS (If Used)

- Verify phone number in **Amazon SNS** or **SES**

- Ensure IAM role used by Cognito has `sns:Publish` permission

- Set SMS region and default message templates

```
aws cognito-idp set-user-pool-sms-
configuration \
  --user-pool-id <user-pool-id> \
  --sns-caller-arn arn:aws:iam::<account-
id>:role/<sns-role> \
  --external-id <external-id>
```

Step 3: Implement TOTP Enrollment Flow

Client-side flow (e.g. using Amplify or SDK):

1. Call `associate-software-token`

2. Show QR code to user

3. Call `verify-software-token` with user's 6-digit code

4. Store `PreferredMfaSetting = SOFTWARE_TOKEN_MFA`

Step 4: Update User MFA Preference

```
aws cognito-idp set-user-mfa-preference \
  --software-token-mfa-settings
Enabled=true,PreferredMfa=true \
  --access-token <access-token>
```

Step 5: Update Lambda Triggers (if used)

If using custom auth:

- Ensure your `DefineAuthChallenge`, `CreateAuthChallenge`, and `VerifyAuthChallengeResponse` explicitly include MFA logic, or fallback to default Cognito handling.

What You Probably Missed

- **MFA settings must be stored per user.** Enabling MFA on the pool isn't enough—you must record it in each user's profile.

- **Custom auth flows must explicitly invoke MFA.** If you override the flow, Cognito's MFA challenge logic is bypassed unless reimplemented.

- **SMS fallback isn't automatic.** If TOTP fails or isn't set, Cognito won't magically fall back to SMS—you must handle the error path.

- **Device remembered settings impact future challenges.** Devices marked as "trusted" can bypass MFA—this is configurable.

Chapter 56: *Fast Track Login — Optimizing Cognito for High-Scale Authentication*

🔍 Quick Skim Checklist

- ☑ Minimize **cold start latency** in Lambda triggers (e.g., pre-token or auth challenge)

- ☑ Reduce reliance on **custom auth flows** unless necessary

- ☑ Enable **caching** of user metadata or tokens where possible

- ☑ Optimize **app client token lifetimes** for balance between speed and security

- ☑ Monitor and stay within **API request rate quotas**

- ☑ Use **Amazon CloudFront + custom domain** to accelerate Hosted UI response times

How This Happens in the Real World

1. **Black Friday Bottlenecks**
   A large ecommerce site using Cognito Hosted UI experiences login delays and timeouts under peak traffic. Investigation reveals that cold-started

506

Lambda triggers and token generation lag were
throttling throughput.

2. **Mobile Login Latency**
   A mobile banking app reports sluggish sign-in UX
   in areas with poor network. Cognito tokens are
   short-lived, and the app re-authenticates too often.
   Without refresh token reuse or caching, logins take
   multiple seconds even on decent connections.

3. **Burst Traffic from Marketing Campaigns**
   A SaaS platform launches a campaign and sees
   50,000 users hit login endpoints in minutes. Half
   experience 5xx errors due to API throttling
   (`TooManyRequestsException`) from hitting
   Cognito's soft quota on `InitiateAuth`.

Root Causes

- **Unoptimized Lambda Triggers (Cold Starts)**
  Custom auth flows or token generation triggers
  (e.g., `DefineAuthChallenge`) add latency when
  scaled across multiple AZs without warm-up
  routines.

- **Frequent Token Expiration**
  Short access token durations and aggressive
  session revocation policies cause excessive re-
  authentication requests.

- **API Quota Bottlenecks**
  Cognito limits requests per second per user pool. Without batching or backoff logic, apps can trip these limits under load.

- **Poor Hosted UI Placement**
  Using the default Cognito domain without CloudFront results in regional DNS resolution and extra hops for static content.

- **Chatty Client Apps**
  Some mobile apps call `InitiateAuth` or `GetUser` too frequently—without local caching or session reuse.

✳ Compliance & Financial Fallout

- **PCI-DSS — Delayed Auth Increases Risk**
  Slower logins may force developers to cache credentials improperly to avoid latency, weakening security.

- **SOC 2 — Availability SLA Violations**
  Outages from API rate limits or login bottlenecks can break commitments under high-availability agreements.

- **User Churn and Reputation Loss**
  High friction in login processes, especially in mobile apps, often leads to user abandonment and

negative NPS scores.

- **Increased Operational Cost**
  Excessive Lambda invocations and retry loops increase AWS bills and cloud inefficiencies.

How Developers Misread the Situation

- "Cognito scales automatically—I don't need to tune anything." → Cognito **scales well**, but your **customizations don't**.

- "Token expiration doesn't affect speed." → It **does** when users are forced to refresh often or reauthenticate frequently.

- "Lambda triggers are fast enough." → Cold starts on Node.js or Python Lambdas with large dependencies can add **400ms+** per request.

- "The Hosted UI is fast everywhere." → Not without **CloudFront** and a **custom domain** to bring it closer to global users.

🦴 Detection Steps (AWS CLI preferred)

```
# Check current token validity durations
aws cognito-idp describe-user-pool-client \
```

```
  --user-pool-id <your_user_pool_id> \
  --client-id <app_client_id> \
  --query
"UserPoolClient.{AccessToken:AccessTokenVal
idity, RefreshToken:RefreshTokenValidity,
IdToken:IdTokenValidity}"

# View CloudWatch metrics for throttling
and latency
aws cloudwatch get-metric-statistics \
  --namespace AWS/Cognito \
  --metric-name ThrottledRequests \
  --dimensions
Name=UserPoolId,Value=<user_pool_id> \
  --start-time <start_time> \
  --end-time <end_time> \
  --period 60 \
  --statistics Sum

# Check Lambda cold starts
aws logs filter-log-events \
  --log-group-name /aws/lambda/<trigger-
function> \
  --filter-pattern '"Init Duration"' \
  --limit 5
```

Diagram

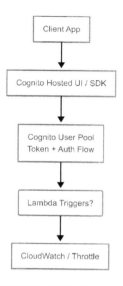

✂️ Fix Instructions

Step 1: Tune Token Lifetimes

In most apps, the defaults are too short. Extend lifetimes cautiously:

```
aws cognito-idp update-user-pool-client \
  --user-pool-id <user_pool_id> \
  --client-id <client_id> \
  --access-token-validity 60 \
  --id-token-validity 60 \
  --refresh-token-validity 1440 \
  --token-validity-units
AccessToken=minutes,IdToken=minutes,Refresh
Token=minutes
```

Step 2: Reduce Trigger Latency

- Use **Lambda Power Tuning** to benchmark optimal memory settings (512MB–1024MB often hits sweet spot).

- Keep warm with **scheduled warmers** or **provisioned concurrency** on critical flows.

- Trim dependencies. Avoid large libraries unless necessary.

Step 3: Add CloudFront to Hosted UI

1. Set up a **custom domain** in your user pool settings.

2. Create a CloudFront distribution pointing to the Cognito Hosted UI.

3. Use it in your app instead of the default `*.auth.region.amazoncognito.com`.

Step 4: Implement Local Token Caching in Clients

In Amplify:

```
Auth.currentSession().then(session => {
  const accessToken =
session.getAccessToken().getJwtToken();
```

```
    // Use or cache this
});
```

Avoid calling `signIn` or `getUser` unnecessarily.

Step 5: Avoid Unnecessary API Calls

- Avoid calling `InitiateAuth` unless truly needed.

- Cache user metadata post-login.

- Batch user attribute updates.

What You Probably Missed

- **Refresh tokens are valid across devices**, so you can reuse them in multi-tab or background sessions.

- **Hosted UI loads fonts and styles from Cognito's regional servers**—CloudFront reduces DNS latency and improves TLS negotiation speed.

- **Token revocation only applies to Refresh Tokens** (via `RevokeToken`). Access and ID tokens are stateless.

- **API rate quotas are per second, per user pool, not per client**—multiple apps sharing a pool increases risk of throttling.

Chapter 57: *The Silent Timeout — Fixing Token Expiration & Refresh Issues in Cognito*

🔍 Quick Skim Checklist

- ☑ Understand Cognito token types: **Access, ID, and Refresh tokens**

- ☑ Know the **default expiration** times for each token and when they apply

- ☑ Ensure clients **cache and reuse** tokens correctly during session

- ☑ Implement **refresh logic** using the refreshToken grant type or SDK built-ins

- ☑ Detect and handle NotAuthorizedException caused by expired tokens

- ☑ Use **CloudWatch Logs** and browser dev tools to identify silent failures

How This Happens in the Real World

1. **Users Randomly Logged Out**
   A streaming media app using Cognito reports sporadic logout issues. Turns out the ID token

expires after 1 hour, and the app doesn't refresh it—forcing full re-auth when trying to access resources secured by the token.

2. **API Requests Failing Without Clarity**
   A React-based dashboard suddenly stops displaying data after 60 minutes. API Gateway rejects the request due to an expired access token, but the frontend doesn't show a login prompt—just a blank screen.

3. **Mobile App Token Confusion**
   A health app built on Amplify logs users in properly, but refresh logic fails silently. Amplify's auto-refresh works in web, but not in native iOS due to incorrect session management across app launches.

Root Causes

- **Misunderstanding Token Lifecycles**
  Access tokens and ID tokens expire by default in **1 hour**, while refresh tokens may last **30 days or more**. Many developers assume tokens persist longer than they do.

- **Missing or Broken Refresh Logic**
  If your frontend/backend doesn't request a new session before token expiry, you'll encounter silent failures or forced logouts.

- **Relying Only on Access Tokens Without Refresh Support**
  Using Cognito in API mode without refresh logic means once the token expires, the client is stuck unless it reauthenticates fully.

- **Improper Token Caching Across Sessions**
  Mobile and SPA apps sometimes lose track of token state on refresh, navigation, or app restart.

- **Silent Failures on Expiration**
  Cognito will return `NotAuthorizedException` with little detail; UI often doesn't show clear errors.

✸ Compliance & Financial Fallout

- **GDPR — Incomplete Session Management**
  Failing to expire or manage tokens properly can violate data protection principles.

- **HIPAA — Session Timeouts Not Enforced**
  Healthcare apps must enforce strict expiration and secure session refresh.

- **Poor User Experience = Lost Revenue**
  If users are silently logged out or apps fail unpredictably, abandonment rates increase.

- **Increased Support Burden**
  Troubleshooting unclear errors from expired

tokens adds overhead and user frustration.

How Developers Misread the Situation

- "Cognito auto-refreshes tokens." → Only if **you implement it** or use **Amplify Auth** correctly.

- "Tokens last as long as the session." → **ID and Access tokens expire in 1 hour**—session != token.

- "My app doesn't need the refresh token." → If you don't use it, **you're forcing full re-authentication**.

- "The SDK handles everything." → Only **some** SDKs (like Amplify Web) handle refresh logic; others require manual setup.

🔧 Detection Steps (AWS CLI preferred)

```
# Check token validity periods for your app
client
aws cognito-idp describe-user-pool-client \
  --user-pool-id <your_user_pool_id> \
  --client-id <app_client_id> \
  --query
"UserPoolClient.{AccessToken:AccessTokenVal
```

```
idity, IdToken:IdTokenValidity,
RefreshToken:RefreshTokenValidity}"

# Attempt token refresh with refresh_token
grant type
curl --request POST \
  --url
https://<your_domain>.auth.<region>.amazonc
ognito.com/oauth2/token \
  --header 'Content-Type: application/x-
www-form-urlencoded' \
  --data
'grant_type=refresh_token&client_id=<client
_id>&refresh_token=<refresh_token>'
```

Monitor Token Errors in CloudWatch Logs

```
# Filter logs for NotAuthorizedException
(expired token or invalid)
aws logs filter-log-events \
  --log-group-name /aws/lambda/<your-
backend-function> \
  --filter-pattern
'"NotAuthorizedException"' \
  --limit 5
```

Diagram

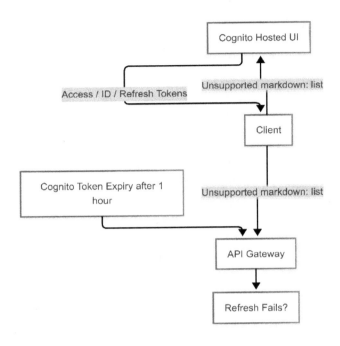

🛠 Fix Instructions

Step 1: Extend Token Lifetimes (Optional for smoother UX)

```
aws cognito-idp update-user-pool-client \
  --user-pool-id <pool_id> \
  --client-id <client_id> \
  --access-token-validity 60 \
  --id-token-validity 60 \
  --refresh-token-validity 1440 \
```

```
  --token-validity-units
AccessToken=minutes,IdToken=minutes,Refresh
Token=minutes
```

Step 2: Use the Refresh Token in OAuth2 Flow

To get a new ID and Access token, call:

```
POST /oauth2/token
Content-Type: application/x-www-form-
urlencoded

grant_type=refresh_token
client_id=YOUR_CLIENT_ID
refresh_token=REFRESH_TOKEN
```

Step 3: Enable Automatic Refresh in Amplify (Web)

```
import { Auth } from 'aws-amplify';

async function getSession() {
  try {
    const session = await
Auth.currentSession();
    const accessToken =
session.getAccessToken().getJwtToken();
    return accessToken;
  } catch (err) {
```

```
    console.error('Token expired or refresh
failed', err);
    // Trigger re-auth
  }
}
```

Step 4: Add Refresh Fallback Logic in Native SDKs

Native SDKs may not auto-refresh. On
`NotAuthorizedException`, catch and retry with
`refreshToken` or re-sign-in logic.

Step 5: Monitor and Handle Errors Gracefully

- Always inspect the error code from Cognito
  SDK/API

- Display a user-friendly prompt to re-authenticate if
  refresh fails

- Log `NotAuthorizedException` events to help
  spot trends in silent failures

What You Probably Missed

- **Refresh tokens don't update ID/Access tokens
  unless used explicitly.**

- **Tokens from the Hosted UI are NOT refreshed by default**—you must handle it on your app side.

- **Access/ID token expiration happens silently in most clients**, especially in SPAs unless monitored or handled proactively.

- **Refresh tokens can be revoked** with RevokeToken, but access/ID tokens can't—once issued, they're valid until expiry.

Chapter 58: *The Federation Frustration —*
Debugging Broken Logins with Google and
Facebook in Cognito

🔍 Quick Skim Checklist

- ☑ Ensure **App client ID and secret** match exactly between Cognito and the IdP (Google/Facebook)

- ☑ Double-check **redirect URIs** in both Cognito and the identity provider console

- ☑ Confirm **OAuth scopes** (e.g. `email`, `profile`) are set correctly

- ☑ Validate **identity provider is enabled** for the correct app client in Cognito

- ☑ Inspect **JWT tokens and OAuth responses** for errors

- ☑ Use **CloudWatch logs** and browser dev tools to trace failures in Hosted UI

How This Happens in the Real World

1. **Login Works in Dev, Fails in Prod**
   A social media analytics platform integrates Facebook login. Everything works in the

development environment, but fails in production due to an incorrect callback URI in the Facebook developer console. Cognito returns a blank screen with no error, frustrating both users and developers.

2. **Silent Failures in Hosted UI**
   A gaming app adds Google login. Users click the "Sign in with Google" button and are redirected back to the login page with no explanation. Turns out the Cognito app client had the wrong Google client ID, and the OAuth handshake failed silently.

3. **SAML Overrides Breaking Federation**
   A multi-tenant platform mixes SAML and social IdPs, but forgets to isolate callback URLs. Google login fails for some users because the same Cognito client is configured with incompatible identity provider settings.

Root Causes

- **Mismatched App Client ID/Secret**
  If the Google or Facebook credentials in Cognito don't match the ones configured in the identity provider console, authentication fails without a meaningful error.

- **Missing or Incorrect Redirect URI**
  The identity provider redirects users back to Cognito—but if the URI isn't explicitly allowed in their console config, the login will silently fail or

show "redirect URI mismatch".

- **Wrong or Incomplete OAuth Scopes**
  If required scopes like `email` or `profile` are missing, the identity provider may authenticate the user, but Cognito can't retrieve enough info to complete the sign-in.

- **Federated IdP Not Enabled on App Client**
  Even if you configure the provider in Cognito, it must also be explicitly **enabled per app client**.

- **Browser Cookies or Local Storage Issues**
  Cognito stores state during the OAuth flow. Cross-origin issues or cookie policy restrictions can disrupt this and break the return handshake.

✳ Compliance & Financial Fallout

- **GDPR — Consent Tracking Failures**
  Federated logins often provide access to user data from external providers. Failure to correctly enforce and log consent can breach GDPR Article 7.

- **CCPA — Untracked Data Collection**
  Incorrect scope handling or failure to disclose third-party sign-in behavior may violate CCPA disclosure rules.

- **Broken Auth = Lost Conversions**
  Each failed social login attempt is a lost signup,

affecting acquisition funnels.

- **Customer Trust Erosion**
  Users expect Google/Facebook login to "just work." A failed flow damages trust and brand perception.

How Developers Misread the Situation

- "I added the IdP in Cognito, so it should work." → You also need to **configure the IdP**, **enable it in the app client**, and match all callback settings.

- "Hosted UI will show me the error." → Not always. Many federation errors **redirect silently** or show ambiguous error codes.

- "OAuth scopes are optional." → Not for Cognito. Without email or profile, **Cognito can't map user identities** correctly.

- "Cognito handles everything." → It facilitates the handshake, but **you're responsible for proper configuration on both sides**.

🦴 Detection Steps (AWS CLI preferred)

```
# 1. Verify the identity provider is
created and configured
aws cognito-idp describe-identity-provider
\
  --user-pool-id <user_pool_id> \
  --provider-name Google

# 2. Check which identity providers are
enabled on the app client
aws cognito-idp describe-user-pool-client \
  --user-pool-id <user_pool_id> \
  --client-id <app_client_id> \
  --query
"UserPoolClient.SupportedIdentityProviders"

# 3. Review redirect URLs
aws cognito-idp describe-user-pool-client \
  --user-pool-id <user_pool_id> \
  --client-id <app_client_id> \
  --query "UserPoolClient.CallbackURLs"

# 4. Test hosted UI login manually
open
"https://<your_domain>.auth.<region>.amazon
cognito.com/login?client_id=<app_client_id>
&response_type=code&scope=email+openid+prof
ile&redirect_uri=<your_redirect_uri>"
```

Diagram

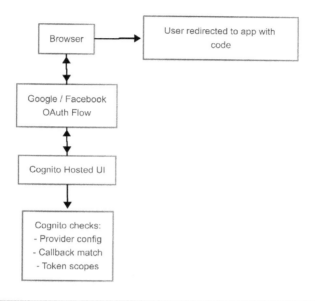

🛠 Fix Instructions

Step 1: Set Up Identity Provider Credentials Properly

In Google or Facebook developer console:

- Create an OAuth 2.0 Client

- Copy **Client ID** and **Client Secret**

Whitelist **redirect URI**:

```
https://<your_domain>.auth.<region>.amazonc
ognito.com/oauth2/idpresponse
```

•

Step 2: Configure the Identity Provider in Cognito

Via AWS Console or CLI:

```
aws cognito-idp create-identity-provider \
  --user-pool-id <user_pool_id> \
  --provider-name Google \
  --provider-type Google \
  --provider-details
client_id=GOOGLE_ID,client_secret=GOOGLE_SE
CRET,authorize_scopes="openid email
profile" \
  --attribute-mapping email=email,name=name
```

Step 3: Enable the IdP in App Client Settings

```
aws cognito-idp update-user-pool-client \
  --user-pool-id <user_pool_id> \
  --client-id <app_client_id> \
  --supported-identity-providers Google
Facebook
```

Step 4: Validate Redirect URIs Match Exactly

Both Cognito and the IdP must agree on the redirect URI down to the **scheme, casing, and trailing slash**.

```
aws cognito-idp update-user-pool-client \
  --user-pool-id <user_pool_id> \
  --client-id <client_id> \
  --callback-urls
https://yourapp.com/callback
```

Step 5: Debug With Browser Dev Tools

- Watch network requests to `oauth2/authorize` and `oauth2/idpresponse`

- Check for `error=access_denied`, `invalid_request`, or `unauthorized_client`

- Confirm that `state` and `code` query params are present in the redirect

---

What You Probably Missed

- **Cognito's Hosted UI doesn't show descriptive errors** for OAuth failures—often just redirects silently to the login page.

- **Facebook requires App Review** to access certain fields like `email`; missing this step will cause the login to fail silently.

- **Google OAuth apps need to be published** (OAuth consent screen) to work for non-Google

Workspace users.

- **Multiple social IdPs share the same** `/idpresponse` **redirect URI**, so mixing callback URLs across app clients can break routing.

- **Custom domains need valid SSL certificates** or the redirect will fail entirely with a browser security error.

Chapter 59: *Brand Your Auth — Custom Domains in Cognito the Right Way*

🔍 **Quick Skim Checklist — Practical checks for the reader**

- ☑ Register your domain and verify DNS control (Route 53 or external provider)

- ☑ Issue an **ACM SSL certificate** in the **same region** as your Cognito user pool

- ☑ Use the **AWS CLI or console** to assign the certificate to a **custom domain** in Cognito

- ☑ Update your DNS to point to the **Cognito-provided CloudFront endpoint**

- ☑ Add matching **callback and logout URLs** to your app client settings

- ☑ Watch for **certificate region mismatches, CloudFront propagation delays**, and **redirect URI typos**

How This Happens in the Real World

1. **The Unbranded Login Page**
   A fintech startup launches using Cognito's default

`*.auth.region.amazoncognito.com` domain. Their login page works—but looks generic. Early testers worry it's phishing. The team rushes to add a custom domain but hits setup errors and propagation delays that cause downtime during launch week.

2. **Redirect Loop Madness**
   A React SPA integrates Cognito Hosted UI via a branded subdomain. After clicking "Log In," users enter a redirect loop between the app and Cognito. The issue? A stale DNS record and a certificate created in the wrong region—an all-too-common pairing.

3. **The Hidden Propagation Trap**
   An engineer deletes and recreates a Cognito custom domain after changing certs. They immediately try to reassign the same domain—only to get a "Domain already exists" error. Turns out Cognito needs time to fully deprovision the old CloudFront stack.

Root Causes

- **SSL Certificate Region Mismatch**
  The certificate must be in the **same region** as your Cognito user pool—if it's not, domain assignment fails silently or throws vague errors.

- **DNS Not Pointing to CloudFront**
  If your custom domain doesn't resolve to the

correct Cognito-hosted CloudFront distribution, users hit redirect loops or blank login screens.

- **Domain Still "Attached" in Background**
  Even after deleting a custom domain, Cognito holds on to backend resources (e.g., CloudFront) for 15–30 minutes, making it **temporarily unavailable for reuse**.

- **Callback/Logout URLs Not Updated**
  After switching to a custom domain, devs often forget to change the **callback URLs** to match it, breaking the OAuth flow.

- **Cross-Origin or Cookie Policy Issues**
  Especially in SPAs or mobile apps, mismatched domains (e.g., login.yoursite.com vs. app.yoursite.com) can lead to CORS errors or broken cookies if not configured for secure cross-domain access.

✳ Compliance & Financial Fallout

- **GDPR / CCPA — Confusing Consent Interfaces**
  Login UIs without clear branding or secured domains may violate informed consent expectations for data collection.

- **SOC 2 — Availability Failures**
  Broken login flows from improper domain setups can cause service disruptions, impacting audit

readiness and uptime guarantees.

- **Brand Damage**
  A confusing or unbranded login experience hurts user trust—especially in fintech, healthcare, or e-commerce sectors.

- **Security Confusion = Phishing Risk**
  Users who expect to see `login.yoursite.com` but land on an unfamiliar domain may distrust even legitimate login flows.

How Developers Misread the Situation

- "The certificate is in ACM—it's good to go." → ☑
  But **it must be in the same region** as the Cognito user pool.

- "Once I delete a domain, I can reassign it immediately." → 🗐 No—you must wait ~30 minutes for CloudFront deprovisioning.

- "Cognito creates DNS records for me." → ✗ DNS management (e.g., CNAME) is **your responsibility**, even in Route 53.

- "I updated the domain—everything should work." → You also need to update your **callback and logout URLs**, or token handoff will fail.

🔧 Detection Steps (AWS CLI preferred)

```
# Check current custom domain configuration
aws cognito-idp describe-user-pool-domain \
  --domain login.yoursite.com \
  --region us-west-2

# Check CloudFront target you need to point
to
aws cognito-idp describe-user-pool-domain \
  --domain login.yoursite.com \
  --query
'DomainDescription.CloudFrontDistribution'
\
  --region us-west-2

# List certificates and confirm region
aws acm list-certificates \
  --region us-west-2

# Confirm callback and logout URLs match
new domain
aws cognito-idp describe-user-pool-client \
  --user-pool-id <your_user_pool_id> \
  --client-id <your_app_client_id> \
  --query
"UserPoolClient.{Callbacks:CallbackURLs,Log
outs:LogoutURLs}"
```

Diagram

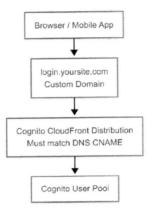

🔧 Fix Instructions — Step-by-step code and config fixes

Step 1: Issue ACM Certificate in the Correct Region

```
aws acm request-certificate \
  --domain-name login.yoursite.com \
  --validation-method DNS \
  --region us-west-2
```

⚠ **Important:** This must be in the **same region** as your Cognito user pool (e.g., `us-west-2`, `eu-central-1`, etc.).

Step 2: Create a Custom Domain in Cognito

```
aws cognito-idp create-user-pool-domain \
  --domain login.yoursite.com \
  --user-pool-id <user_pool_id> \
  --custom-domain-config
CertificateArn=arn:aws:acm:us-west-
2:123456789012:certificate/<cert_id>
```

🔁 **Domain reuse warning:** If this fails with `Domain already exists`, the domain may still be "detaching." Wait **15–30 minutes** after deletion before reusing.

Step 3: Set Up DNS (Route 53 or external)

Create a **CNAME** record:

```
login.yoursite.com - abc123.cloudfront.net
```

   ●

☑ Use the `CloudFrontDistribution` value from `describe-user-pool-domain`.

Step 4: Update App Client Callback and Logout URLs

```
aws cognito-idp update-user-pool-client \
  --user-pool-id <pool_id> \
  --client-id <client_id> \
```

```
--callback-urls
https://login.yoursite.com/callback \
  --logout-urls
https://login.yoursite.com/logout
```

Ensure they **match exactly** (including `https://` and any trailing slashes).

Step 5: Test the Hosted UI

```
https://login.yoursite.com/login?client_id=
<app_client_id>&response_type=code&scope=em
ail+openid+profile&redirect_uri=https://log
in.yoursite.com/callback
```

Try the full flow—including sign-in, callback, token retrieval, and logout.

What You Probably Missed — Lesser-known edge cases, hidden pitfalls

- **Deleting a domain doesn't free it up immediately.** CloudFront and DNS propagation takes time.

- **Region mismatch is the #1 silent failure.** The CLI won't always tell you the cert is from the wrong region—it just won't work.

- **OAuth flow breaks if `redirect_uri` doesn't match.** Even `https://login.yoursite.com` vs `https://login.yoursite.com/` can cause hard-to-debug failures.

- **Using Cognito's default domain alongside a custom domain?** Not a good idea. Stick to one domain per app client to avoid state conflicts.

- **Custom domain login breaks on Safari if `SameSite=None` cookies aren't set.** Make sure your browser environment allows secure, third-party cookies for auth.

Chapter 60: *When SSO Meets AWS — Taming Cognito + Enterprise Identity Providers*

🔍 **Quick Skim Checklist — Practical checks for the reader**

- ☑ Use **OpenID Connect (OIDC)** for Azure AD, Okta, and other modern enterprise IdPs

- ☑ Register **Cognito as a client app** in the enterprise IdP

- ☑ Match **redirect URIs exactly** between Cognito and the IdP

- ☑ Ensure the IdP sends **standard claims** (like `sub`, `email`, `name`)

- ☑ Map user attributes correctly in Cognito's identity provider settings

- ☑ Test the entire flow through the **Cognito Hosted UI**, not just token endpoints

How This Happens in the Real World

1. **The Azure AD Integration That Wouldn't Work**
   A B2B SaaS startup wants to let corporate customers sign in using Azure AD. They follow

AWS's docs but hit constant errors like
`invalid_request` or `missing_token`. After
weeks of back and forth, they realize their Azure
redirect URI didn't match what Cognito expected—
and their token mapping was missing the `email`
claim Cognito needs.

2. **The Okta Setup That Broke on Production**
   A team configures Okta as an OIDC IdP in Cognito
   and tests everything in dev using `localhost` as
   the callback URI. Once deployed to
   `app.company.com`, logins break due to a
   mismatch in the allowed redirect URIs in the Okta
   admin panel.

3. **Custom Claim Chaos**
   An enterprise health platform integrates an internal
   IdP using OIDC. The IdP uses a custom claim
   (`user_identifier`) instead of `sub` for user ID.
   Cognito can't link the user identity properly, leading
   to broken federation and duplicated users.

Root Causes

- **Strict OIDC Spec Adherence**
  Cognito expects standard OIDC behavior.
  Enterprise IdPs often deviate or require special
  setup to return the correct claims and scopes.

- **Redirect URI Mismatch**
  If the IdP's registered redirect URI doesn't exactly

match what Cognito uses (including case, slashes, or HTTPS), the login will fail silently or with cryptic errors.

- **Missing Required Claims**
  Cognito expects at minimum `sub`, `email`, and sometimes `name`. If these aren't returned in the Id token, user mapping will fail.

- **Attribute Mapping Left Unconfigured**
  Even if tokens are valid, Cognito won't know how to assign values to its internal user model without explicit mapping of claims to user pool attributes.

- **App Client Configuration Confusion**
  Developers often forget to enable the new IdP in their app client settings, or fail to adjust the OAuth scopes to request the right data.

✳ Compliance & Financial Fallout

- **SAML/OIDC Misconfiguration = Security Exposure**
  If your login provider misrepresents user identity or doesn't enforce MFA, it weakens your security posture and audit trail.

- **GDPR / HIPAA — Poor User Mapping or Data Exposure**
  Incorrect claim mappings may expose sensitive identity data to the wrong roles or leave audit logs

fragmented.

- **Customer Frustration in B2B Flows**
  Enterprise clients expect SSO to "just work."
  Broken or inconsistent login behavior can block
  contracts and raise trust issues.

- **Support Cost Surge**
  Every failed login integration leads to dev time,
  escalated support tickets, and tension with IT
  security teams at client organizations.

How Developers Misread the Situation

- "Cognito supports OIDC—it should just work with
  Azure or Okta." → ☑ It does **if the IdP fully
  complies with the spec**—which they often don't
  out of the box.

- "Cognito auto-detects user claims." → ✘ You
  must explicitly **map IdP claims to Cognito
  attributes**.

- "Redirect URI is flexible." → ✘ It must **exactly
  match** on both Cognito and the IdP side—including
  trailing slashes and scheme.

- "I don't need Hosted UI for OIDC." → ⚠ If you're
  using Cognito's OIDC federation, you **must** use the
  Hosted UI to initiate the login flow—it won't work

from custom frontends alone.

🔧 Detection Steps (AWS CLI preferred)

```
# 1. Describe the identity provider to
verify claim mappings
aws cognito-idp describe-identity-provider
\
   --user-pool-id <user_pool_id> \
   --provider-name <OIDC_Provider_Name>

# 2. Check which identity providers are
enabled for your app client
aws cognito-idp describe-user-pool-client \
   --user-pool-id <user_pool_id> \
   --client-id <app_client_id> \
   --query
'UserPoolClient.SupportedIdentityProviders'

# 3. Verify callback URLs
aws cognito-idp describe-user-pool-client \
   --user-pool-id <user_pool_id> \
   --client-id <app_client_id> \
   --query 'UserPoolClient.CallbackURLs'
```

Bonus CLI test: Try using `curl` with a known good `id_token` to simulate OIDC exchange behavior and view raw claims.

Diagram

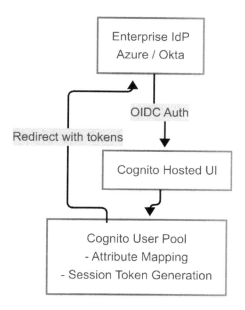

⚒ Fix Instructions — Step-by-step code and config fixes

Step 1: Register Cognito in the IdP

In Azure AD, Okta, or any OIDC-compliant IdP:

- Register a new **client application**

Set the **redirect URI** to:

```
https://<your_domain>.auth.<region>.amazonc
ognito.com/oauth2/idpresponse
```

-
- Note the **Client ID**, **Client Secret**, and **well-known OIDC endpoint**

Step 2: Add the OIDC Provider to Cognito

```
aws cognito-idp create-identity-provider \
  --user-pool-id <user_pool_id> \
  --provider-name "MyOIDCProvider" \
  --provider-type OIDC \
  --provider-details
client_id=<CLIENT_ID>,client_secret=<CLIENT
_SECRET>,attributes_request_method=GET,oidc
_issuer=<OIDC_ISSUER_URL>,authorize_scopes=
"openid email profile" \
  --attribute-mapping
email=email,username=sub,name=name
```

Step 3: Enable IdP on Your App Client

```
aws cognito-idp update-user-pool-client \
  --user-pool-id <user_pool_id> \
  --client-id <client_id> \
```

```
  --supported-identity-providers
MyOIDCProvider
```

Step 4: Add Correct Callback and Logout URLs

```
aws cognito-idp update-user-pool-client \
  --user-pool-id <user_pool_id> \
  --client-id <client_id> \
  --callback-urls
https://yourapp.com/callback \
  --logout-urls https://yourapp.com/logout
```

Step 5: Test the Login via Hosted UI

```
https://<your_domain>.auth.<region>.amazonc
ognito.com/login?client_id=<client_id>&resp
onse_type=code&scope=email+openid+profile&r
edirect_uri=https://yourapp.com/callback
```

Ensure your IdP logs show a completed exchange, and validate the Cognito user has mapped attributes.

What You Probably Missed — Lesser-known edge cases, hidden pitfalls

- **Azure AD may require admin consent** for scopes like email and profile—you must configure the app for multi-tenant or request elevated permissions.

- **OIDC claims are case-sensitive.** `Email` ≠ `email` in attribute mappings.

- **You must use the Hosted UI for OIDC federation.** Direct API-based flows will fail unless initiated via Hosted UI.

- **Token signature validation errors can occur** if Cognito's metadata cache is stale. A new IdP might take a few minutes to propagate.

- **Multiple IdPs using the same redirect URI can cause confusion**—use different Cognito app clients for each integration where possible.

Chapter 61: *Mind the Map — Getting Identity Provider Attributes Right in Cognito*

🔍 **Quick Skim Checklist — Practical checks for the reader**

- ☑ Define **attribute mappings** explicitly when configuring each identity provider

- ☑ Map **standard claims** like `email`, `sub`, and `name` to Cognito attributes

- ☑ Use **custom attributes** (`custom:*`) for non-standard IdP claims

- ☑ Confirm that the IdP returns **all required claims** in the token

- ☑ Avoid case mismatches in claim keys (`Email` ≠ `email`)

- ☑ Validate mappings using **admin-get-user** and **token inspection**

How This Happens in the Real World

1. **The "Email Not Found" Mystery**
   A healthtech platform connects Azure AD to Cognito using OpenID Connect. Users authenticate

successfully, but no email is stored in their Cognito profile. After digging through logs, the team finds out that Azure AD returned `userPrincipalName` instead of `email`, and no attribute mapping was set to handle it.

2. **Custom Roles That Vanished**
   A B2B SaaS app tries to use a `department` claim from Okta to apply user-specific roles. Cognito silently ignores the attribute because it wasn't mapped to a custom field like `custom:department`.

3. **User Pool Chaos**
   An internal tool uses SAML to federate employee access from multiple business units. One group uses `uid`, another uses `sub`, and neither group has consistent mappings. As a result, users are misidentified or duplicated across sessions.

Root Causes

- **Missing or Incorrect Attribute Mappings**
  Cognito does not automatically infer mappings from IdP claims—you must configure them explicitly.

- **Case Sensitivity in Claims**
  Cognito's mapping is case-sensitive. A claim named `Email` won't match `email`.

- **Non-Standard Claim Names**
  Enterprise IdPs often use custom field names (like `employeeId`, `department_code`) that need to be mapped to custom attributes.

- **Using Reserved Attribute Names Incorrectly**
  You can't use `custom:*` names for built-in Cognito attributes like `email` or `sub`.

- **Mismatched or Incomplete Token Claims**
  If the IdP doesn't send a required claim, Cognito can't populate the user profile—even if the mapping is correct.

✳ Compliance & Financial Fallout

- **GDPR — Incomplete User Profiles**
  Missing email or identity claims may result in data that's unusable for GDPR subject access or portability requests.

- **HIPAA — Risk of Identity Misattribution**
  Misconfigured attributes could cause users to access another patient or clinician's data.

- **SOC 2 — Auditing and Accountability Gaps**
  Improper mapping can lead to inconsistencies in logs and session identity tracking.

- **Revenue Impact from Login Failures**
  If users can authenticate but have incomplete

profiles, app logic tied to roles or billing entitlements may break silently.

How Developers Misread the Situation

- "Cognito will pick up the IdP attributes automatically." → ✖ Not unless you **explicitly map** them during IdP setup.

- "The token has the value, so it's stored." → ✖ If there's **no mapping**, Cognito **ignores it**—no matter what's in the token.

- "All IdPs return `email` and `name`." → ⚠ Azure AD, SAML, and custom OIDC providers often **return different field names**.

- "I can map any claim to any Cognito field." → ✖ Mappings must align with **valid Cognito attribute types**—custom values go into `custom:*` fields only.

🔧 Detection Steps (AWS CLI preferred)

```
# 1. Describe the identity provider to
review mappings
aws cognito-idp describe-identity-provider
\
```

```
  --user-pool-id <user_pool_id> \
  --provider-name <provider_name> \
  --query
"IdentityProvider.AttributeMapping"

# 2. Inspect user attributes post-login
aws cognito-idp admin-get-user \
  --user-pool-id <user_pool_id> \
  --username <cognito_user_id>

# 3. Decode the IdP's token manually
(base64 decode JWT) to view claims
# Look for expected claims like 'email',
'sub', 'department', etc.
```

Diagram

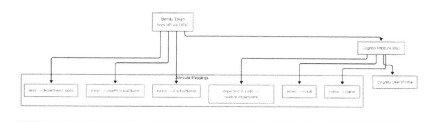

🛠 Fix Instructions — Step-by-step code and config fixes

Step 1: Identify the Token Claims from the IdP

- Use browser tools or decode the JWT to view IdP claims (e.g., `email`, `userPrincipalName`, `department_code`).

- Note exact casing and key names.

Step 2: Add or Update Attribute Mapping in Cognito

```
aws cognito-idp update-identity-provider \
  --user-pool-id <user_pool_id> \
  --provider-name <provider_name> \
  --attribute-mapping
email=userPrincipalName,name=displayName,cu
stom:department=department_code
```

Step 3: Confirm the Mapping Took Effect

```
aws cognito-idp describe-identity-provider \
  --user-pool-id <user_pool_id> \
  --provider-name <provider_name> \
  --query
"IdentityProvider.AttributeMapping"
```

Step 4: Test User Login and Inspect Result

- Log in using the Hosted UI or federated flow

- Use `admin-get-user` to verify that expected attributes are populated

- Confirm role or group assignment logic based on custom attributes works correctly

---

What You Probably Missed — Lesser-known edge cases, hidden pitfalls

- **Mapping `sub` is not required**—Cognito uses it automatically as the unique user ID from the IdP.

- **You can't remap reserved fields** like `sub`, `username`, or `cognito:groups`.

- **Custom attributes must be prefixed with** `custom:`, or they're ignored completely.

- **Order of operations matters**—users federated before you fixed mappings may have incomplete profiles. You'll need to clear and reauthenticate those accounts.

- **Token claim values must be strings**—claims returned as arrays or objects may silently fail to map.

Chapter 62: *Trapped in Limbo — Fixing "Confirm Sign Up" State in Cognito*

🔍 **Quick Skim Checklist — Practical checks for the reader**

- ☑ Check if user status is stuck at UNCONFIRMED in the user pool

- ☑ Confirm if email/SMS delivery is failing (SES/SNS verification, bounce rates)

- ☑ Ensure frontend properly calls `confirmSignUp()` after user receives code

- ☑ Use **admin-confirm-sign-up** only after verifying intent

- ☑ Consider building a **resend + reset flow** with expiry-aware UX

- ☑ Handle edge cases like **expired confirmation codes** or deleted emails

How This Happens in the Real World

1. **The One-Time User Never Returns**
   A user signs up, doesn't get the confirmation email (due to typo or SES bounce), and quietly abandons

the app. Their record sits forever in `UNCONFIRMED` state, blocking re-registration with the same email.

2. **SMS Gone Wrong**
   A rideshare app using SMS for sign-up sees dozens of users stuck in the registration flow. SNS delivery fails due to region or permission issues. Developers don't notice until a spike in support tickets.

3. **No Confirm Logic in Frontend**
   A dev team builds a beautiful sign-up form, but forgets to call `Auth.confirmSignUp()` in the React app. Users receive codes—but nothing happens when they enter them.

Root Causes

- **Confirmation Step Not Triggered**
  Cognito requires explicit confirmation (code + confirmSignUp API call) after sign-up unless auto-confirm is enabled via trigger.

- **Email/SMS Not Delivered**
  If Cognito uses SES/SNS and these aren't correctly set up or verified, confirmation messages may silently fail.

- **Expired or Invalid Codes**
  Confirmation codes expire (typically in 24 hours). Users who try after expiry see "CodeMismatchException" or

"ExpiredCodeException".

- **Resend Not Implemented**
  If the UI lacks a resend link/button, users have no way to recover from a missed message.

- **Pre Sign-up Lambda Blocking Confirmation**
  Custom logic may allow sign-up but conditionally block confirmation by returning error or not auto-confirming based on user attributes.

✳ Compliance & Financial Fallout

- **GDPR / CCPA — Orphaned Data**
  Partially created accounts may contain identifiable user data but never complete the sign-up, raising data minimization concerns.

- **SOC 2 / ISO 27001 — Broken Authentication Flows**
  Systems that can't ensure a consistent and functional sign-up process create audit flags for reliability and account security.

- **Customer Abandonment**
  If users get stuck during sign-up, especially on mobile, they rarely retry—impacting activation and retention metrics.

- **Spam / Bot Risk**
  Failure to complete or clean up unconfirmed sign-ups may leave your user pool full of unused,

potentially malicious records.

How Developers Misread the Situation

- "Cognito confirms users automatically." → ✗ Only if **you configure Lambda triggers** or bypass confirmation for trusted flows.

- "If they didn't confirm, they can just try again." → ✗ Cognito blocks duplicate emails—**even if the user is unconfirmed**.

- "SNS/SES just works." → ✗ Not unless **you verify domains, regions, and IAM permissions**.

- "I can safely use `admin-confirm-sign-up` any time." → ⚠ This is only appropriate **if you've confirmed user intent** (e.g., via support ticket, known identity).

🔧 Detection Steps (AWS CLI preferred)

```
# Check user status
aws cognito-idp admin-get-user \
  --user-pool-id <user_pool_id> \
  --username <email or sub>
```

```
# Expected output
# UserStatus: UNCONFIRMED

# Manually confirm user (use with caution)
aws cognito-idp admin-confirm-sign-up \
  --user-pool-id <user_pool_id> \
  --username <email or sub>

# Resend confirmation code
aws cognito-idp resend-confirmation-code \
  --client-id <app_client_id> \
  --username <email>
```

☑ You can also **filter by status** using `list-users`:

```
aws cognito-idp list-users \
  --user-pool-id <user_pool_id> \
  --filter "status=\"UNCONFIRMED\""
```

Diagram

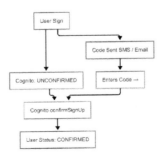

🛠️ Fix Instructions — Step-by-step code and config fixes

Option 1: Trigger Manual Confirmation (Admin Flow)

Use this only if user identity is verified (e.g., through support or internal staff):

```
aws cognito-idp admin-confirm-sign-up \
  --user-pool-id <user_pool_id> \
  --username <email>
```

Option 2: Resend Confirmation Code

Prompt the user to retry:

```
aws cognito-idp resend-confirmation-code \
  --client-id <app_client_id> \
  --username <email>
```

In Amplify (JS):

```
Auth.resendSignUp(email)
  .then(() => console.log("Code resent
successfully"))
  .catch(err => console.error(err));
```

Option 3: Auto-Confirm on Sign-Up (Trusted flows only)

Use a Pre Sign-Up Lambda trigger:

```
exports.handler = async (event) => {
  event.response.autoConfirmUser = true;
  event.response.autoVerifyEmail = true;
  return event;
};
```

☑ Only do this if you trust the identity source (e.g., internal employee portal, federated users).

Option 4: Clean Up Unconfirmed Users Periodically

Script to remove users who've remained UNCONFIRMED for too long:

```
aws cognito-idp list-users \
  --user-pool-id <user_pool_id> \
  --filter "status=\"UNCONFIRMED\"" \
  --query "Users[?UserCreateDate<'2024-01-01'].[Username]"
```

Follow with admin-delete-user for cleanup.

What You Probably Missed — Lesser-known edge cases, hidden pitfalls

- **Email delivery failures are silent** unless you monitor SES/SNS bounce and complaint notifications.

- **SES sandbox mode limits email delivery** to verified addresses only.

- **Cognito won't resend confirmation automatically**—the user or app must trigger it explicitly.

- **Using federated IdPs (Google, SAML)** bypasses the confirmation state entirely—no `confirmSignUp` is needed.

- **Username can be email or alias**—make sure your `admin-confirm-sign-up` and filters are using the correct field.

Chapter 63: *Fortify the Front Door — Securing the Cognito Hosted UI from Phishing and Clickjacking*

🔍 Quick Skim Checklist — Practical checks for the reader

- ☑ Use a **custom domain** to avoid untrusted Cognito default URLs

- ☑ Add **Content Security Policy (CSP)** and **X-Frame-Options** via CloudFront or reverse proxy

- ☑ Enable **HTTPS only** and force redirection from HTTP

- ☑ Set **OAuth redirect URIs** to known, validated URLs only

- ☑ Monitor for **spoofed domains** using tools like AWS Route 53 or external DMARC monitoring

- ☑ Implement **short-lived tokens** and **state parameter validation** in OAuth flows

---

How This Happens in the Real World

1. **The Branded Login Page That Isn't**
   A fintech app links users to Cognito's default

Hosted UI
(`*.auth.region.amazoncognito.com`). An
attacker clones the page and sends a phishing
email with a nearly identical-looking domain. Users
enter real credentials into the fake page, and the
breach begins.

2. **Iframe Exploit on Embedded Login**
A travel booking company embeds Cognito's
Hosted UI inside a `<iframe>` in their app. A
security review reveals the flow is vulnerable to
clickjacking—where attackers overlay invisible
buttons to trick users into clicking "Approve" or
"Sign In" without realizing.

3. **OAuth Redirect Hijack**
A React SPA includes a redirect URI in Cognito
pointing to a misconfigured subdomain. An attacker
exploits the loose validation to inject their own
redirect target, harvesting ID tokens after sign-in.

Root Causes

- **Use of Default Cognito Domain**
The default Cognito domain is generic and easier
to spoof—making it a weak point in phishing
defense.

- **Missing Security Headers**
Cognito's Hosted UI by default does not include
`Content-Security-Policy` or `X-Frame-`

`Options`, leaving it open to clickjacking.

- **Redirect URI Whitelist Loopholes**
  If wildcard domains or unvalidated URLs are accepted, attackers can hijack OAuth redirection to steal tokens.

- **Lack of State Parameter Validation**
  Without verifying the `state` parameter returned by Cognito during OAuth, the client cannot prevent token leakage or forged sessions.

- **No Custom Branding or Domain Ownership**
  Without a custom domain, users have no visual way to distinguish legitimate login pages from fakes.

✳ Compliance & Financial Fallout

- **GDPR / CCPA — Credential Theft**
  Phishing or token theft caused by misconfigured Hosted UI flows may lead to unauthorized access and regulatory breaches.

- **PCI-DSS — Auth Flow Integrity**
  If payment user flows are vulnerable to redirection or session hijack, your PCI compliance is at risk.

- **SOC 2 — Security and Confidentiality Violations**
  Failure to secure authentication interfaces can

trigger SOC 2 exceptions during audits.

- **User Trust & Brand Damage**
  If customers fall victim to phishing from spoofed
  Cognito domains, they lose trust—regardless of the
  actual fault.

How Developers Misread the Situation

- "Cognito handles security automatically." → ✖
  While Cognito protects backend authentication,
  you are responsible for UI exposure, domain
  spoofing, and redirect integrity.

- "My redirect URI is secure because it uses
  HTTPS." → ⚠ **Only whitelisted, tightly scoped
  redirect URIs** prevent token leakage—not just
  HTTPS.

- "I can't change headers on the Hosted UI." → ☑
  Not directly, but **you can use CloudFront or a
  reverse proxy** to inject headers and block
  clickjacking.

- "Only advanced attackers care about clickjacking."
  → ✖ This is **commonplace in phishing kits** and
  takes minutes to automate.

🔧 Detection Steps (AWS CLI preferred)

```
# 1. List callback (redirect) URLs
aws cognito-idp describe-user-pool-client \
  --user-pool-id <user_pool_id> \
  --client-id <app_client_id> \
  --query "UserPoolClient.CallbackURLs"

# 2. Check if using default Cognito domain
aws cognito-idp describe-user-pool-domain \
  --domain <your_auth_domain> \
  --region <region>

# 3. Validate token request origin using
OAuth state
# (Use this to check client behavior,
manually or with logs)

# 4. List hosted UI custom domain config
aws cognito-idp describe-user-pool-domain \
  --domain <your_custom_domain>
```

Diagram

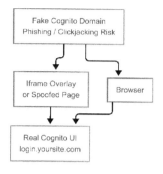

⚒ Fix Instructions — Step-by-step code and config fixes

Step 1: Use a Custom Domain for the Hosted UI

```
aws cognito-idp create-user-pool-domain \
  --domain login.yoursite.com \
  --user-pool-id <user_pool_id> \
  --custom-domain-config
CertificateArn=arn:aws:acm:<region>:<accoun
t_id>:certificate/<cert_id>
```

- Ensure DNS (e.g., Route 53) points
  login.yoursite.com to the CloudFront
  distribution.

Step 2: Secure the OAuth Redirect URIs

```
aws cognito-idp update-user-pool-client \
```

571

```
--user-pool-id <pool_id> \
--client-id <client_id> \
--callback-urls
"https://yourapp.com/callback" \
  --logout-urls
"https://yourapp.com/logout"
```

- 🚩 Avoid wildcards. Do **not** allow redirects to
  `*.yourapp.com`.

Step 3: Add CSP and Frame Options via CloudFront

Since Cognito doesn't let you set headers directly, use a
CloudFront behavior with Lambda@Edge:

```
exports.handler = (event, context,
callback) => {
  const response =
event.Records[0].cf.response;
  const headers = response.headers;

  headers['content-security-policy'] = [{
    key: 'Content-Security-Policy',
    value: "default-src 'self'; frame-
ancestors 'none';"
  }];
  headers['x-frame-options'] = [{
    key: 'X-Frame-Options',
    value: 'DENY'
```

```
  }];

  callback(null, response);
};
```

Step 4: Validate OAuth State in Client

When initiating login:

```
const state = crypto.randomUUID();
localStorage.setItem('oauth_state', state);

// redirect to Cognito Hosted UI with
&state=state
```

When user is redirected back:

```
const returnedState = new
URLSearchParams(window.location.search).get
('state');
const expected =
localStorage.getItem('oauth_state');

if (returnedState !== expected) {
  alert('Possible tampering detected');
}
```

What You Probably Missed — Lesser-known edge cases, hidden pitfalls

- **You can't modify Cognito Hosted UI headers**, but **CloudFront + Lambda@Edge** lets you inject security controls.

- **Clickjacking works silently.** Users don't realize they've been redirected or clicked malicious buttons.

- **Unconfirmed domains in callback URLs enable phishing**—especially in B2B multi-tenant flows.

- **Tokens from OIDC flows can be replayed** if state and redirect are not locked down tightly.

- **You can monitor referrers and failed sign-in attempts via CloudTrail**, but you'll need to parse logs for high-traffic Hosted UI misuse.

Chapter 64: *Ghost in the Pool — Fixing the 'AliasExistsException' in Cognito Sign-Up Flows*

🔍 **Quick Skim Checklist — Practical checks for the reader**

- ☑ Check if the **email or phone number is configured as an alias** in the user pool

- ☑ Understand that **aliases must be unique**, even across unconfirmed users

- ☑ Implement proper **resend confirmation logic** for users stuck in UNCONFIRMED state

- ☑ Detect AliasExistsException in your app and handle it with **recovery logic**

- ☑ Use admin-delete-user cautiously in cleanup flows

- ☑ Avoid race conditions with **parallel sign-up attempts** from same device/session

---

How This Happens in the Real World

1. **Stuck at Sign-Up**
   A new user tries to register with their email, but

gets an error: `AliasExistsException`. They never received the confirmation email, and now can't sign up again or log in. The email is held by a zombie user in `UNCONFIRMED` state.

2. **Mobile App Retry Loops**
   A Flutter app fires off two sign-up requests when a user taps "Create Account" twice. The second request returns `AliasExistsException` because the first one reserved the alias. The app doesn't catch it and crashes.

3. **Support Inbox Flooded**
   A social platform sees a wave of support requests like "I can't register—it says my email is in use." Investigation shows these users previously signed up but never confirmed, and Cognito still treats the alias as taken.

Root Causes

- **Email or Phone Configured as an Alias**
  Cognito aliases (email, phone) must be unique across all users, including those in `UNCONFIRMED` state.

- **Incomplete Confirm Sign-Up Flow**
  If a user signs up but never confirms (e.g., due to delivery failure or user drop-off), their alias is still reserved.

- **No Cleanup or Retry Logic**
  Without proper logic to resend confirmation codes or delete unconfirmed users, aliases become permanently blocked.

- **Alias Cannot Be Claimed Twice**
  You cannot sign up a second user with the same alias—even if the first account was never confirmed.

- **Simultaneous Sign-Up Requests**
  Multiple requests from the same client (e.g., double-taps or retries) can trigger conflicts mid-flight.

✳ Compliance & Financial Fallout

- **GDPR — Orphaned User Data**
  Data tied to unconfirmed aliases may persist without clear consent, violating data minimization and right-to-erasure principles.

- **User Frustration & Abandonment**
  Users blocked from signing up due to alias errors are unlikely to retry—hurting activation and growth metrics.

- **SOC 2 — Weak Account Recovery**
  Lack of clear sign-up recovery paths may expose your org to audit scrutiny and usability concerns.

- **Increased Support Cost**
  Manual intervention to delete or troubleshoot unconfirmed users adds friction and operational overhead.

How Developers Misread the Situation

- "That alias isn't in use—they never confirmed." →
  ✘ Even unconfirmed aliases **count as used** if the user hasn't been deleted.

- "We can just try again." → ⚠ Not without handling the exception—Cognito **won't overwrite** an alias automatically.

- "AliasExists means the user confirmed already." →
  ✘ It may just mean the alias is reserved, **not that the user is active**.

- "Deleting the user solves it." → ☑ Sometimes—but deletion must be **done carefully**, and only if identity can be verified.

🔧 Detection Steps (AWS CLI preferred)

```
# Check user existence by email
aws cognito-idp list-users \
  --user-pool-id <user_pool_id> \
```

```
  --filter "email = \"user@example.com\""

# Check user status (CONFIRMED vs
UNCONFIRMED)
aws cognito-idp admin-get-user \
  --user-pool-id <user_pool_id> \
  --username <sub or username>

# If UNCONFIRMED, consider resending code
or deleting user
aws cognito-idp resend-confirmation-code \
  --client-id <app_client_id> \
  --username <email>

# Cautiously delete user if recovery is
verified
aws cognito-idp admin-delete-user \
  --user-pool-id <user_pool_id> \
  --username <email>
```

Diagram

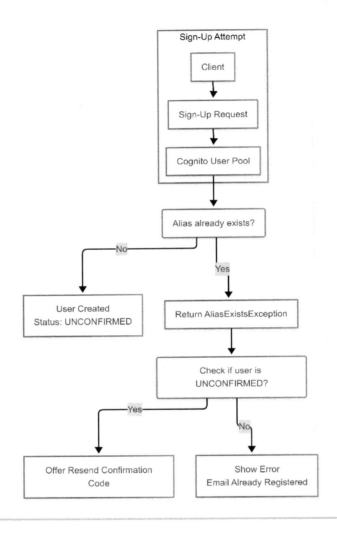

✂️ Fix Instructions — Step-by-step code and config fixes

Step 1: Catch and Handle AliasExistsException in Your Frontend

```
try {
  await Auth.signUp({
    username: email,
    password: password,
    attributes: { email }
  });
} catch (error) {
  if (error.code ===
'AliasExistsException') {
    // Trigger resend flow or support
message
    showRecoveryPrompt(email);
  } else {
    throw error;
  }
}
```

Step 2: Offer Resend Confirmation Code in UI

```
Auth.resendSignUp(email)
  .then(() => alert("Confirmation code sent
again."))
  .catch(err => console.error(err));
```

Step 3: Optionally Auto-Delete Unconfirmed Users After N Hours (Admin Flow)

Build an automated script or support tool:

```
# Find UNCONFIRMED users older than 24h
aws cognito-idp list-users \
  --user-pool-id <pool_id> \
  --filter "status=\"UNCONFIRMED\"" \
  --query "Users[?UserCreateDate<'2024-04-
01'].[Username]"
```

Then:

```
aws cognito-idp admin-delete-user \
  --user-pool-id <pool_id> \
  --username <username>
```

Step 4: Prevent Double Submissions in UI

Disable sign-up buttons after first tap, and debounce API calls.

What You Probably Missed — Lesser-known edge cases, hidden pitfalls

- **AliasExistsException can happen even if user doesn't appear in the console.** Unconfirmed users are still stored unless deleted.

- **Email aliases are case-insensitive, but Cognito usernames are not.** This can cause confusion in lookup and error handling.

- **You can't update an alias post sign-up**—if a user signed up with the wrong email, they need a full account deletion + re-registration.

- **This issue can affect federated users too.** If Cognito tries to create a new user after SAML/OIDC login and the alias is already taken, login will fail silently.

Chapter 65: *One Pool to Rule Them All —*
Scaling Cognito for Multi-Tenant and Region-
Aware Architectures

🔍 **Quick Skim Checklist — Practical checks for the reader**

- ☑ Use **groups, custom attributes**, or **identity provider contexts** to separate tenants logically within a single user pool

- ☑ Implement **scoped access** using fine-grained IAM and tokens with custom claims

- ☑ Use **custom domains** per tenant or region for better branding and UX

- ☑ Avoid duplicating user pools unless strict **compliance or data residency** requires it

- ☑ Use **Pre Token Generation Lambda** to inject tenant context into tokens

- ☑ Implement **region-aware routing logic** at the app layer, not in Cognito

How This Happens in the Real World

1. **The 15-User-Pool Monster**
   A startup launches its SaaS platform in multiple
   countries and creates a separate user pool for
   each. A year later, managing sign-in, tokens, and
   user roles across pools becomes a nightmare.
   They also hit rate limits and can't share sessions
   across regions.

2. **Enterprise Tenant Explosion**
   A multi-tenant CRM app provisions a separate pool
   per customer. When the app hits 200 customers,
   onboarding slows, user management becomes
   inconsistent, and cost monitoring is impossible.

3. **Token Blindness in API Gateway**
   A team uses separate user pools by region but
   routes all API traffic through a global API Gateway.
   Their backend has no way to know which tenant or
   region a token came from—breaking role-based
   access and audit logging.

Root Causes

- **Overuse of Separate User Pools**
  Developers often think each tenant or region must
  have its own pool—but that limits scalability and
  multiplies management overhead.

- **Lack of Tenant Context in Tokens**
  By default, Cognito tokens don't include tenant
  identifiers unless explicitly injected via Lambda

585

triggers.

- **Confusion Between Auth Boundaries and Logical Boundaries**
  Cognito user pools are authentication boundaries, but tenants are usually logical boundaries handled at the app level.

- **IAM and Token Validation Conflicts Across Pools**
  Verifying tokens across multiple pools introduces complexity in identity propagation and access control.

- **No Custom Domain or Hosted UI Routing Strategy**
  Without custom domains or domain-aware routing, users are confused by non-branded login pages or cross-region redirects.

✳ Compliance & Financial Fallout

- **GDPR / CCPA — Regional Segmentation Misfires**
  Misrouting EU user traffic to a US user pool may violate regional data storage laws.

- **SOC 2 / ISO 27001 — Inconsistent Access Controls**
  Inconsistent user pool policies across tenants may lead to security configuration drift.

- **Tenant Lock-In Failure**
  If user tokens don't indicate tenant identity, it becomes easy for one tenant to access another tenant's data—breaking isolation.

- **Cost Inefficiency at Scale**
  Multiple pools increase operational overhead, duplicate cloud costs, and break monitoring visibility.

How Developers Misread the Situation

- "We need one user pool per tenant." → ✖ In most SaaS models, you can scale with a **single user pool + custom claims**.

- "Cognito can route by region automatically." → ✖ Cognito is **region-bound—you must handle routing at the app level**.

- "Groups are for access control, not tenancy." → ☑ But you can **repurpose them for tenant separation** when scoped correctly.

- "A custom domain means a separate user pool." → ✖ One user pool can support **multiple domains or custom branding strategies**.

🔧 Detection Steps (AWS CLI preferred)

```
# List user pool groups (which can
represent tenants)
aws cognito-idp list-groups \
  --user-pool-id <user_pool_id>

# View a user's attributes and group
membership
aws cognito-idp admin-get-user \
  --user-pool-id <user_pool_id> \
  --username <username>

# Describe a user pool's domain setup
aws cognito-idp describe-user-pool-domain \
  --domain <custom_domain_name>

# View token claims (after login, locally)
# Decode your JWT and check for
"custom:tenant_id" or "cognito:groups"
```

Diagram

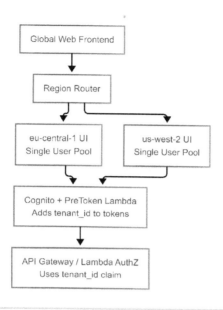

🛠️ Fix Instructions — Step-by-step code and config fixes

Step 1: Use a Single User Pool + Groups or Custom Claims

- Create a group per tenant (optional):

```
aws cognito-idp create-group \
  --user-pool-id <user_pool_id> \
  --group-name tenant_alpha
```

- Add user to the group:

```
aws cognito-idp admin-add-user-to-group \
  --user-pool-id <user_pool_id> \
  --username <username> \
  --group-name tenant_alpha
```

Step 2: Add Tenant Metadata During Sign-Up (Option A: Custom Attributes)

During sign-up, pass `custom:tenant_id`:

```
Auth.signUp({
  username: email,
  password,
  attributes: {
    email,
    "custom:tenant_id": "alpha"
  }
});
```

Step 3: Use Pre Token Generation Lambda to Inject Claims (Option B)

```
exports.handler = async (event) => {
  const tenantId =
event.request.userAttributes['custom:tenant
_id'];
  event.response.claimsOverrideDetails = {
```

```
      claimsToAddOrOverride: {
        'tenant_id': tenantId
      }
    };
    return event;
};
```

Step 4: Secure Your Backend Using Token Claims

In your API or Lambda authorizer, validate the `tenant_id` from token:

```
claims =
event['requestContext']['authorizer']['clai
ms']
tenant_id = claims.get('tenant_id')
```

Match it against the resource access context for authorization logic.

Step 5: Add Region- or Tenant-Aware Hosted UI Entry Points

Use subdomain routing or query parameters like:

```
https://login.company.com/us-
west?tenant_id=alpha
```

Redirect users to:

```
https://yourcustomdomain.auth.us-west-
2.amazoncognito.com/login?client_id=...&sta
te=alpha
```

What You Probably Missed — Lesser-known edge cases, hidden pitfalls

- **Cross-region sign-ins aren't supported**—a token issued in `us-east-1` is invalid in `eu-west-1`.

- **Tokens don't include group membership unless you enable** `tokenScopes = groups`.

- **Hosted UI branding is global per pool**—you can't brand per tenant unless using custom domains.

- **Federated identity tokens won't include tenant data unless mapped via Lambda or attribute mapping.**

- **Admin APIs don't respect group access**— you'll need to enforce tenant-level access in your app logic.

📎 Appendix: Useful AWS Links for Developers

These resources will help you go beyond this book and stay up to date with the AWS ecosystem.

🔐 Security & IAM

- IAM Policy Simulator:
  https://policysim.aws.amazon.com/
- AWS IAM Best Practices:
  https://docs.aws.amazon.com/IAM/latest/UserGuide/best-practices.html
- Service Control Policies (SCPs):
  https://docs.aws.amazon.com/organizations/latest/userguide/orgs_manage_policies_scps.html

---

📦 Amazon S3

- S3 Security Best Practices:
  https://docs.aws.amazon.com/AmazonS3/latest/userguide/security-best-practices.html
- Block Public Access overview:
  https://docs.aws.amazon.com/AmazonS3/latest/userguide/access-control-block-public-access.html
- S3 Lifecycle Configuration:
  https://docs.aws.amazon.com/AmazonS3/latest/userguide/lifecycle-configuration-examples.html
- S3 Storage Classes comparison:
  https://aws.amazon.com/s3/storage-classes/

⚙️ AWS Lambda

- Lambda Best Practices:
  https://docs.aws.amazon.com/lambda/latest/dg/best-practices.html
- Lambda Execution Role Permissions:
  https://docs.aws.amazon.com/lambda/latest/dg/lambda-intro-execution-role.html
- Optimizing Lambda performance:
  https://aws.amazon.com/blogs/compute/operating-lambda-performance-optimization/

🧠 Amazon Cognito

- Cognito Developer Guide:
  https://docs.aws.amazon.com/cognito/latest/developerguide/cognito-user-identity-pools.html
- MFA and Password Policies:
  https://docs.aws.amazon.com/cognito/latest/developerguide/user-pool-settings-mfa.html
- OAuth 2.0 in Cognito:
  https://docs.aws.amazon.com/cognito/latest/developerguide/cognito-userpools-server-contract-reference.html

💡 Monitoring & Cost Control

- AWS Pricing Calculator:
  https://calculator.aws.amazon.com/

- AWS Cost Explorer:
  https://docs.aws.amazon.com/cost-management/latest/userguide/ce-what-is.html
- S3 Storage Lens:
  https://docs.aws.amazon.com/AmazonS3/latest/userguide/storage-lens.html
- CloudWatch Logs Insights:
  https://docs.aws.amazon.com/AmazonCloudWatch/latest/logs/AnalyzingLogData.html

---

🛠️ Other Useful Tools

- AWS CLI Command Reference:
  https://docs.aws.amazon.com/cli/latest/index.html
- AWS Well-Architected Framework:
  https://aws.amazon.com/architecture/well-architected/
- AWS Documentation Hub:
  https://docs.aws.amazon.com/

🎯 You've Made It!

Congratulations—you've reached the end of *Mastering AWS: Solving the Top Developer Challenges with S3, IAM, EC2, Lambda, and Cognito*. If you've made it this far, you're not just reading documentation—you're becoming the person your team turns to when everything breaks and no one knows why.

Remember, mastery doesn't mean knowing everything. It means knowing how to troubleshoot, ask the right questions, and build with clarity under pressure. Keep this book close, but more importantly—keep experimenting, breaking things (safely), and building better every day.

If this book helped you, consider leaving a review. Your feedback keeps books like this alive and useful.

Until next time—build smart, secure everything, and automate the boring parts.

www.ingramcontent.com/pod-product-compliance
Lightning Source LLC
LaVergne TN
LVHW022332060326
832902LV00022B/3992